THE CALCULUS OF LINGUISTIC OBSERVATIONS

JANUA LINGUARUM

STUDIA MEMORIAE
NICOLAI VAN WIJK DEDICATA

edenda curat

CORNELIS H. VAN SCHOONEVELD

STANFORD UNIVERSITY

SERIES MAIOR

IX

1962

MOUTON & CO · 'S-GRAVENHAGE

THE CALCULUS OF LINGUISTIC OBSERVATIONS

by

GUSTAV HERDAN

LECTURER IN STATISTICS
UNIVERSITY OF BRISTOL

1962

MOUTON & CO · 'S-GRAVENHAGE

PREFACE

The aim of this book is to give an outline of the mathematical structure of language, developing the subject systematically with illustrative material from a wide range of languages. Thus, what in each of the author's previous books, LANGUAGE AS CHOICE AND CHANCE and TYPE-TOKEN MATHEMATICS, was relegated to Part V, has here been made the 'Leitmotif' of the whole book.

Whereas Part V of LANGUAGE AS CHOICE AND CHANCE is a succinct exposition of the general theory of mathematical statistics in its application to language, and Part V of TYPE-TOKEN MATHEMATICS stresses the peculiarity of statistical linguistics as a branch of statistics in its own right, this book, apart from being a systematic exposition of all these methods, takes the quantitative description of language a step further by introducing *Bose-Einstein* statistics as the appropriate type of statistics when dealing with language on the morphemic level, and so develops the *Quantum Theory of Language* as the necessary complement of information theory on the phonemic and alphabetic level.

The complete picture of the calculus of linguistic observations provides a new criterion for language classification, reveals the close similarity between language structure and thought form, and shows the relation between language and mathematics in a new light. It will, so one hopes, not be regarded as only a minor by-product of this exposition of the calculus that it shows up 'Linguistic Philosophy' as resting upon one of the most grotesque misunderstandings of the working of language. This is the object lesson of what is bound to happen if one makes language the central concept of philosophy, neglecting at the same time the study of linguistics.

The sequence of subjects in this book, which is dictated by the systematic exposition of the calculus of linguistic observations, need not be the order in which the linguist might find it easiest to proceed. He might wish to start with empirical facts of language, and I would advise in this case to read first Chpts. 10, 11 (Part III) and Chpts. 16-19 (Part V), and follow this up with Parts II, I, IV, VI and VII, in this order.

I am greatly indebted to Dr. D. W. Moore of the Department of Mathematics, University of Bristol, for checking the mathematical formulae, and to my wife Innes Herdan for her patient help with proofreading and checking the Chinese writing in Chpt. XV.

Bristol, Feb. 1962   G. HERDAN

ERRATA

p. 30, formula (4): for $p\,'$ read p'_i

p. 46, 6th line from below: for v^r_i read v'_i

p. 51, 11th line from top: after 'table 1-3' insert (Tables 2-4)

p. 60, line 8 from below: for $\frac{1}{10\,\mathrm{R}}$ read $\frac{1}{10\mathrm{R}}$

p. 67, line 8 from top: instead of (4), it should be (1)

p. 67, line 3 from top: the 1st term on the right of (4) is $\int_0^1 \lambda^{i-1}(1-\lambda)^\rho\,d\lambda$

p. 78, Table 13, heading of col. 4: instead of % read 'd '

p. 79, line 8 of Sect. 8.3: after 'scores' insert 'd'

p. 85, line 5 from top: after X2X should follow: and X4X, X6X for Q.

p. 89, Table 18 last column heading: for '*sj*' read '*s*'

p. 99, line 12 from below: for 'Chpt. 11' read 'Chpts. 16, 17'

p. 102, formula (7): first term on the right in brackets should be $\left(\dfrac{S_2}{N} - \dfrac{S_1{}^2}{N^2} - \dfrac{S_1}{N}\right)$

p. 116, formula (A): instead of S_{l_2} read $S_i{}^2$

p. 123, line 8 from top: instead of 'of' read 'for'

p. 124, formula (1a): the term in brackets on the right should be $\left(\dfrac{N}{r}!\right)^r$

p. 155, line 10 from top: after 'wordadd' 'sound'

p. 157, line 17 from top: after 'symbol' put '(Chpt. 12)'

p. 171, column headings of table should be: 'av. b' and 'av. stroke no'

p. 206, formula (17), nominator in 1st term on the right should be $(A\beta\gamma\delta\varepsilon)$

p. 225, 1st line from top: for 'medical' read 'practical'

p. 225, from 5th line below: for 'promoted' read 'prompted'

p. 251, line 17 from bottom: for 'concepts' read '(concepts)'

p. 252, line 9 from top: for 'theologists' read 'theologians'

p. 261, 3rd para. from top, last line: for 'expression' read 'experience'

p. 263, line 5 from end of Sect. 24.5: delete 'thus'

p. 265, insert reference: Cambon, G., "Dante's Francesca and the Tactics of Language", *Modern Language Quarterly*, 196.

TABLE OF CONTENTS

PART III
SPECTROGRAPHY OF SPEECH ON THE MORPHEMIC LEVEL

BOOK TWO:
THE RELATION BETWEEN LANGUAGE IN THE MASS AND LANGUAGE IN THE LINE

PART IV
THE STATISTICAL THEORY OF LINGUISTIC CODING—INFORMATION
THEORY

PART V
QUANTUM THEORY OF LANGUAGE

BOOK THREE:
LANGUAGE IN THE LINE—THE UNIVERSES OF LANGUAGE DISCOURSE

PART VI
THE UNIVERSE OF DISCOURSE AS A LINE—LINGUISTIC DUALITY

PART VII
LANGUAGE AND MATHEMATICS

LANGUAGE IN THE MASS – THE UNIVERSES OF LANGUAGE STATISTICS

PART I

STATISTICS OF PHONEMIC (ALPHABETIC) SYSTEMS

I

FUNDAMENTAL CONCEPTS OF THE CALCULUS OF LINGUISTIC OBSERVATIONS

1.1   THE DEFINITION OF THE CALCULUS

1.   There are two great fields for the use of statistical methods in the study of language: one in which statistics is used as an auxiliary tool, mainly for the purpose of testing hypotheses, and the other in which the problems themselves are of a quantitative nature, and therefore require statistical methods.[1]

Statistical methods can on any level of language study contribute to evaluating the evidence in favour of one or the other hypothesis. In these questions or problems themselves there is nothing statistical, e.g. when we ask which of two languages is closer related to a third one, or which of two writers is to be regarded as the author of a particular book. For such purposes, the statistical methods as used in other branches of knowledge are, as a rule, sufficient and, if not, could be made so by suitable alterations. They form what the English mathematician, E. Whittaker, has called the *Calculus of Observations*.

A very different situation arises if the question or problem itself is of a quantitative nature. In such a case, the linguists themselves operate with concepts which require for their precise use statistical methods. Statistics is thus here not something super-imposed upon an essentially qualitative or non-mathematical structure, but forms a part of linguistic thought and method, and as such is already needed for the very use of language itself. The mathematical methods required for this I call the *Calculus of Linguistic Observations*. Mathematically, there is, of course, no clear-cut distinction between the two types of the Calculus, and our presentation comprises both.

2.   We now ask what are the essential features of that calculus.

The distributionalist's method of determining the system of phonemes in a language is, as such, non-statistical—or, at least, this is what the distributionalist believes. It is true that the determination of the phonemic system as such does not require statistics, but only so long as the question of corpus versus language does not arise. If it does, then there is great need for mathematical statistics, for the simple reason that the opposition corpus versus language is nothing else but that between sample versus

---

[1]   H. Karlgren, "Die Tragweite lexikalischer Statistik", in *Språkstatistika Symposiet 1960* (Uppsala, 1962).

statistical population. Thus, as Karlgren l.c. rightly says, even though statistics is not openly used by the distributionalist, it creeps in surreptitiously.

How highly advantageous it is from the mere theoretical angle to make here deliberate use of statistical methods can be seen from Spang-Hanssen's book on *Probability and Structural Classification* (1959). This valuable exposition is marred by the effort the author makes to develop the relation between 'observed' and 'open' material from scratch, so to speak, instead of making full use of what mathematical statistics has to say on this point, the relation in question being nothing else but that between sample and statistical population.

But even so, and as a matter of principle, the distributionalist is concerned only with the presence or absence of phonemes in a language, or with yes-no answers about particular phonemes. Clearly, this is not the whole answer to the question. The description of the phonemes in a language could hardly be regarded as complete if we knew only *which* phonemes are comprised in its phonemic system, without knowing *how much* a particular phoneme is used, not only in the dictionary, but also by the members of the speech community or, briefly, without knowing their functional burdening. And this immediately brings out the need for both lexical and text statistics.

The importance of the functional burdening of a phoneme, or any other linguistic form, for strictly linguistic questions, need hardly be emphasized, since it is obvious. It is the first step for establishing tendencies in the language for the use or non-use of certain phonemes or other linguistic forms. A significant decrease in functional burdening with time is a pointer to the complete disappearance of the linguistic form in the near future and, generally, a systematic change in the system of functional burdening of phonemes points to an impending alteration of the phonemic system itself.

3. Not only do we require both, running text statistics as well as lexical statistics, for answering linguistically relevant questions, but the relation of the two may be regarded as the prototype of a linguistic relation of a quantitative nature. It forms the basis for the explanation of the remarkable stability of relative frequencies of linguistic forms. This brings us to the very heart of quantitative linguistics: with the recognition of that relation between the two types of count as a statistical one stands and falls the science of quantitative linguistics.

This is what I set out to show in *Language as Choice and Chance*, Sect. 5.3 where I formulated it as follows.

"The phenomenon of the stability of relative frequencies of linguistic forms leads to the statistical view of de Saussure's fundamental distinction between 'la langue' and 'la parole'. According to de Saussure, 'la langue' is the total of linguistic habits which make communication between the members of the speech community possible. It is a social reality, existing for the mass of people. Roughly, it represents the lexicon of the language in question. 'La parole', on the other hand, is the individual utterance. Whereas 'la langue' is independent of the individual, 'la parole' as the realisation of parts of 'la langue' through speech is dependent upon the individual. So far, it was thought that the former comprised the engrams of the language in the sense of 'lexical forms' (including here, of course, also grammar forms listed in the lexicon), and the latter the words of actual speech. However, the stability of the relative frequencies which we find attached to the various items of a given series of linguistic forms leads inevitably to the conclusion that what 'la langue' comprises are not only engrams as lexical forms, but *these engrams plus their respective probabilities of occurrence*. This is what I have called the statistical view of de Saussure's dichotomy. The basic law of linguistic communication as stated above is then tantamount to the statement that language is the collective term for linguistic engrams (phonemes, word engrams), together with their particular probabilities of occurrence. The engram concept is thus inseparably connected with that of frequency of occurrence, and if by linguistic normative laws we understand something which regulates the relative frequency of linguistic forms belonging to a certain class, then our statistical conception of 'la langue' implies such normative laws, as whose realisation we must regard the empirically determined frequencies of 'la parole'.

This seemingly small modification of de Saussure's conception has the important consequence that 'la langue' now has the essential characteristic of a statistical population. Such a population is characterised by definite probabilities for the categories of the variable, here the linguistic forms belonging to a particular linguistic level, to materialise in random samples. 'La parole' then appears as it ought to according to its meaning, as a term for statistical *samples* withdrawn from 'la langue' as the *population*".[2]

Since then, great progress has been made in establishing the relation between the functional burdening of phonemes in the dictionary and their utilisation in speech (writing) as being of the nature of the relation between statistical population of events at risk and their occurrence through random sampling.

The frequency of occurrence of phonemes in a language may be derived from dictionary material or from continuous texts, viz., as the ratio of occurrence numbers to text length (in terms of total phoneme number) and as the ratio of their incidence in the dictionary to the total of phonemes there. As a rule, the two distributions are regarded as basically different; even so unsurpassed an expert in matters of phonology as Trubetzkoy seems to have taken this for granted, since otherwise he would not have used the term "double relativity" (Trubetzkoy, 1939). However, statistical analysis has shown that the utilisation of phonemes in speech, according to place of production, is closely similar to their functional burdening in the dictionary or in 'la langue', the functional burdening of the phoneme group in use being only a random sample of that in the dictionary. This means that Trubetzkoy's "double relativity" is an illusion in this case.[3]

[2] G. Herdan, *Language as Choice and Chance* (P. Noordhoff, Groningen, 1956), Sect. 5.3.
[3] G. Herdan, *Type-Token Mathematics* (Mouton & Co., The Hague, 1960), Sect. 8.1-8.4.

It is quite instructive in this connection to mention a study on 'Frequency Studies of English Consonants'[4] by W. S.-Y. Wang and J. Crawford, in which the authors found that the relative frequency of consonants in English is not seriously affected by the type of literary content or by the dialect of the sample, and that even a relatively small sample yielded typical values. This is in full accordance with my hypothesis that such counts are random samples of a statistical universe of consonant probabilities in the language (la langue). The authors claim, however, to have established differences in this respect between a dictionary count and counts from running texts. This is not borne out by their numerical results. They have overlooked the fact that the coefficients of correlation between the count from the dictionary and from running texts are also highly significant. It follows that there cannot be significant discrepancies between them, nor have the authors proved anything of the sort. The slight differences between the dictionary count and some of the running text counts—by no means all—are easily explained by the former comprising only consonants from mono- and dis-syllables, a fact completely overlooked by the authors. In a word, as Trubetzkoy says: "Man darf sich die Sache nicht zu leicht vorstellen.'

The dependence of the count from running texts upon that in the dictionary need not always be that between sample and statistical population. While remaining indicative of a close statistical relation, it changes in form from one language level to another. Thus, the distribution of word length in 'la parole' was shown to follow from that in the dictionary as a higher *moment distribution*[5] of word length for its functional burdening in the dictionary (Ref. 3, Chpt. IX).

That the relation between the vocabulary and the occurrence distribution with regard to word length should turn out to be one between *different moments of a statistical variate*, must be regarded as one of the most remarkable facts so far established about the statistical nature of language.

The relation between dictionary and running text counts could also be established in terms of the intensity of correlation. Karlgren l.c. has given the frequency distribution of Swedish mono-syllables according to initial letter in both, the dictionary and in running texts. I obtained the rank correlation coefficient between the two as $r = .9567$, which means that $r^2\%$, or approximately 92%, of the text count is accounted for by the dictionary count.

These are just a few instances of the statistical nature of the relation between the two types of count, dictionary and running text statistics.

The remarkable stability of the three types of distribution mentioned above, i.e. that of the phonemes in a language, of word length and of words according to their initial letter, can also be explained, partly at least, by the well-established stability of relative frequency of particular vocabulary items. From an extensive word count

---

[4] *Language and Speech*, Vol. 3, Part 3, p. 131-139.
[5] In general, the moment is the mean value of a power of the variate; in particular, the r'th moment of a variate x with distribution $dF(x)$ is given by $\mu_r = \int_{-\infty}^{\infty} x^r \, dF(x)$, and the moment about a particular fixed value, α, e.g. the arithmetic mean, by $\int_{-\infty}^{\infty} (x - \alpha)^r \, dF(x)$.

of Russian in three chronologically different periods it was found that such word counts show a considerable overlap in vocabulary items and their frequency of occurrence (20-50% in that case according to whether by overlap we mean the strictly identical part, or whether we admit a $\pm$ 10% deviation), and this produces the part of the phoneme distribution which is common to the two independent samples; also, that part of the word length distribution and the distribution according to initial letter of words, which is common to both samples (Sect. 6.1, ref. footnoot 2).

The stability of relative frequency of vocabulary forms one of the central topics of this book.

The calculus of linguistic observations, apart from comprising the mathematical procedures by which the smallest units of language, phonemes and letters, are combined into words, and the words into sentences etc., is mainly concerned with establishing how much the speaker's (writer's) utterance is language-conditioned, that is, dependent upon the code, and how much style-conditioned, that is, his own. In other words, *it is concerned with establishing how hide-bound the speaker or writer is by the linguistic code he uses or, briefly, how code-bound he is.*

For a somewhat different conception of the Calculus, see Chapter XXII.

1.2 THE GEOMETRIZATION OF LINGUISTICS

1.   One of the difficulties of getting mathematical linguistics across to an audience of linguists is to make it clear at the outset—that is, before any practical results could be shown—, what is to be gained by it, or rather, why the linguist should be asked to abandon his time-honoured methods, or some of them, in favour of so "outlandish" a method. The answer can be given in one sentence: we simply follow the general trend of modern science, with all the advantages which should accrue from it.

Let us look at the development of classical into modern physics. The trend I am referring to is known as the *geometrization* of physics. The main—and profound—difference between classical and modern, i.e. Einsteinian physics, is this. According to the former, the mathematician was to confirm and analyse the properties of space and time, building up the primary sciences of geometry and kinematics; then, when the stage had thus been prepared, the physicist was to come along with the dramatis personae—material bodies, magnets, electric charges, light, and so forth—and the play was to begin. The geometry was that of Euclid as the only possible one, and the behaviour of the dramatis personae had to be in conformity with it, no matter what the difficulties and contradictions were in which one got involved.

In Einstein's revolutionary conception of general relativity, it was the characters which created the stage as they walked about on it; geometry was no longer antecedent to physics, nor was it any longer exclusive, but was indissolubly fused with physics into a single discipline. Euclidian geometry was deposed from its old position of propriety, if not uniqueness, and from being accepted as a valid representation of space.

The transition from classical to modern physics appeared to turn on the question whether we prefer to have an easily intelligible geometry with complicated physical laws, different according to the branch of physical science, or a less intelligible geometry with simple physical laws, unified for the various fields of the physical universe. The concensus of opinion now is that geometry should be regarded as part of physics, and, therefore, our system of geometry should be one in which the rest of physics can be expressed as simply as possible: it is this consideration which led ultimately to the curved space of general relativity.

Generally speaking, the development consisted in realising that much of what was regarded as physics, or space and time content, could be conceived as geometry, and this also characterises the transition from classical to structural linguistics. The three-fold system of phonetics—vocabulary—grammar of a particular language was for classical linguistics what Euclidian geometry was for classical physics: the form or the stage on which the ideas as the dramatis personae appeared. Differences between works of literature in a given language could only be accounted for in terms which had nothing to do with the general stage of language.

The development towards structural linguistics consists in reclaiming more and more linguistic features as part of the stage, just as more and more physical features were claimed to be part of geometry. The advantage this has in linguistics is again parallel to that in physics. We may have simple or easily intelligible linguistics of the old type, but with rather complex laws—if any—governing the actual linguistic events in la parole, or we may have the less intelligible and more complex structural linguistics of today, but with rather simple laws for the relation of literary events. The concensus of opinion is now very much in favour of the latter.

Take style, for instance, and suppose that a literary scholar of the old school had been asked to describe the differences in style between, say, Gibbon and Macaulay. We can well imagine the number of volumes required for doing the job in a comprehensive and thorough way if the writer started with the assumption, appropriate to the old-time conception of literary criticism, that the question of structure or of linguistics did not enter at all, because style had nothing to do with language as the subject of linguistics. Not only will his answer be of very great length, but the more so, the less objective will it be, nor will it be free from contradictions. Thus, we have all the disadvantages from using simple or easily intelligible linguistics—the same for both writers—which does not regard style as being within its precincts. On the other hand, suppose that the matter had been dealt with by a structural linguist versed in mathematical methods. For him, style has different characteristics, some of which, like word frequency, are partly language-conditioned, and therefore belong to language structure. Using the information provided on this point by structural linguistics, he will be able to describe the style of each, Gibbon and Macaulay, in terms of what they have in common as regards the use of vocabulary, namely as far as their style is language-conditioned, and in terms of their difference in this respect—namely insofar as their use of vocabulary is style-conditioned—, and so give the required answer to the problem, all in quantitative terms and in a completely objective way. This is the result of working with the more complex form of structural linguistics as 'geometry', which has the advantage of making the laws or the relations in which the literary scholar is interested simple, general and objective.

1.3 THE UNIVERSES OF STATISTICAL LINGUISTICS

1.3.1 Population Probabilities of Statistical Linguistics

Phonemic (alphabetic) and quantitative characteristics (word length in terms of letter, phoneme or syllable number) of language are, on the whole, independent of individual style, and thus language-conditioned, whereas qualitative characteristics such as vocabulary, and sentence length are to a great extent style-conditioned, with grammar characteristics occupying a medium position while inclining more strongly to being independent of style, and thus to being language-conditioned.

For truly quantitative style characteristics and for phonemes (letters) it was found that even small samples (of say 1000 letters or phonemes) appear to be representative of the statistical population, provided that due care is taken to spread the sample in a random way over a great part of the text. We say in this case that the universe is one of "simple sampling", and mean by it that a specified linguistic form, say a specified phoneme, has a constant probability, independent of the length of the text samples. It is a comparatively simple matter to ascertain these quantities, and that is why the universe is called one of "simple sampling".

Grammar style characteristics, although more closely related to quantitative characteristics than to vocabulary, may show significant variations with individual style, if the field of observation is sufficiently extended. This means that we cannot speak of the probabilities of such characteristics as strictly constant throughout the universe, though some of them can still be considered as constant (e.g. relative frequency of nouns, adjectives and pronouns), to a greater extent than others (e.g. verbs). Since a reasonably small sample will no longer give an adequate picture of the universe of grammar forms, sampling must extend over a field large enough to include possible "outliers", i.e. writers having certain idiosyncracies in the use of grammar forms. In addition to the variation of constant probabilities due to fluctuations of random sampling, there is variation of these basic probabilities due to assignable causes. The variation of a given language unit which in the universe of simple sampling is governed by a simple law of chance, such as the Binomial law or the Poisson law, consists now of two parts: an aleatoric part governed by a law of chance and a "physical" part, representing the element of choice. We may speak here, in contradistinction to the phonemic universe discussed above, of the tagmemic universe. This type of universe is known in statistical theory as a Lexian universe (see *LCC*, sect. 6.4, 18.6).[6]

The element of choice assumes greater importance when sampling for vocabulary style characteristics. It is important to remember that language data are peculiar in this, that they show gradual transitions from simple sampling to sampling from which the limitations of simple sampling have been removed, and sampling for vocabulary characteristics is just one further step in that direction compared with sampling for grammar characteristics.

The choice element has become so powerful that we cannot any longer aim at separating it in a simple manner from the aleatoric effect, the chance element. We therefore do not aim at a description of the universe with the choice element eliminated, but rather at an integration of such styles which together might give an adequate picture of the use of vocabulary in the speech community. In place of the conventional parameters for describing universes like that of quantitative and grammar style characteristics (mean, standard deviation), we now have to use a complex parameter, the Characteristic "K", or v_m as an overall index of the type-token relation in the universe. We may speak here of the vocabulary universe of language. A related type is what might be called the taxonomic universe of content.

Instead of aiming at a stratified sample from a great number of texts and writers, we may also regard each writer as a universe. This will be the correct procedure when individualisation of style has become pronounced.

The basis for the application of statistical methods to linguistic data is the quantitative interpretation of the "langue-parole" dichotomy (Sect. 1.3, 5.3, *LCC*). According to it, "la langue" is the total of the linguistic forms shared by the members of a speech community plus their probabilities of occurrence, and "la parole" represents samples of that population.

1.3.2 *The 'Sample Space' of Statistical Linguistics*

Random sampling as an operational concept was defined by Kendall and Babington Smith (1938) as a method of sampling for a specified characteristic such that the method is independent of the characteristic itself. They add: "There is no such thing as a random method of selection per se considered apart from the universe whose members are being selected. ... Within the same universe, a method which is random in respect of one characteristic is not necessarily random in respect of another."

It follows that provided the method of sampling was independent of the characteristic for which we sample, it does not matter how regular or systematic the procedure

---

[6] The author's previous books on mathematical linguistics, *Language as Choice and Chance* (Groningen, 1956) and *Type-Token Mathematics* (The Hague, 1960), are referred to as *LCC* and *TTM* respectively.

is by which the individual samples are selected. This is what von Mises (1939) has called the "Prinzip des ausgeschlossenen Spielsystems" (the principle of the impossibility of a gambling system), which he regards as the most important criterion of a random series. If the universe is a random aggregate of events which may occur in two alternatives, say *A* and *B*, then no matter what elaborate system one were to devise for getting the better of chance, provided only that the method did not imply a knowledge of the characteristics *A* and *B* themselves, the resulting selection of items would again be a random series or random sample. (Objections against Mises' principle as a criterion of randomness rest, as far as I have noticed, upon an incomplete knowledge of his definition, mostly forgetting the proviso.)

My contention is that the linear sequences of linguistic forms in written texts or speech are random series with respect to certain quantitative characteristics, and any sampling procedure, be it by disconnected linguistic units, or by continuous pieces of text, by pages or by chapters etc., will give a random sample of such a quantitative characteristic, provided only that the sampling method is in no way connected with the characteristic; that is, provided that it does not consist in a direct or indirect selection of categories of just the characteristic we are sampling for.

How to take samples from a linguistic text in order that the principles of geometrical probability should give the desired results, and how large to make them, depends very much upon the type of linguistic form. In general, the less the occurrences of 'type' for which we sample are connected with the content of the text, the less need we trouble about superimposing a random sampling scheme upon the natural occurrence of the 'type' in the text, for the simple reason that it will, by and large, be already random. This is, for instance, true for letters and phonemes. These views will be substantiated in the following paragraphs.

1.3.3 *The Ergodicity of Word Masses*

1. It is a characteristic of linguistic distributions that their properties may be interpreted in terms of either number statistics or statistical physics (*LCC*, Sect. 1.5). According to the former, the properties of empirical linguistic distributions are derived from those of a hypothetical statistical universe of which the empirical distribution is conceived to be a random sample. According to the latter, the universe is not primary, but represents the limiting form to which the linguistic system will, under certain circumstances, tend. We describe below some of the essential features of linguistic systems, using both types of interpretation.

2. We start with the fundamental tenet of de Saussure, viz., that the signs of language are independent of their content or meaning. Now let us review the results of the quantitative study of language in the light of the definition of random sampling (as given by Kendall) as a method of selecting specimens of an event which is independent

of the event itself, or, briefly, as a method of sampling in which the units selected for examination are independent of what we are sampling for. Linguistic sampling, no matter how varied, is essentially one of words. If our purpose is to make a dictionary count or a text count of letters, of phonemes, or letter or phoneme groups, of word length in terms of letter or phoneme number or syllable number, the units selected directly are words, since the sample is given in terms of the number of words examined. We may, of course, sample in a different way, e.g. by counting the items in which we are interested in a specified length of the linear sequence of letters, say, plus spaces between words and punctuations, but nothing is gained by it, since, as we have seen, samples in terms of word number are random samples of the smaller units, such as letters, phonemes, word length, etc. Indeed, this forms an important characteristic of language statistics.

In the light of the definition of random sampling given above, we must conclude that what we select or sample by, namely words, is independent of what we sample for, be it the primary linguistic units such as letters and phonemes, or the secondary linguistic characteristics such as word length. Considering now that words have meaning, and in texts are arranged according to meaning, our conclusion is in full agreement with the fundamental tenet of de Saussure mentioned at the beginning of this paragraph, namely, that the signs of language are independent of their content or meaning.

The main results of statistical linguistics as described above, namely, the independence of the quantitative characteristics of language from content or meaning, is fundamental—though seldom recognised to be so—for the whole concept of information theory. Only because of that independence is it possible that the smaller code units can be manipulated with a view to reducing the time, and with it the cost, needed for transmitting a message, without interfering with the content of the message. We may express this by using the term "Ergodicity" which originated in statistical physics.

"Ergodicity" denotes a property of certain systems which develop through time according to probabilistic laws. Under certain circumstances a system will tend in probability to a limiting form which is independent of the initial position from which it started. This is the Ergodicity Property. It may be regarded as a form of the Law of Large Numbers when applied to stationary processes.

Applied to the linguistic distributions we have in mind, we may say that no matter what the content of the message, that is no matter what the initial conditions, as time goes on the masses of words used in the message will show a sensibly stable distribution of the smallest units, letters or phonemes, in any part of the message.

3. The same applies when we sample a text—not a dictionary—for frequency of occurrence of vocabulary items. No matter which part of the text we sample, or which text by a particular writer, the Characteristic K epitomising the vocabulary-occurrence, or type/token relation, is sensibly constant, which means that the frequency

property of vocabulary is again independent of the content which necessarily differs somewhat between different parts of the text, and much more between different texts.

The above statement about independence of word length from content, although true to a large extent, is not so general as is that of the independence of letter or phoneme occurrence. Subject and style begin to exert some influence upon the use of words of different length. Such a qualification of the statement about independence is still more important in the case of frequency of occurrence of vocabulary items, indeed so much more that the Characteristic K was originally regarded as a style characteristic. However, with these provisos it is true to say that even word length and frequency of use of words—not particular ones, though—are also largely independent of content, and thus support de Saussure's tenet about the independence of sign and meaning. This does, of course, not mean that a particular word will always have the same frequency in different samples from a given text, let alone in different texts. It is only the group of vocabulary items occurring with a specified frequency which will represent approximately the same proportion of the total vocabulary in different samples or texts. Members of that group may be different vocabulary items, though a good many will be the same.

All this may seem to be more exciting to the statistician than to the linguist, until we realise what the fact that our word samples are random as regards the relative frequency of letters, phonemes, word length and vocabulary items with specified occurrence frequencies means for the use of words in speech and writing. Briefly, we may say that although speech requires primarily the choice of words to fit the thoughts we wish to express, yet its characteristic sound pattern, its speed, and with it that of thought, and its uniformity and diversity of expression are language-conditioned, and thus largely outside individual choice. Deviations from the language-conditioned pattern of sound, speed of thought, and uniformity and diversity of expression, are largely governed by chance, that is they are, as a rule, not greater than what might, with a high probability, occur on pure chance. This provides us with a standard of comparison for such language-conditioned characteristics of expression in speech and writing against which to judge a deviation which is possibly in excess of what may still be reasonably attributed to chance.

The probabilities of events of language are, as a rule, what is called "composite probabilities", i.e. consisting of (1) particular combinations of the basic probabilities, the "likelihood" of linguistic units belonging to one level ·of language structure multiplied by (2) the number of possible combinations in a sample of a given size. The statistical distribution of *language in the mass* is the series of these composite probabilities. As a rule, there is no compelling reason in *statistical linguistics* to split the probabilities up into their component parts (Book I).

Two other parts of the calculus deal each with one of these components. In statistical *information theory* (Book II), where we are still concerned with language in the mass, but now as a succession of linguistic code symbols in time, we are primarily interested in the possible number of messages that can be formed out of a given multivariate frequency distribution of such units. This means that it is not the particular pattern of the elements which mainly interests us here, but the *number of possible combinations* of joint occurrence of these units.

In the last part of the calculus (Book III), on the other hand, it is precisely the different patterns in which the units belonging to a given level of language structure may occur "in situ" or "*in the line of language*", and thus their *distribution in the linguistic sense*, which form the subject matter. The possible number of particular pattern combinations, i.e. the combinatorial coefficients of the likelihood is here a matter of minor importance.

The partition of the Calculus as outlined above is reflected in the historical development of mathematical linguistics.

After its inception as just another branch of *statistics*, viz., one dealing with problems of word frequency and style by Zipf and Yule, it was Shannon who introduced the study of the *combinatorial*, i.e. frequency component of the probabilities of stylostatistics for its own sake with his information theory, which represents the second stage of the subject. The logical completion of information theory by my theory of linguistic duality as the general *pattern of distribution* in the linguistic sense may be regarded as the third stage in the development of mathematical linguistics.

II

THE PHONEMIC FREQUENCY DISTRIBUTION

2.1 THE MULTINOMIAL THEOREM AS THE GENERAL DISTRIBUTION LAW OF PHONEMES

The statistical universe of language at each structural level is that of a multinomial population, that is a universe in which the probabilities of the different categories of the variable are given by the multinomial theorem. Basically, these are universes of qualitative linguistic variables. The probabilities according to the multinomial theorem are calculated as follows.[1]

If n is a positive integer, the expression $(x_1 + x_2 + \ldots + x_m)^n$ may be expanded as follows. To distribute the product of n factors

$$(x_1 + x_2 + \ldots + x_m)(x_1 + x_2 + \ldots + x_m) \ldots (x_1 + x_2 + \ldots + x_m)$$

we have to find the coefficients of any given term, for example:

$$x_1{}^{n_1} x_2{}^{n_2} \ldots x_m{}^{n_m}$$

where $n_1 + n_2 + \ldots + n_m = n$.

Evidently, the number of times that this particular term arises in the product is the number of n-permutations of the n units in which n_1 are alike, n_2 are alike $\ldots$ and so on. Hence by the theorem due to Montmort (1708) according to which $P = n! / p! q! r! \ldots$, the coefficient of the given term is $n! / n_1! n_2! \ldots n_m!$

Thus, finally we obtain

$$(x_1 + x_2 + \ldots + x_m)^n = \sum \frac{n!}{n_1! n_2! \ldots n_r!} x_1{}^{n_1} x_2{}^{n_2} \ldots x_m{}^{n_m} \tag{1}$$

where $n_1, n_2, \ldots n_m$ take all positive integral values for which

$$n_1 + n_2 \ldots + n_m = n$$

This result is the multinomial theorem for a positive integral index.

For the purpose of applying the multinomial theorem to linguistics, it is often advantageous to use formula (1) with the population probabilities of the linguistic units in question as the terms of the multinomial. We thus consider a random variable which can take on one of r different values, each with probability p_r, $\sum_{i=1}^{r=1} p_r = 1$. If a sample of n observations is taken from such a population,

---

[1] H. Levy and L. Roth, *Elements of Probability* (Oxford, 1936).

and $n_1, n_2 \ldots n_r$ are the numbers of observations falling into each of the r categories, and $n_1 + n_2 + \ldots + n_r = n$, then

$$(P \, n_1, n_2 \ldots n_r) = \frac{n!}{n_1! \, n_2! \ldots n_r!} \, p_1{}^{n_1} p_2{}^{n_2} \ldots p_r{}^{n_r} \qquad (2),$$

This is the probability that a sample of n phonemes from a running text with $n_1, n_2 \ldots n_r$ occurrences of phonemes 1, 2, $\ldots$ r respectively represents a random sample from the dictionary population of these phonemes with probabilities $p_1, p_2 \ldots p_r$.

It is characteristic for language that at any level or stratum of language structure there is a number of categories. If one category, say A, is considered versus all the other categories together as non-A, the multinomial is reduced to the binomial and the probability according to (2) becomes that of finding A in specified parts of literary texts, such as lines, pages, volumes. This acquires importance for the problem of linguistic sampling from literary texts.

The smaller the linguistic units, that is the more the linguistic units are removed from, or independent from, meaning, the more will their frequency distribution (in the statistical sense) conform with the probabilities calculated according to the multinomial theorem. As an illustration may serve the distribution of phoneme occurrences as used in Information theory for calculating H.

2.2   THE DERIVATION OF THE ENTROPY FROM THE MULTINOMIAL THEOREM

Let $p_1, p_2 \ldots p_r$ be the probabilities of r categories of a linguistic form and $n_1, n_2, \ldots n_r$ the frequencies with which the categories occur, and $n_1 + n_2 + \ldots + n_r = n$ where $n_1/n = p_1$, $n_2/n = p_2 \ldots n_r/n = p_r$.

By the multinomial theorem,

$$(p_1 + p_2 + \ldots + p_r)^n = \sum \frac{n!}{n_1! \, n_2! \ldots n_r!} \, p_1{}^{n_1} p_2{}^{n_2} \ldots p_r{}^{n_r}$$

The probability of a particular distribution is then given by

$$P = \frac{n!}{n_1! \, n_2! \ldots n_r!} \, p_1{}^{n_1} p_2{}^{n_2} \ldots p_r{}^{n_r} \qquad (3)$$

Denoting the relative frequencies n_1/n in the sample by p_i', we have, using Sterling's approximation to the factorial

$$\log P = -n\Sigma \, p_i' \log p_i' + n\Sigma \, p' \log p_i \qquad (4)$$

For the population value of n_i, i.e. for $p_i' = p_i$, $\log P = 0$ and $P = 1$, as it must be. For sample values of n_i, $n_i/n \neq p_i$.[2] Since the logarithm of a probability is negative, it follows that the first term of (4) taken absolutely must be greater than the second. This means that the *entropy H* calculated according to information theory from the

---

[2] $\neq$ is the symbol for "not equal to".

sample and representing the first term of our fundamental equation (3) will be, taken absolutely, greater than the second term.

In (4) the probability by the multinomial theorem is therefore shown to be the sum of two entropies, the sample entropy and the modified population entropy, and consequently we have derived the formula for the entropy according to information theory from the multinomial theorem.

Apart from the theoretical interest, this affords the possibility of new computational methods for P according to the multinomial theorem by using tables of information values of p_i (see Sect. 14.2)

III A

THE POSITION OF CHI-SQUARE IN THE SYSTEM
OF STATISTICAL LINGUISTICS

3.1   THE CHI-SQUARE DISTRIBUTION AS THE LIMITING FORM
OF THE MULTINOMIAL THEOREM

The limiting form of the probability according to the multinomial theorem can be shown (von Mises, pp. 415-8) to be for very great n

$$P = C e^{-x^2/2} \tag{5}$$

This means that the probabilities are distributed like χ^2 or that their distribution conforms to that of χ^2. The statistical parameter χ^2 is much used in practical work for characterizing deviations from the expected values or probabilities of the categories of a linguistic variable. The formula for the probability as given above means that all distributions, that is all sets of occupation numbers, for which the statistical parameter χ^2 calculated by formula (5) has the same value, will have the same probability.

Corollary: having by the multinomial theorem calculated P for a sample from a certain linguistic distribution, we can, by equating it to the limiting form for P, calculate its χ^2, and thus the probability of its having arisen from the population of the linguistic form in question through random sampling. In other words, formula (3) enables us to obtain χ^2 for testing the significance of differences between sample and linguistic population.

The relation between Chi-square and the entropy is as follows. On the one hand we have by (4) according to the multinomial theorem

$$\log P = -n \sum_1^r p_i{}' \log p_i{}' + n \sum_1^r p_i{}' \log p_i$$

On the other hand, we have by formula (5)

$$P = C \cdot e^{-x^2/2}$$

and
$$\log P = \log C - \chi^2/2$$

Equating the two expressions for $\log P$, we have

$$\chi^2/2 = \log C + n\Sigma p_i{}' \log p_i{}' - n\Sigma p_i{}' \log p_i \tag{5a}$$

How to calculate Chi-square, using information statistics, is shown in the following paragraphs.

3.2   THE RELATION BETWEEN CHI-SQUARE AND THE ENTROPY

As a rule, we are not so much interested in the precise probability of a given sample from the multinomial distribution, as in the question whether the deviations in the sample from the populations are such as to exceed certain multiples of the standard deviation corresponding to specified probabilities, and even more often in a statistic such as Chi-square, i.e. in the proportion of *all possible* random samples from a given population which would yield a Chi-square like our particular sample, or greater.

For this purpose, the relation (5a) is of great importance, since it suggests the use of information statistics for the purpose of significance testing. As will be seen, this has great advantages from the computational point of view. In general, the formula for Chi-square in terms of information statistics for a contingency table with r rows and c columns is, writing ln for the natural logarithm $\log_e$

$$2I = 2 \left[\sum_{i=1}^{r} \sum_{j=1}^{c} f_{ij} \ln f_{ij} + n \ln n - \sum_{i=1}^{r} f_i \ln f_i - \sum_{j=1}^{c} f_j \ln f_j \right] \qquad (6)$$

which is derived as follows. We start with the formula

$$R = H(i) + H(j) - H(i,j) \qquad (7)$$

as derived in Section 13.4.

R is the contingency per observation and thus a mean contingency. In order to obtain the contingency measure for the whole sample we multiply by n, and considering that χ^2 is a two-sided test, referring to both tails of the distribution, we also multiply by 2 and have, writing the terms in (7) explicitly,

$$2n \, (\Sigma \, \Sigma \, p_{ij} \ln p_{ij} - \Sigma \, p_i \ln p_i - \Sigma \, p_j \ln p_j). \qquad (8)$$

We now add and subtract within the bracket $2 \ln n$ and multiply throughout by n:

$$2 \, (\Sigma \, \Sigma \, n p_{ij} \ln p_{ij} + n \ln n + n \ln n - (\Sigma \, n p_i \ln p_i + n \ln n) - (\Sigma \, n p_j \ln p_j + n \ln n); \qquad (9)$$

$$\text{Since } n = \sum_{i} \sum_{j} n p_{ij} = \sum_{i} n p_i = \sum_{j} n p_j,$$

the expression in the bracket can be written as

$$\Sigma \, \Sigma \, n \, p_{ij} \ln p_{ij} + \Sigma \, \Sigma \, n \, p_{ij} \ln n + n \ln n - (\Sigma \, n \, p_i \ln p_i + \Sigma \, n \, p_i \ln n) -$$
$$- (\Sigma \, n \, p_j \ln p_j + \Sigma \, n \, p_j \ln n)$$

but $\ln n + \ln p = \ln n \, p$, and writing f_{ij} for $n \, p_{ij}$, f_i for $n \, p_i$, f_j for $n \, p_j$, we get finally

$$2 \, (\Sigma \, \Sigma \, f_{ij} \ln f_{ij} + n \ln n - \Sigma \, f_i \ln f_i - \Sigma \, f_j \ln f_j) \qquad (10)$$

which is the formula for $2I$ and, as has been shown, is asymptotically distributed like *Chi-square* with $(r-1)(c-1)$ degrees of freedom (Wilks, 1935, Kullback, 1959).

3.3   ADVANTAGES OF THE RELATION EXPLAINED IN SECT. 3.2
FOR COMPUTATIONAL PURPOSES

If a table of values $n \log n$ is available, it saves much labour to calculate χ^2 according to formula (6). There are certain requirements for the calculation of χ^2 as regards the theoretical numbers in the different cells of the table, none of which should be less than 5 if the χ^2 result is to be depended on (*LCC*, Sect. 5.5.2).

As a numerical illustration for using formula (6) we take 30 words of Biblical Greek which can be regarded as favourite expressions ("Vorzugswörter") in the Gospel according to Luke selected as such by R. Morgenthaler,[1] and compare their use in terms of frequency of occurrence in that Gospel with their use in the shorter Gospels according to Matthew and Mark. A negative testing result, i.e. non-significance of χ^2 would point to these words as having been used in all three Gospels to sensibly the same extent; a positive result, i.e. a significant χ^2 would lead to the conclusion that favourite expressions in Luke were not, by and large, also favourite ones to that extent in Matthew and Mark.

TABLE 1

	ἄγγελος	ἁμαρτωλός	ἀνήρ	ἀπολλύναι	γίνεσθαι	δεῖ	ἑαυτοῦ	εἰπεῖν	ἔτι	ἑτοιμάζειν	εὐλογεῖν	εὑρίσκειν	ζητεῖν	ἡγεμών	ἡμέρα
Mt.	10	5	8	19	75	8	32	182	8	7	5	27	14	19	45
Mk.	7	6	4	10	55	6	24	84	5	6	5	11	10	24	27
Lk.	20	18	27	27	129	18	58	294	16	14	13	45	25	69	83
Total	37	29	39	56	259	32	114	560	29	27	23	83	49	142	155

Continued

	θαυμάζειν	θεός	καλεῖν	κύριος	μέσος	οἶκος	ὄνομα	ὅς	οὗτος	περί	πόλις	ποῦς	πρός	τις	φωνή	
Mt.	7	51	24	80	7	10	22	122	147	28	26	10	41	21	7	1097
Mk.	4	48	11	18	5	12	15	85	78	22	8	6	63	33	7	699
Lk.	12	122	43	103	14	33	34	182	230	45	39	19	164	78	14	1989
Total	23	221	78	201	26	55	71	389	455	95	73	35	269	132	28	3785

By formula (6) we obtain Chi-square as

$$\chi^2 = 2(16{,}264.941 + 31{,}180.830 - 27{,}366.747 - 20{,}031.222) = 95.594$$

Since for $(r-1)(c-1)$ degrees of freedom, that is 58 for our illustration, Chi-square

---

[1] R. Morgenthaler, *Statistik des Neutestamentlichen Wortschatzes* (Zürich, 1958).

at the 0.01 level of probability is 88.379, it follows that the three writers differ in their use of the particular 30 words in question more than can be accounted for by random sampling, and, in particular, that favourite expressions (Vorzugswörter) of Luke were not, on the whole, also favourite expressions of Matthew and Mark.

Chi-square in terms of information statistics, that is as $2I$, can also be shown to equal $-2 \ln$ (likelihood ratio). In information-statistical terms this amounts to deriving $2I$ from the *conditional* entropy instead of from the *bivariate* entropy, the basic relations being $H_x(y) = H(x, y) - H(x)$ and $H_y(x) = H(x, y) - H(y)$. We must combine $H_x(y)$ and $H_y(x)$ because of the two-sidedness of Chi-square. This gives the quantity $H(x, y) - H(x) - H(y)$. But this is $-R$ which, as we have shown above, is transformed into Chi-square through multiplication by $2n$. Furthermore, the conditional entropy can be shown to be the information statistic corresponding to the log-likelihood ratio, from which the above relation between $2I$ or Chi-square and the likelihood ratio follows (Chpt. 14).

Attention is drawn to the difference between (5) and (6); the former relates Chi-square to a multinomial probability comprising combinatorial and likelihood components, the latter relates Chi-square to a quantity based upon the frequency component only.

The advantages of using the information statistics for calculating Chi-square are considerable from the practical point of view, since if tables of $n \ln n$ are available, only summation is required and we escape the squarings, multiplications and divisions that plague the calculator of Chi-square.[2]

The information statistic $2I$ is very simply calculated by using the table of $n \log_e n$, as given in Kullback's book on *Information Theory and Statistics* (1959).

<hr>

[2] M. Kupperman, *Applied Statistics*, IX (1960), 37—42.

III B

THE REPEAT RATE OF LINGUISTIC FORMS IN ITS RELATION TO OTHER STATISTICAL PARAMETERS

3.4   THE CHARACTERISTIC K (AND v_m) AS THE SAMPLE STATISTIC
OF THE REPEAT RATE

The repeat rate of linguistic forms is defined as the sum of the squared probabilities of the different categories belonging to that form type, and thus as the sum of the squared terms in the expression $(P_1 + p_2 + \ldots p_r)^n$ whose expansion was given in terms of the multinomial theorem in formula (2).

$$\varkappa = \sum_1^r p_i^2 \tag{11}$$

For instance, we may represent a printed language with r different alphabetic symbols as a point P in r-dimensional space with probabilities p_i as co-ordinates. Geometrically, $\sum_1^r p_i^2$ represents the square of the distance of the point P from the origin. That point lies also in the hyperplane $\sum_1^r p_i = 1$.

It follows from the definition that the repeat rate is not uniquely specified. All points which lie on the intersection of the $(n-1)$-dimensional sphere with $r^2 = \sum_1^n p_i^2$ and the plane $\sum_1^n p_i = 1$ have the same distance from the origin.

This means that the parameter would be the same for any language in which the frequency distribution of alphabetic symbols was only a permutation of the original one, i.e. any language with identically the same frequencies, but attached to different letters, which property the repeat rate has in common with Chi-square.

In the case of an equi- or rectangular distribution $p_i = \frac{1}{r}$, and we have for the repeat rate

$$\varkappa_r = \sum_1^r \left(\frac{1}{r}\right)^2 \tag{12}$$

The distribution of the repeat rate in this case approaches that of the non-central χ^2-distribution. In all other cases it is dependent upon the parameter p_i. Sometimes the repeat rate is called the coincidence constant.

Denoting by r_i the frequency of an alphabetic symbol or a phoneme ($i=1,2,3\ldots s$), by N the sum ($r_1+r_2+\ldots+r_s$) and by p_i the ratio r_i/N, a sufficient estimate of the repeat rate is given by the statistical quantity

$$K = \sum \frac{r_i(r_i-1)}{N(N-1)} \tag{13}$$

Proof:

We denote by c_m a measure of heterogeneity of the statistical population such that $c_m=p_1{}^m+p_2{}^m+\ldots+p_s{}^m$, where p_μ is the probability of occurrence of the μ-th word. Then the expectation of that parameter for which we will write $\hat{c}_m$ is given by:

$$\hat{c}_m = \frac{1}{N^{[m]}} \sum_r r^{[m]}n_r = \frac{1}{N^m} \sum_r r^{[m]} \sum_{\mu=1}^{s} \binom{N}{r} p_\mu{}^r (rp_\mu)^{N-r}$$

$$= \sum_{\mu=1}^{s} \sum_r \frac{1}{N^{[m]}} r^{[m]} \binom{N}{r} p_\mu^r (1-p_\mu)^{N-r}$$

$$= \sum_{\mu=1}^{s} \sum_r \frac{(N-m)!}{(r-m)!\,[N-m-(r-m)]!} p_\mu{}^{r-m}(1-p_\mu)^{N-m-(r-m)}\, p_\mu^m$$

$$= \sum_{\mu=1}^{s} p_\mu^m [p_\mu + (1-p_\mu)]^{N-m}$$

$$= \sum_{\mu=1}^{s} p_\mu{}^m = C_{m,\,o} \tag{14}$$

In other words $\hat{c}_m$ is an unbiased estimate of c_m.

For our case $m=2$, and we write

$$\hat{c}_2 = \frac{1}{N^2} \sum r(r-1)n_r = \frac{\Sigma_r^2 - N}{N(N-1)} \tag{15}$$

Multiplying by $(1-1/N)$ we get

$$\hat{c}\,(1-1/N) = \sum \frac{r^2}{N^2} - \frac{1}{N} \tag{16}$$

which we recognise as Yule's Characteristic. The variance of K is (de Vries, 1962)

$$\sigma_K^2 = \frac{4N\,[\Sigma p_i^3 - (\Sigma p_i^2)^2] + 6\,(\Sigma p_i^2)^2 - 8\,\Sigma p_i^3 + 2\,\Sigma p_i^2}{N\,(N-1)} \tag{17}$$

In order to use the parameter K for describing vocabulary distribution—for which purpose it was in fact originally designed by Yule—certain modifications of the original formula are advisable. The great number of vocabulary items occurring in a literary text made Yule adopt the grouped distribution of vocabulary according to frequency of occurrence, and calculate K from the grouped frequencies. Following his method, we define

$$S_1 = \Sigma\, r\, n_r$$
$$S_2 = \Sigma\, r^2\, n_r \tag{17a}$$

where n_r is the number of different words occurring with frequency r, and write Yule's constant as

$$K = \frac{S_2 - S_1}{S_1{}^2} \tag{17b}$$

In formula (17) both r and n_r are the frequencies of word occurrences and vocabulary respectively, and may by division through the corresponding totals be transformed into relative frequencies. For great samples, these relative frequencies are sensibly stable and may be regarded as estimates of the corresponding probabilities, $p_r = r/N$ and $\pi_r = n_r/n$ $(n = n_1 + n_2 + \ldots n_s)$ respectively.

Using the first transformation, we have

$$K^* = S_2/N^2 = \sum_{r=1}^{s} \frac{r^2}{N^2} n_r = \sum_{r=1}^{s} p_r^2 n_r \tag{17c}$$

and summing over the individual p_r instead of over their groups, n_r, we may write

$$K^* = \sum_{\mu=1}^{n} p^2$$

which shows K to be the repeat rate of particular words. (For a more satisfactory proof see above, formula 14.) Using the second transformation we write

$$K^* - \frac{1}{n} = S_2/N^2 - 1/n = \frac{n\Sigma r^2 n_r - [\Sigma r n_r]^2}{n\,[\Sigma r n_r]^2} \tag{17d}$$

Dividing numerator and denominator by n^3, the expression on the right becomes

$$\frac{\{\Sigma r^2 \pi_r - [\Sigma r \pi_r]^2\}/n}{[\Sigma n \pi_r]^2} = \frac{\sigma_r^2/n}{M_r^2} \tag{17e}$$

which shows K (more precisely K^*) for great n, to be equal to the coefficient of variation of the mean of the variable r.

3.5 RESTRICTIVE CONDITION OF THE GEOMETRICAL INTERPRETATION OF THE REPEAT RATE WHEN APPLIED TO LINGUISTIC DISTRIBUTIONS

The geometrical interpretation of the Repeat Rate was given without any restrictive condition. It is, however, of the greatest importance for the sensible application of geometrical methods to language structure to realise that there *is* a restrictive condition.

There exists a linkage between frequency of occurrence of words and meaning (*LCC*, pp. 97 ff). The term "words" includes here grammar words and relations. It follows that a statistic such as K, which is based directly upon frequency of vocabulary items only, derives its stylo-statistical qualities from the linkage between occurrence frequency and meaning, or between frequency pattern and particular vocabulary. That the linkage is only a statistical one, not a functional relationship, goes without saying.

It has been empirically established that the relative frequencies attached to particular words in a literary text are characteristic, to a greater or lesser extent, according to the type of words, not only of the particular text, but of the use of the vocabulary items as such. It follows that the Repeat Rate for a text will, to a great extent, depend upon its particular vocabulary. Since different writers and texts will, in general, differ in their vocabulary, they will be characterised by different repeat rates. It is this empirical fact of the sensible uniqueness of that parameter for the vocabulary comprised in a given text which justifies its use as a characteristic of style.

3.6   AN INEQUALITY RELATION BETWEEN THE ENTROPY AND THE REPEAT RATE (AND ITS SAMPLE STATISTIC K)

The entropy $H = -\Sigma\, p_i \log_2 p_i$ and the repeat rate stand to one another in an important *inequality relation* which can be used for estimating the Characteristic K from the data required for the calculation of the entropy, and thus ultimately by the multinomial theorem.

The negative entropy $-H = \Sigma\, p_i \log_2 p_i$ is the arithmetic mean of the logarithmic variable $\log_2 p$. Its antilog is, therefore, the geometric mean G of p_i. In symbols:

$$\text{Antilog}\,(-H) = G. \tag{18}$$

The arithmetic mean A of p, as a weighted average, or the expectation of p, is

$$A = \Sigma\, p_i\, p_i. \tag{19}$$

$\Sigma\, p_i^2$ is the repeat rate, i.e. the probability that two particular linguistic events, say words, selected at random from the text under consideration should turn out to be the same word.

Using the inequality between arithmetic and geometric mean

$$G \leqslant A, \tag{20}$$

we obtain the following inequality between the entropy and the repeat rate of particular events:

$$\text{Antilog}\,(-H) = G \leqslant A = \Sigma\, p_i^2. \tag{21}$$

On the other hand, it was shown above that Yule's Characteristic K is an unbiased estimate of the sum of the repeat rates for particular linguistic events $\Sigma\, p_i^2$, and equal to

$$\hat{c}_2\left(1-\frac{1}{N}\right) = \frac{S_2-N}{N(N-1)} \cdot \frac{N-1}{N} = \frac{S_2-N}{N^2} = K, \tag{22}$$

and thus tends to $p_1^2+p_2^2+\ldots$ as $N \to \infty$. It appears thus to be the repeat rate of the linguistic events in question.

We write therefore:

$$\text{Antilog}\,(-H) \leqslant K. \tag{23}$$

The essence of the result as given in formula (23) is that from a knowledge of the entropy we can obtain an estimate of the repeat rate in the form of a lower limit of that parameter. Considering now that the entropy—as shown in Section 2.2—can be derived from a set of linguistic data by the multinomial theorem, it follows that the preceding derivation amounts to the estimation of the repeat rate, or the Characteristic K by applying the multinomial theorem to a set of linguistic data.

The inequality

$$K \leqslant \text{antilog}\,(-H)$$

reveals the duality between the two fundamental measures of language statistics, K, the measure of concentration of vocabulary and H the measure of information.

We know from the structure of H that it will be the smaller, the steeper the gradient of probabilities of the unit symbols, say vocabulary items of specified occurrence frequency, the gradient being understood to have as its highest point the probability of symbols most often needed, and as its lowest that of the rarest symbols.

K, on the other hand, is the greater, the steeper the gradient of the probabilities of words with different numbers of occurrence, the highest point of the gradient being here the probability of words used once only, the hapax legomena, and its lowest point that of words used most often. It follows that K and H must be reciprocal, or dual, to one another, and since H is calculated from log p_i, whereas K from p_i (K being the repeat rate), it must be the antilog of $-H$ which stands in the inequality relation (23) to K.

The essential sameness of structure of the two parameters, H and K, consists in this that whereas H is the (negative) sum of products $p_i \log p_i$, K as the repeat rate is the sum of products $p_i p_i$, and both, H and K as sums of probabilities represent alternative probabilities. It is this essential sameness in the structure of the two parameters which led to the setting up of the inequality relation (23).

And the third important linguistic parameter, the random partitioning constant V, is again of the same form, since it is the alternative probability of a vocabulary item belonging to one part of the text only or to all such parts. The only difference from H and K in this respect is that the alternative is here one between the extremes only of the series.

IV

TWO MODIFICATIONS OF THE MULTINOMIAL THEOREM

4.1 THE BINOMIAL DISTRIBUTION

The first modification is one of reducing the number of categories of the variable in formula (1) to two only, or, more precisely, to one category, say A and another of all non-A events. In this case, the multinomial theorem goes over into the binomial theorem, and the distribution into the Bernoullian.

We assume that the events in a number of trials are all independent, i.e. that the chances p of the event happening and q of its not happening are the same for each event and remain constant throughout the trials. The case corresponds to the tossing of perfect coins. For the case of single events we expect in N trials to get N_p successes and N_q failures. In general, for N events the frequencies of successes in N sets are given by the successive terms in the binomial expansion of $N (q + p)^n$, i.e.

$$N \left\{ q^n + nq^{n-1} p + \frac{n(n-1)}{1.2} q^{n-2}p^2 + \frac{n(n-1)(n-2)}{1.2.3} q^{n-3}p^3 + \ldots \right\} \qquad (24)$$

The form of the binomial distribution depends (1) on the values of p and q, and (2) on the value of the exponent n.

If p and q are equal, the distribution is evidently symmetrical, for p and q may be interchanged without altering the value of any term, and consequently terms equidistant from the two ends of the series are equal. If, on the other hand, p and q are unequal, the distribution is skew.

If $p = q$, the effect of increasing n is to raise the mean and increase the dispersion. If p is not equal to q, however, not only does an increase in n raise the mean and increase the dispersion, but it also lessens the asymmetry; the greater n for the same values of p and q, the less the asymmetry.

This distribution provides the test function whenever we are dealing with an alternative like A and non-A events.

The Bernoullian Law enables us to state the range of variation on either side of the mean together with the probability of occurrence of deviations from the mean. If the proportion of occasions in which an event, say the letter e, is present is denoted by p, and that in which it is absent by q, so that $p + q = 1$, the average number of occasions of e occurring in a sample of n will be np, that of e not occurring nq, and the standard deviation as the measure of dispersion or variation npq. In terms of relative frequencies, the average proportion of e occurring will be p, of e not occurring q, and the standard error $\sqrt{pq/n}$.

According to the Bernoullian Law, there is a chance of $1:3$ that a deviation from the mean lies beyond once the standard error, and a chance of $1:20$ that it lies beyond twice the standard error, and finally a chance of $1:370$ that it lies beyond three times the standard error. However, we like to draw the line between probable and improbable at the .05 level of probability or at 5 times in 100, which corresponds to twice the standard deviation, since $1:20$ means that of 20 cases, one will be outside twice the standard deviation, and of 100 cases 5. Our method of testing the differences between sample and population relative frequencies consists therefore in comparing such differences with twice the standard deviation $\sqrt{pq/n}$.

4.1.1 The Poisson Distribution

As the limiting form of the binomial for a very small probability of one of the alternative events, the Bernoullian distribution goes over into the Poisson distribution.

Just as Laplace developed an approximate formula for the limiting case when numbers are very great, so Poisson arrived at the formula for the limiting case when the probability p is very small, which means that one of the alternatives (the "positive") of the event is very rare. This formula, as Bortkiewicz (1898) has shown, may fitly be called the Law of Small Numbers.

Whereas in Laplace's development p and q remain constant while n grows to infinity, Poisson assumes that p decreases with increasing n in the ratio $1/n$, that is, he assumes $a=np$ constant with increasing n. Substituting $p=a/n$, $q=1-a/n$ in the Bernoullian formula

$$W(r) = \binom{n}{r} p^r p^{n-r} \tag{25}$$

we get

$$W(r) = \left(1-\frac{a}{n}\right)^n \frac{a^r}{r!} \frac{1\left(1-\frac{1}{n}\right)\cdots\left(1-\frac{r-1}{n}\right)}{\left(1-\frac{a}{n}\right)^r} \tag{26}$$

Letting now n grow to infinity while a and r remain constant, all the single factors in numerator and denominator of the last fraction tend towards unity, and so the value of the fraction becomes unity. On the other hand, since $\left(1-\frac{a}{n}\right)^n \to e^{-a}$, we have in the limit for n

$$W(r) = a^r e^{-a}/r! \tag{27}$$

This is Poisson's formula for the occurrence of rare events. In words: The probability $W(r)$ that the alternative of the event, whose probability p is very small, will in n cases occur r times, is, for great n governed by the Poisson law, provided that $a=np$ is not great. It is to be observed that the number of possible cases n no longer enters in the equation.

This formula enables us to calculate the frequency of the event in samples of n if its basic probability p in the population is known.

The Poisson distribution occurs in linguistics in the field of language as the simple and as the compound distribution. The former is the appropriate distribution, for instance, for the gap length between occurrences of grammatical forms, the latter has been proposed by Yule as the theoretical model for the distribution of vocabulary according to occurrence frequency.

4.2 THE LOGNORMAL DISTRIBUTION OF LINGUISTIC UNITS

The transition from the multinomial theorem to the Gaussian distribution, or the normal law, is given by the fact that the multinomial theorem was used by Maxwell, and Boltzmann, for the derivation of the distribution of molecules according to energy in an ideal gas. The transition from the Gaussian distribution, or the normal law, to the lognormal distribution is outlined in the next paragraphs.

According to the Gaussian law, the probability density is given by

$$p(x) = \frac{1}{\beta\sqrt{2\pi}} e^{-\frac{(x-a)^2}{\beta}}$$
$$= \frac{1}{\beta\sqrt{2\pi}} \exp\left[-\tfrac{1}{2}\left(\frac{x-\alpha}{\beta}\right)^2\right] \tag{28}$$

($e = 2.71828 \dots .$

$\pi = 3.14159 \dots .$)

where α and β are the arithmetic mean and standard deviation, respectively.

The graph of the function shows a bell-shaped symmetrical curve with the greatest probability density around $x = \alpha$, that is around the arithmetic mean of x. Two values of x which are equally distant from the mean on the positive and negative side have the same probability density $p(x)$ which value diminishes rapidly with distance from the mean.

The cumulative distribution of the normal law (that is the sum of individuals measuring less than a stated value of the variable plotted against that value) is an s-shaped (sigmoid) curve which can be transformed into a straight line by plotting it on a grid whose horizontal ordinate is equidistant and whose vertical ordinate is spaced according to the error function (probability paper). On such a grid the arithmetic mean is obtained by projecting onto the base line the crossing point of the straight line graph for the distribution with the horizontal at $P(x) = .50$, and the standard deviation is the difference between that point of the base line and the projection of the crossing point of the straight line graph with the horizontal erected at either $P(x) = .84$ or $P(x) = .16$.

Apart from the distribution of individuals, we may be interested in that of the product of values of x by the corresponding frequency f_x and, in general, of powers of x by the frequencies f_x, that is in the distributions of xf_x, x^2f_x .... and so on. These are called the *moment distributions* of x.

Symmetrical distributions are not the rule in nature; more often distributions are skewed, that is humped to the right or to the left. A certain class of these skew distributions can, however, be transformed into symmetrical ones by using a logarithmic transformation of the variable, with all the advantages normality of distribution entails in theoretical and practical work. Such variables are called lognormal. The transformed distribution, that is the logarithmic distribution, is then a normal distribution with all the properties of the normal law. Certain modifications in the assumption for the normal law lead to the so-called lognormal distribution law.

The general, somewhat picturesque, development of the normal law and the law of elementary errors has been subjected to criticism. Even if we admit the concept of elementary errors, it is unlikely that these errors would combine purely by addition. At least, we could not assume that they would always do so. As an alternative to the hypothesis of addition, we might presume that each elementary cause merely gives an impulse to change the value of the variable. This is introducing an element of order since the value of the variable will now depend upon the immediately preceding one. The effect of this impulse might be taken as proportional to the strength of the impulse and the value of the variable at the instant the impulse is given. Under these assumptions we obtain the probability density $p(x)$ according to the lognormal distribution law as in (29).

According to the lognormal law, it is not differences of equal amount in excess or defect from a mean value which are equally likely, but ratios of equal amount in excess or defect from a mean value. Let x_1, x_2, x_3 .... x_n be a set of values of a chance variable, and y_1, y_2, y_3 .... y_n be the transformation $y = \log x$. Then if

$$p(y) = \frac{1}{\sigma\sqrt{2\pi}}\exp\left[-\frac{(y-\mu)^2}{2\sigma^2}\right] \tag{29}$$

where μ is the arithmetic mean of y and σ its standard deviation, we say that the variable x is lognormally distributed.

What is important for us is to remember that the lognormal distribution is no longer a pure chance distribution. The element of order which is interfering with mere chance is the influence of the immediately preceding event upon the following event. This being so, it is not surprising that the emergence of the lognormal distribution in the linguistic field, and more so its great importance in that field, could also be arrived at from the other end, so to speak. The lognormal law in linguistics can also be derived by starting with the order element of language in the line, mitigated by an admixture of chance.

The distribution of vocabulary according to frequency of occurrence occupies, in a way, a medium position between the distributions appropriate to qualitative and quantitative variables, insofar as it can be conceived either as a complex Poisson distribution, that is as a distribution of a qualitative variable, or as a lognormal distribution which is most appropriate for quantitative variables.

4.3 THE VOCABULARY DISTRIBUTION

Let us now apply the model for the occupancy according to the Maxwell-Boltzmann law, that is virtually according to the multinomial theorem (Herdan, 1953), to the distribution of vocabulary according to frequency of occurrence. The subsidiary conditions become in this case

$$n_1 + n_2 + \ldots + n_m = V$$
$$n_1 x_1 + n_2 x_2 + \ldots + n_m x_n = N \tag{30}$$

and

where $n_1, n_2 \ldots n_m$ are the frequencies of vocabulary items with occurrence x_1, x_2, x_n respectively; $V = $ total vocabulary and $N = $ total occurrence number or length of sample.

If we were, for instance, interested in whether by the criterion of the vocabulary frequency distribution a particular Pauline Epistle might be regarded as a random sample of the total of Paul's contribution to the New Testament, we would calculate the probability of a combination of vocabulary frequencies as in the given letter occurring on random sampling from that in the total of Paul. In doing this we neglect the question—and intentionally so—whether vocabulary items with a specified occurrence frequency x_i in the sample were identical with those having the same frequency x_i in the population. Our subsidiary conditions do not take the meaning or identity of the vocabulary items into account, only the quantitative characteristic of occurrence frequency.

If, on the other hand, we wish to answer questions which require taking into account the identity of vocabulary items in different samples from a universe, we must introduce certain alterations in the models used so far for applying the multinomial theorem to language.

Since, by supposition, we are now interested in whether two or more parts of a given total of text overlap in vocabulary, it is evident from what we know about the effect of sample length upon frequency of occurrence that we must work with equal parts or equal sample size. We then ask what is the probability of the vocabulary item occurring in one part only, of its being common to 2, 3, ... r parts into which the total is supposed to have been divided. There are thus two further subsidiary conditions for the solution of the problem, viz. that the parts into which the total of a text is divided be equal, and that the vocabulary of a part is the sum of words peculiar to it and those it has in common with 1, 2, 3 ... $r-1$ parts. In accordance with these subsidiary conditions we now develop the formula of the random partitioning function.

$$(A)+(B)+(C)+\ldots(R)=N \tag{31}$$

where (A), (B) ... are the samples of equal length in terms of number of words; and

$$v_1+v_2+\ldots v_r=n \tag{32}$$

are the words peculiar to one part (or sample), common to 2, 3 ... r parts and n the total vocabulary in the r parts together.

Denoting the population probabilities of the word categories of (32) by $\gamma_1=v_1/n$, $\gamma_2=v_2/n \ldots$, the occupancy numbers in a given, i.e. observed, vocabulary partition in a part of a literary text with probabilities γ_1, $\gamma_2 \ldots \gamma_r$ by v_1', $v_2' \ldots v_r'$ and the relative frequencies of these events in a total of n by $p_i=v_i^r/n$, we have for the probability of the observed combination of v_i'

$$P=\frac{n!}{v_1'!\,v_2'!\,\ldots\,v_r'!}\,\gamma_1^{v_1'}\,\gamma_2^{v_2'}\,\ldots\,\gamma_r^{v_r'} \tag{33}$$

and

$$\log P=-n\,\Sigma\,p_i\,\log p_i+n\,\Sigma\,p_i\,\log\gamma_i$$

Herewith we have defined the *probability* of a given vocabulary distribution in samples withdrawn from literary texts in terms of the multinomial theorem.

V

THE COMBINATORIAL STRUCTURE OF MORPHEMES

5.1 THE PATTERNING OF SEMITIC VERBAL ROOTS

This chapter is meant to be a contribution to the subject of the "Patterning of Semitic Verbal Roots" as the problem was formulated in the title of the fundamental paper by H. J. Greenberg of 1950.[1] Greenberg's paper in applying statistical methods to the data of tri-literal root patterning in the Semitic languages did not leave anything to be desired according to the state of statistical linguistics at the time when he wrote it, but Greenberg himself has stressed the need for further work when he said: "It is obvious that this is in many ways merely a preliminary attempt in a very neglected field. The conclusions stated here are, in many cases, quite tentative. The general subject of the patterning of consonantal phonemes within the morphemes in Hamito-Semitic languages would seem to be a promising subject of investigation and one whose results must be kept in mind for their bearing on the historical analysis of this family of languages."

In 1948 C. E. Shannon published his epoch-making paper on the mathematical theory of information, which it took some years to penetrate even to the statistical world, let alone that of linguists. This theory must be regarded as a valuable addition to current statistical methods when we are dealing with data from the area of language. Since Shannon's theory may be regarded as the quantification of de Saussure's treatment of language as a code and, therefore, of linguistics as a part of semiology, we shall really be applying, in the last resort, de Saussure's ideas. In the wake of information theory there came the application of combinatorial mathematics to word formation, and it is the application of these ideas to the problem of patterning of the verbal root morphemes in Arabic which forms the subject of the present chapter.

5.2 CONSONANT FREQUENCIES IN ARABIC VERBAL ROOTS

In his paper of 1950, Greenberg uses the statistical device of comparing the observed frequencies of consonant combinations in any two of the positions of tri-literal

---

[1] H. J. Greenberg, "Patterning of Semitic Verbal Roots", *Word*, VI (1950), No. 2, and the literature cited there.

TABLE 2 (Greenberg 1950)

II	?	h	ḥ	q̲	x	γ	q	k	g	r	l	n	š	ḍ	s	z	ṣ	t	d	ṭ	ṯ	ḏ	ṱ	f	b	m	w	y	
I ?	0	3	2	0	3	0	1	4	5	13	9	8	2	0	9	9	3	5	6	2	5	2	0	5	11	8	7	9	131
h	0	0	0	0	0	0	0	1	10	12	5	1	3	3	0	7	2	6	10	3	1	5	0	4	10	11	13	15	122
ḥ	0	0	0	0	0	0	8	7	10	17	11	12	9	5	9	8	9	5	9	4	3	7	4	9	10	11	16	13	196
q̲	0	3	0	0	0	0	10	8	9	15	12	12	5	6	9	9	8	9	7	9	6	7	2	8	12	11	15	14	206
x	0	0	0	0	0	0	0	0	1	15	13	8	9	6	7	7	7	4	9	8	1	3	0	8	11	9	11	7	144
γ	0	1	0	0	0	0	0	0	0	13	11	7	4	7	5	3	3	2	5	6	4	3	0	6	10	13	7	12	122
q	1	3	6	11	0	0	0	0	1	18	15	11	8	5	7	0	8	4	9	7	2	6	0	10	12	12	14	10	180
k	3	5	4	5	0	0	0	0	0	13	11	8	6	0	10	2	0	6	9	0	4	2	4	7	11	10	15	6	141
g	3	7	6	5	0	0	0	0	0	16	9	10	6	0	6	8	1	0	10	0	5	7	1	6	9	8	13	6	142
r	7	9	7	10	4	7	13	10	13	0	0	5	9	7	10	9	5	8	12	5	6	2	0	13	15	12	14	16	228
l	3	8	12	8	5	6	11	9	8	0	0	0	1	0	4	6	3	3	2	7	4	2	2	10	14	8	16	8	160
n	6	14	10	12	10	11	21	15	15	0	0	0	18	9	13	12	10	11	11	8	2	1	3	16	20	9	18	8	283
š	4	7	8	7	5	5	7	8	6	15	2	8	0	0	1	2	3	4	6	5	0	4	3	7	11	9	14	12	163
ḍ	3	4	4	3	1	3	0	0	4	10	2	5	0	0	0	0	0	0	1	0	0	0	0	3	10	5	9	8	75
s	5	8	12	8	9	1	6	6	10	12	17	14	0	0	0	0	0	4	10	5	0	0	0	13	14	12	14	8	188
z	1	5	4	7	2	2	1	4	4	7	6	8	0	0	0	0	0	0	0	0	0	0	0	4	7	7	6	9	84
ṣ	3	6	7	6	4	3	4	2	0	9	13	6	0	0	0	0	0	0	11	0	0	0	0	8	8	8	14	8	120
t	2	1	1	2	2	0	1	0	1	9	6	3	0	0	1	0	0	0	0	0	0	0	0	4	5	3	5	4	50
d	4	6	6	8	3	3	3	2	6	11	12	6	0	0	4	0	0	0	0	0	2	0	0	7	10	9	13	8	123
ṭ	0	3	6	2	2	3	0	0	0	12	10	7	1	0	1	0	0	0	0	0	0	0	0	8	8	9	10	8	90
ṯ	2	0	0	2	1	3	3	1	2	5	6	2	0	0	0	0	0	0	1	1	0	0	0	4	6	5	6	0	50
ḏ	6	3	0	4	1	0	1	2	0	9	4	2	0	0	0	0	0	0	0	0	0	0	0	2	4	4	6	6	54
ṱ	1	1	0	1	0	0	0	0	0	3	4	1	0	0	0	0	0	0	0	0	0	0	0	1	0	2	1	0	15
f	8	5	9	4	5	4	8	4	7	21	11	7	7	6	8	2	7	12	8	6	4	1	2	0	0	0	13	12	181
b	2	9	4	7	7	6	5	5	5	15	11	3	4	2	7	7	4	5	8	9	3	6	1	0	0	0	11	6	152
m	3	6	10	10	5	5	4	6	5	17	16	5	7	5	8	8	9	5	4	7	3	3	0	0	0	0	10	10	171
w	4	9	5	8	7	4	11	13	11	14	13	3	8	7	9	8	8	4	8	4	5	3	3	6	9	4	0	0	188
y	1	1	0	0	0	0	2	0	0	0	0	1	1	0	1	1	0	2	0	1	0	0	0	1	2	2	0	0	16
	72	127	123	130	76	66	120	107	133	301	229	163	108	68	129	108	90	99	156	97	60	64	25	170	239	201	291	223	

TABLE 3 (Greenberg 1950)

III	?	h	ḥ	q̱	x	γ	q	k	g	r	l	n	š	ḍ	s	z	ṣ	t	d	ṭ	ṯ	ḍ̱	ṭ̣	f	b	m	w	y	
I ?	0	6	1	0	2	0	6	5	3	14	11	10	1	3	3	1	0	2	9	4	3	1	0	8	10	10	7	11	131
h	10	1	0	6	0	0	2	3	7	12	8	4	5	3	5	2	0	7	6	2	3	1	0	4	11	9	5	6	122
ḥ	7	0	1	0	0	0	11	10	6	17	11	11	6	4	7	7	4	2	10	4	4	3	2	12	13	13	17	14	196
q̱	1	5	0	0	0	0	12	5	9	18	17	13	5	3	9	5	4	2	13	5	4	1	0	15	15	16	16	13	206
x	5	0	0	7	0	0	7	0	3	15	13	8	5	2	5	3	6	5	6	5	2	0	0	10	10	11	7	9	144
γ	0	0	0	0	1	0	5	0	2	10	9	6	2	4	5	2	4	3	4	6	5	1	3	7	7	8	14	14	122
q	6	1	10	11	2	0	1	0	0	15	9	8	4	5	9	5	8	5	11	10	3	1	2	9	14	14	7	10	180
k	8	2	9	4	1	0	1	1	1	11	8	7	6	0	6	3	0	9	11	1	5	2	1	10	14	8	5	7	141
g	8	3	6	7	0	0	1	0	0	15	11	5	7	2	5	6	1	0	11	0	2	3	2	11	11	10	8	7	142
r	10	2	12	12	5	6	11	4	3	1	15	13	4	7	8	4	5	3	14	4	8	2	1	12	16	18	16	12	228
l	11	0	8	7	3	2	9	4	9	1	0	9	4	0	6	4	4	6	7	5	10	3	4	7	12	13	4	8	160
n	11	5	16	9	8	2	9	6	11	24	17	2	13	7	13	9	6	14	9	8	8	4	2	11	18	13	14	14	283
s	5	6	5	9	5	0	9	4	3	18	8	7	1	0	5	1	4	3	5	6	2	4	1	7	14	9	15	7	163
ḍ	4	0	4	7	1	0	1	2	2	8	4	6	0	0	1	2	0	0	3	3	2	0	0	4	3	6	6	6	75
š	5	3	10	9	4	3	8	7	8	18	14	8	0	0	4	0	0	7	11	9	0	0	0	13	12	11	12	12	188
z	2	0	2	2	4	2	9	0	4	13	9	5	0	0	0	0	0	2	5	0	0	0	0	5	4	8	4	4	84
ṣ	2	1	8	10	5	5	4	4	0	11	7	5	0	0	0	0	1	3	8	0	0	0	0	8	10	9	10	9	120
t	1	4	3	4	1	0	2	2	0	6	3	3	0	0	3	0	0	0	1	0	1	0	0	3	5	6	1	1	50
d	4	2	2	7	3	2	6	5	7	14	10	10	1	1	6	0	2	0	3	0	3	0	0	5	4	8	8	10	123
ṭ	3	0	7	5	4	0	5	0	0	6	5	6	3	0	5	2	0	0	2	1	1	0	0	6	5	5	9	10	90
ṯ	1	0	0	0	0	0	0	0	4	7	7	5	0	0	0	0	0	0	1	2	3	1	0	1	6	4	4	4	50
ḍ̱	2	0	2	2	0	0	3	0	0	9	6	7	0	0	0	0	0	0	1	0	0	0	0	6	7	3	2	4	54
ṭ̣	1	0	0	1	0	0	0	0	0	4	1	2	0	0	0	0	0	0	0	0	0	0	0	3	1	1	0	1	15
f	8	6	13	9	10	3	6	5	7	14	12	4	5	4	6	3	6	6	10	1	3	3	3	1	0	11	12	10	181
b	8	4	6	10	4	2	13	2	4	20	15	6	5	4	4	2	3	6	6	3	4	1	1	0	1	5	8	5	152
m	6	1	12	8	5	2	7	3	10	16	12	11	4	5	6	3	4	8	12	8	7	2	0	0	0	0	9	10	171
w	14	2	9	10	4	2	9	5	5	17	7	4	5	3	4	6	3	5	16	3	5	1	2	7	15	11	0	14	188
y	0	0	0	1	1	0	0	1	0	1	0	3	0	0	2	0	0	1	0	0	0	0	1	0	2	3	0	0	16
	143	54	146	157	73	31	157	78	108	335	249	188	86	57	127	70	65	100	196	91	86	33	25	185	240	243	220	232	

TABLE 4 (Greenberg 1950)

III \ II	?	h	ḥ	q̱	x	ɣ	q	k	g	r	l	n	š	ḍ	s	z	ṣ	t	d	ṭ	ṯ	ḏ	ẓ	f	b	m	w	y	
?	0	0	0	0	0	0	0	2	2	11	6	5	2	0	4	0	0	2	7	0	1	0	0	3	10	8	3	6	72
h	3	3	0	0	0	0	6	2	7	16	11	7	4	2	1	2	0	4	11	2	1	0	1	2	13	12	11	6	127
ḥ	0	0	13	0	0	0	4	1	4	6	12	7	3	3	3	1	2	5	5	3	2	1	2	8	7	12	10	9	123
q̱	0	0	0	4	0	0	5	4	6	12	9	6	2	2	4	2	1	3	8	3	7	0	3	8	15	6	11	9	130
x	0	0	0	2	8	0	1	0	2	10	4	4	1	1	3	1	4	4	2	3	0	2	0	2	5	9	5	3	76
ɣ	0	0	0	0	0	0	0	0	0	8	7	1	2	2	1	2	2	1	4	2	4	0	0	1	7	8	8	6	66
q	3	2	6	7	1	0	10	0	0	10	10	5	3	1	2	1	6	3	6	5	2	3	1	6	9	6	6	6	120
k	6	1	3	3	0	0	0	9	0	12	10	5	2	1	6	5	1	4	8	0	4	0	1	4	4	9	5	4	107
g	6	2	5	8	0	0	0	0	14	17	12	10	1	0	8	5	0	0	6	0	1	2	0	6	8	10	9	3	133
r	11	6	13	16	6	2	15	9	13	23	1	6	13	8	16	7	6	6	19	10	8	1	1	15	21	17	12	20	301
l	5	5	9	13	5	4	15	9	11	0	22	1	1	1	13	0	4	10	10	8	5	2	1	16	15	15	17	12	229
n	11	2	6	7	6	0	12	3	3	3	0	24	1	0	5	5	1	4	6	3	3	1	1	10	10	8	11	17	163
š	4	0	5	7	1	1	6	3	3	11	3	3	14	0	0	1	0	0	4	4	0	0	0	6	8	9	9	6	108
ḍ	3	1	5	4	4	1	0	0	1	6	4	2	0	10	0	0	0	0	3	0	0	0	0	3	8	3	6	4	68
s	8	0	6	6	5	1	5	4	2	12	9	5	0	0	11	0	0	0	8	3	0	0	0	6	8	11	12	7	129
z	6	1	3	6	1	3	10	2	3	12	8	4	0	0	0	13	0	0	0	0	0	0	0	4	8	9	7	8	108
ṣ	2	0	3	4	1	0	2	1	0	10	9	3	0	0	0	0	12	2	8	0	0	0	0	7	9	5	5	7	90
t	6	2	5	4	2	0	4	6	2	10	7	6	2	0	0	0	0	13	3	0	0	0	0	4	4	10	6	3	99
d	7	3	9	8	3	4	5	0	5	15	5	8	2	1	8	0	0	0	19	0	2	0	0	9	6	12	12	13	156
ṭ	8	0	6	6	2	0	2	0	0	11	8	7	2	0	4	0	0	0	0	11	2	0	0	6	8	6	6	2	97
ṯ	5	0	0	0	0	1	2	0	2	10	3	2	0	0	0	0	0	0	2	0	15	0	0	2	1	5	5	5	60
ḏ	3	0	2	3	1	0	2	0	0	10	5	2	0	0	0	0	0	0	0	0	0	11	0	5	5	3	5	7	64
ı	0	0	0	1	0	0	0	0	0	4	2	0	0	0	0	0	0	0	0	0	0	0	7	3	2	3	1	2	25
f	7	4	7	7	4	1	11	2	3	19	13	9	2	4	2	3	3	7	7	2	4	1	2	19	0	0	15	12	170
b	10	4	10	9	6	5	12	6	5	20	17	14	7	4	8	3	5	9	8	12	10	3	0	0	22	1	15	14	239
m	7	2	7	10	5	2	5	4	5	20	17	13	7	4	10	9	4	9	14	4	3	0	1	0	0	23	5	11	201
w	11	9	12	12	7	4	14	7	11	21	19	14	8	6	10	7	8	9	13	7	5	6	1	16	16	12	3	23	291
y	11	7	11	10	5	2	9	4	4	16	16	15	7	7	8	3	6	5	15	9	7	0	3	14	11	11	0	7	223
	143	54	146	157	73	31	157	78	108	335	249	188	86	57	127	70	65	100	196	91	86	33	25	185	240	243	220	232	

verbal roots in Arabic, and other Semitic (Hamitic) languages, with the corresponding expected frequencies. The latter are calculated as the product of the row total (R) and column total (C) for the two consonants in question divided by the total number of roots, 3775, R being the number of roots with one consonant of the pair in question in a specified position, I, II or III, and C the number of roots with the other consonant in another position.

This means that the observed frequency of a particular combination of two consonants in two different positions is judged against the accumulated result of Arabic root formation. On the basis of this procedure, Greenberg arrives at the following conclusions for Proto-Semitic which, however, are essentially identical with what may be inferred from the numerical material for Arabic as set out in Greenberg's tables 1-3.

1. Apart from w and y, there are 4 sections of consonants, back consonants (?, h, ḥ, c, x, γ, q, k, g), liquids (r, l, n), front consonants (š, s, z, ṣ, ḍ, t, d, ṭ, ṭ, ḍ, ṯ) and labials (f, b, m). Consonants of any one section occur freely with those of any other section in the formation of tri-consonantal verb morphemes.

2. Different consonants of the same order tend not to appear in the same tri-consonantal verb morpheme, except that (a) in the section of back consonants, the velars (k, q, g) occur freely both with pharyngeals (x, c) and the laryngeals (?, h); (b) in the front section sibilants occurs fairly freely with the dental stops (ḍ, t, d).

3. The rule of the previous paragraph applies with considerable regard to positions I-II and II-III. It is less marked in I-III. There are no Arabic roots with identical consonants in the first and second position and in the first and third position, though there are a few exceptions. On the other hand, identical second and third consonants are very common.

4. The above statements apply only to the verbal root morphemes. Substantival morphemes frequently violate them.

5.3   COMBINATORIAL ANALYSIS APPLIED TO THE PATTERNING

OF ARABIC VERBAL ROOT MORPHEMES

Provided these rules are exhaustive, it should be possible to account by means of them for the number of roots in Semitic languages in general, and in Arabic in particular. This is the problem with which this chapter intends to deal, and which may briefly be formulated as the question "why are there 3775 verbal roots in Arabic?" Insofar as this chapter aims at arriving at what Greenberg has used as his basic datum, viz., the number of 3775 roots, our method will be dynamical as different from Greenberg's statistical method. We may also express this by saying that our intention is to watch the language at work, i.e. the work of word formation which gave the 3775 verbal roots as its result.

The starting point for our procedure is determined by the following consideration. Greenberg's rule that consonants of any of the four sections: back, front, liquids and labials occur freely with those of any *other* section in the formation of tri-consonantal verb morphemes contains a tacit exemption from the rule of general combinability of 26 consonants (28 minus y, w which remained outside the pattern for consonant combinations in Semitic verbal roots as given by Greenberg) of Arabic, and the starting point for our argument and computation must, therefore, be the number of all possible sets of 3 different items which can be taken from 26 different elements, which is

$$26!/23! = 15,600$$

From this must be subtracted the number of combinations which according to Greenberg's rules do not occur in Arabic, viz. combinations of homorganic consonants from the four sections. There are 9 back consonants from which $9!/7! = 72$ sets of 2 are possible, each of which could conceivably have combined with one of the other 24 consonants in position III, to give sets of 3 different consonants. This gives 1728 combinations. Since this applies to any of the three pairs of positions, I-II, II-III, I-III, the number of combinations to be subtracted on that account is $3 \times 1728 = 5184$.

Proceeding in the same way with the other homorganic sections, we calculate the number of possible, but inadmissible, combinations of the 3 liquidae as

$$(3!/0!) \times 24 = 144$$

and for the three pairs of positions as

$$144 \times 3 = 432;$$

that of possible, but inadmissible, combinations of the 11 front consonants as

$$(11!/9!) \times 24 = 2640$$

and for the three pairs of positions as

$$2640 \times 3 = 7920;$$

that of possible, but inadmissible, combinations of the 3 labials as

$$(3!/0!) \times 24 = 144$$

and for the three pairs of positions as

$$144 \times 3 = 432.$$

Together this gives 13,968 combinations to be subtracted on account of inadmissibility.

This figure is, however, to be reduced by the number of exceptions from the first exception to the general rule of free combinability between all consonants (rules 2a, 2b).

In the section of back consonants, velars (k, g, q) occur freely both with the pharyngeals (x, q) and the laryngeals (?, h) giving $3 \times 2 \times 2 = 12$ combinations each of which may occur with any of the other 24 consonants in position III, which gives 288 combinations. Since this applies to any of the 3 pairs of positions, the number of combinations to be added (or subtracted from the main subtraction item) is 864.

In the front section, sibilants (š, s, z, ṣ) occur fairly freely with the dental stops (ḍ, t, d, ṭ, ṭ, ḍ, ṭ) which gives 4×7 combinations which may combine with the 24 other consonants in position III, which gives 672 combinations. Since this applies to any pair of positions, the number of combinations to be added is 2016.

On the other hand, every one of the 15,600 combinations contains, by definition, three different consonants. In other words, it does not contain combinations with the same sound occurring more than once. Insofar, their formation is in agreement with the rule according to which there are no Arabic roots with identical sounds in position I and II, and also, largely I and III. However, identical sounds in position II and III are very common. Since the 26 combinations with identical sounds in II and III may possibly each combine with any of the 25 other consonants in position I, we must add to the number of combinations so far arrived at,

$$25 \times 26 = 650$$

Finally, the consonants, w, y, so far left out altogether, as being outside the system, and for which, therefore, Greenberg did not give any rules of combination, must also be added. It was thought best in this case, and in the absence of any such rules, to add the observed number of combinations with y, w, in any of the three positions. This gave 1170 roots.

These results set out in table form give the following picture.

TABLE 5

All possible combinations of 3 out of 26 consonants $26! / 23! = 15,600$.
    From this to be subtracted:

$$
\begin{aligned}
9!/7! &= 72 \times 24 = 1728 \\
3!/0! &= 6 \times 24 = 144 \\
11!/9! &= 110 \times 24 = 2640 \\
3!/0! &= 6 \times 24 = 144 \\
\hline
& 4656
\end{aligned}
$$

For all 3 pairs of positions	$4656 \times 3 = 13,968$	
To be reduced by second order exceptions	-864	
and	$-2,016$	
	11,088	4,512
To which must be added		650
and		1,170
which gives the calculated number of tri-literal verb roots as		6,332

5.4   THE RELATION BETWEEN THE THEORETICAL AND OBSERVED NUMBERS OF ROOT MORPHEMES

By applying combinatory mathematics in connection with the rules of formation of Arabic tri-literal verbal roots, we thus arrive at 6332 such morphemes. This means that even with Greenberg's exemptions from free combination applied strictly—which in reality they are not—there would be about $6332/3775 = 1.68$ times as many roots as we actually know. Apart from the not all-too likely possibility of verbal morphemes having been discarded with time to such an extent as to account for the difference $6332 - 3775 = 2557$, or that the rules of consonant combinations as given by Greenberg are not exhaustive, the conclusion may be that for positive reasons only $3775/6332 = 60\%$ of all admissible tri-literal combinations are used in word formation. At the first glance, it would seem that the Semitic languages, and Arabic in particular, were rather wasteful as regards the functional burdening of their phonemes in verbal morphemes. If they were, Arabic would in this respect not be worse than some European languages which very seldom utilise to 100% the available number of combinations. E.g. the number of two-phoneme words in German is 94 as against the theoretically possible calculated number of 311 words, or 30%; in French the number of two-phoneme words is 192 as against the theoretically possible number of 387, or 50%. However, as will be seen, the explanation of the observed difference lies most likely with the differential preference of the Arab tongue for particular sounds, and groups of sounds.

In calculating the number of verbal roots by combinatorial methods without any reference to differential frequency of sounds—as we have done—it is implicitly assumed that the relative frequency of sounds is not essentially different from an equi-distribution. As the following table shows, this is not true, though the gradient from high to low frequencies is not particularly striking.

TABLE 5a

Distribution of relative frequencies (in %) of the consonants in Arabic verbal roots.

r	7.7	f	4.7	d	3.7	x	2.6	z	1.8
w	6.2	c	4.3	g	3.4	ṣ	2.5	ṯ	1.8
l	5.7	y	4.2	s	3.2	ṭ	2.5	ḍ	1.8
b	5.7	ḥ	4.1	?	3.1	t	2.1	ḏ	1.3
n	5.6	š	4.1	k	2.9	σ	1.9	ẓ	.6
m	5.4	q	4.0	h	2.7				

The well-defined gradient of relative frequencies suggests the preference, or otherwise, of particular consonants in the formation of verbal roots to be a factor in their formation. We may express the effect of consonant preference, or otherwise, in terms of the entropy H (the characteristic parameter of information theory) and obtain it as

$$H = 4.480 \text{ "bits" of information}$$

against the entropy for equi-distribution

$$H' = 4.808 \text{ "bits" of information.}$$

The difference, though small, is yet a sufficient pointer to preference of particular consonants against others. The value of H is calculated under the assumption of free combination of consonants. If we were to consider the preferences for joint occurrences of particular consonants, H would be considerably reduced. However, for our argument there is no need to determine its value since the pattern of tri-literal consonant combinations gives all the required information on that point in much greater detail. Only such admissible combinations for which the Arab tongue and ear had a preference materialised as root morphemes, other combinations with less suitable consonants being formed only sporadically, instead of systematically. Whereas the preferred sounds, e.g. liquids, labials, are utilised to the full and thus made to bear the maximum functional burden, the less favoured ones are carrying less of a burden: they are not fully utilised.

All this suggests that the tri-literal combinations which for this reason did not materialise, may account for the difference between observation and expectation according to combinatory mathematics in the number of tri-literal verbal roots.

PART II

VOCABULARY AND STYLO-STATISTICS

$$VI$$

THE STUNTED DEVELOPMENT OF VOCABULARY AND STYLO-STATISTICS THROUGH UNSUITABLE MATHEMATICAL MODELS

According to the reputation which the Zipf law and its modification known as the Zipf-Mandelbrot Canonical law enjoys among many linguists, mathematical or otherwise, one would have expected an upward trend in the development of vocabulary and stylo-statistics since these laws have been promulgated, the Zipf law in 1949[1] and its modification in 1954.[2] It is now a sad fact that just the reverse is true. To the writer's knowledge, hardly any practical application has been made of these laws in the field of vocabulary statistics, in spite of their having been religiously quoted by linguists as the last word in matters concerning word frequency distributions. What is the reason for the almost complete lack of use of these models?

It will be shown that it lies in the unsatisfactory nature of their mathematical interpretation of linguistic facts, and of the mathematical models constructed so as to duplicate such facts. The relevant mathematical formulae by Zipf and Mandelbrot are unsatisfactory from both the theoretical and practical angle, moreover they do not fit the facts.

6.1 THEORETICAL SHORTCOMINGS OF THE ZIPF AND MANDELBROT LAWS

6.1.1 The Zipf law

The *Zipf law* is the supposedly straight line relation between occurrence frequency of words in a language and their rank, if both are plotted logarithmically. Mathematicians believe in it because they think that linguists have established it to be a linguistic law, and linguists believe in it because they, on their part, think that mathematicians have established it to be a mathematical law. As can be shown in a few lines, it is not a law at all in the sense in which the term is used in other sciences. If the words in the sample under consideration are arranged in descending order with regard to frequency, and the other variable is arbitrarily made a sort of inverse

---

[1] G. K. Zipf, *Human Behaviour and the Principle of Least Effort* (Cambridge, Mass., Addison-Wesley, 1949).

[2] B. Mandelbrot, "Structure Formelle des Textes et Communications: deux études", *Word*, vol. 10, pp. 1-27.

function of frequency by giving the word with the highest frequency the lowest rank, continuing with this along the series of the integral numbers, then it follows, as night follows day, that the relation between our "variables" must be an inverse one. It is true, the relation need not have turned out to be such as to approach the bilogarithmic straight line relation, but, as a matter of fact, it does not do so, and even if it did, this would not make it any more a law in the strict sense of the term. That the decrease of frequency should be related to an increase in rank follows, not from any natural property of language structure, but merely from the fact that the word with the highest frequency is given the lowest rank, and as the frequency decreases the words are given correspondingly higher ranks. Thus, the inverse relation between frequency and rank which is at the basis of the Zipf law is one of our own making. Rightly seen, the Zipf law is nothing but the arbitrary arrangement of words in a text sample according to their frequency of occurrence. How could such an arbitrary and rather trivial ordering of words be believed to reveal the most recondite secrets, and the basic laws, of language?[3]

Apart from the fact that it cannot be regarded as a law connecting two linguistic variables, because there is only one independent variable, the other being a mere transformation of it, the form of the Zipf law leads to certain impossible conclusions. It implies that the product of the frequency of occurrence of a word F and its rank R is a constant C. Zipf now claimed that the products $F \times R$ were all of the order $\frac{1}{10}$, and that the law therefore assumes the form $F = 1/10\,R$, at least for English. This statement is repeated in the literature as if it were an established fact, by linguists and scientists alike (Brillouin)[4] although examination on even a limited scale shows that it is simply not true. If it were, it would lead to the absurd conclusion that every word sample contained 12,000 different words regardless of length, since it takes about 12,000 terms of the series $\frac{1}{10} + \frac{1}{20} + \frac{1}{30} \ldots$ to equal unity.

Proof:

$$\frac{1}{10} + \frac{1}{20} + \ldots + \frac{1}{10\,R} = \frac{1}{10}\left(\log_e R_{\max} + \gamma\right) = 1$$

where γ is Euler's constant

$$\log_e R_{\max} = 10 - \gamma = 9.4$$
$$R_{\max} = e^{9.4} \sim 12,000$$

It follows that according to the Zipf law, every sample examined must contain the same vocabulary, 12,000 words! To overcome these contradictions, modifications of the Zipf law were suggested, in particular that R should be raised to some specified power. Neither of these modifications have, so far, proved satisfactory.[3]

---

[3]   *TTM*, Sects. 1.6, 1.7.
[4]   L. Brillouin, *Science and Information Theory* (New York, 1956).

6.1.2 *The Mandelbrot canonical law*

Since *Mandelbrot's canonical law* is originally only a modification of the Zipf law supposed to change the straight line relation into a curve which is more in accordance with the observed facts, all the objections against the bilogarithmic relation between occurrence frequency of words and rank which have been raised against the Zipf law apply fully also to the Mandelbrot law. The unscientific nature, if not futility, of the frequency-rank relation is best brought out by comparison with a physical law of essentially the same form. As is well known, the relation between volume and pressure in an adiabatic gas can be represented as an equi-lateral hyperbola in a co-ordinate system, one of whose co-ordinates, say x, represents the volume, and the other, say y, the pressure. The formula is then $xy = $ const. On a bilogarithmic grid, the relation would, of course, plot as a straight line.

It is easily seen that both formula and graph of the volume-pressure relation are closely similar to those for the word frequency-rank relation. But there is a great difference. The value of the volume-pressure relation consists in this, that it enables us to estimate either the volume for a specified pressure, or the pressure for a specified volume, of the gas under certain conditions. Both, volume and pressure, are independently observed, and a specified value of one enables us to estimate the corresponding measure of the other variable.

Nothing of this is possible according to the Zipf-Mandelbrot law. There is no way of independently obtaining the rank of a word from which to estimate the frequency, simply because the rank of the word results only from having first arranged all the words, including the one we have in mind, according to their frequency. And vice versa, although the frequency of a word can be directly observed by counting the number of occurrences, again we cannot give an estimate of the rank of that word until the frequency observations for all words in the text have been done, and the frequency-rank curve has been properly set up.

All this is a consequence of the "rank" not being a linguistic variable at all, but only a mathematical transformation of the occurrence frequency.

6.1.3 *Substitution of 'Cost' etc. for 'Rank'*

So far, the original version of the Mandelbrot Canonical Law.

But now comes a step in Mandelbrot's modification which is contrary to even the elementary rules of co-ordinate geometry. Feeling that "rank" was not a real variable and, in fact, had no linguistic meaning, Mandelbrot substituted for it first "coût" (cost) and later "word length" and "occurrence frequency", always arguing as if the curve described by the formula remained identically the same in spite of the change in the variable. Now this is against the fundamental ideas of co-ordinate geometry. If the word distribution curve is described by a function of r, $f(r)$, r being the rank of the individual words, then any change in the independent variable, especially any substitution of another variable in place of r will, in general, change the function f, and with it the curve. The "Canonical Law" can, therefore, not be expected to hold any longer.

This is where the great fault of Mandelbrot's argument lies. *His whole argument is based upon the tacit assumption that the substitution of another variable in place of r would leave the formula, and thus the curve, identically the same.*

If in place of such an assumption, the empirical values of word length and occurrence frequency are plotted, it is at once evident that the law does not hold. The resulting empirical curves are toto genere different from the original Zipf law and its modification by Mandelbrot, since instead of the one-to-one correspondence of word frequency and rank, we now have the grouped distribution of vocabulary items with the same length in terms of letter or phoneme or syllable number, and of vocabulary items occurring with the same frequency.

6.2   SHORTCOMINGS FROM THE PRACTICAL ANGLE

(a) Quite apart from the theoretical shortcomings of both the Zipf and the Mandelbrot law, and apart from the fact that neither of these laws agrees with the facts, let us now consider what is required for the application of either of these laws to actual numerical data. The Zipf law has one parameter, and its modification by Mandelbrot has three. The application to numerical data requires the calculation of these parameters, and since the essence of statistics is comparison, it requires the comparison of these parameters as obtained from different masses, e.g. from different languages. But here comes the main defect of both models from the practical angle: *their authors have forgotten to take the possible influence of sample size upon the parameters into account.* It is simply an empirical fact that the word frequency distribution changes its shape with sample size, which must have the consequence of the parameters changing accordingly. Without taking this into account, comparisons are valid only between samples of the same size from the different languages, or different texts, and quite useless for more general comparisons. Until the influence of text length (sample size) upon the parameters, and thus the transformation formulae when changing the sample size, are known, these models are of no practical use. This goes far to explain the absence of numerical work in this field in the last decade, and with it the stunted development of vocabulary and stylo-statistics.

The importance of the neglect of sample size in what is meant to be an essentially statistical model of a linguistic process cannot be over-rated. To anybody acquainted with statistics, it need not be emphasized that the neglect of the influence of sample size upon a statistical relation makes the mathematical model unsuitable. To the linguist not acquainted with statistics, this will not be so obvious. In order to make the importance of sample size in mathematical models of this type clear, let me refer him to the fact that what led to the derivation of one of the best parameters of vocabulary statistics, Yule's Characteristic K, was the desire, and the need, to have a parameter of word frequency which is independent of the sample size (See Sect. 10.4). It was found before that neither the arithmetic mean, nor the standard deviation, had retained that property, characteristic for them, when applied to word frequency distributions.

(b) A brief consideration of the true nature of the pseudo variable "rank" and the variable "word length" shows that the substitution of word length for rank means abandoning the double-logarithmic law. The scale of "rank" is theoretically infinite and even for only a moderately large text extends to over 10,000.

Word length, on the other hand, even if expressed in terms of the ultimate linguistic units of the spoken or written language—phonemes or alphabetic symbols—, does not exceed, at any rate for our Western languages, 12-15 units, and in fact tails off very quickly after a peak at, say, 3-5 units. The discrepancy in dispersion between the two variables, frequency and word length, makes it impossible that their relation should be satisfactorily fitted by the bilogarithmic straight line law. Since each length category comprises a number of items, all of the same length—such numbers being quite appreciable for the lower length categories—, but with different frequencies, the co-ordinate representation of all the items belonging to one category will be a straight line vertical to the word length axis, and instead of a straight line graph for the distribution in that range, we would get a rather pronounced step-wise descent of the line.

Moreover, it is established practice in modern scientific procedure that if a mathematical model is used for the explanation of an observed relation—as in this case—the "goodness of fit" is tested by an appropriate test function, say Chi-square. Yet nowhere in the relevant literature have I come across such a test carried out on the Mandelbrot law, with "cost" or "word length" or "frequency" as the dependent variable.

$$* \ * \atop *$$

That the very serious shortcomings of the Mandelbrot canonical law should have escaped the attention of Mr. Warren Plath, the author of "Trends in European and American Linguistics 1930-1960" (Utrecht, 1961) admits of only one explanation, viz. that Mr. Plath is not really familiar with mathematical statistics and, in particular, with the mathematical technique of curve-fitting. His article, as far as it deals with the Mandelbrot law, is quite uncritical and merely a repetition of the claims which Mandelbrot himself has made for his canonical law, thus treating it with the respect due only to a Pontifical Law.

VII

A CRITICAL EXAMINATION OF SIMON'S MODEL OF CERTAIN DISTRIBUTION FUNCTIONS IN LINGUISTICS

For mathematical models to be of real value it is necessary that (1) the relation of events of which the mathematical structure is to be a model should be as the mathematician believes it to be, (2) that the assumptions needed for constructing the model should be sensible, i.e. in accordance with how the operations in question take place, and (3) that the formulae derived in this way should fit the observed facts. None of these requirements must be neglected if the model is to fulfil its purpose. It is now a sad fact that model construction in mathematical linguistics seems dogged by the neglect of one or the other of these requirements, especially the first, which cannot but have in its wake the neglect of the other two.

Since the mathematics of these model structures are, as a rule, beyond the non-mathematical linguist, such models are often taken on trust, even by linguists with some experience of statistical procedures. If that trust is misplaced because of the model not really being what it purports to be, the model, instead of fulfilling a useful purpose and encouraging practical numerical work on language data will prove sterile. This has happened with the Zipf-Mandelbrot law and, more recently, with Simon's model of certain skew distribution functions in linguistics.[1]

Simon starts with describing the characteristics of the skew distributions for which he wishes to construct a "model". He ascribes to them three main characteristics:

(a) They are j-shaped in reverse or, at least, highly skew, with very long upper tails. The tails can generally be closely fitted by an empirical function of the form

$$f(i) = (a/i^k)^{b^i} \tag{1}$$

where $f(i)$ is the number of words occurring i times and a, b and k are constants, b being usually so close to unity that the final factor has no significant effect on $f(i)$,

[1] Herbert A. Simon, "On a class of skew distribution functions", *Biometrika*, 42 (1955), pp. 425-440.

except for very large values of i. Thus, according to Simon, the number of words that occur exactly i times in James Joyce's *Ulysses* can be fitted by a formula such as a/i^k;

(b) The exponent k is greater than 1, and in the case of word frequencies, is very close to 2; in this case, formula (1) becomes, with b close to unity,

$$f(i) = a/i^2$$
$$i^2 f(i) = a \qquad\qquad (2)$$

In words: the product of the squared frequency of occurrence and the number of vocabulary items with such frequency is a constant for all values of i;

(c) In the case of word frequencies, the function (1) describes the distribution not merely in the tail, but also for very small values of i. In this case, the ratio of *hapax legomena* to total vocabulary, $f(1)/V$, where $V = \sum_{1}^{n} f(i)$ is generally in the neighbourhood of $\frac{1}{2}$, and the rate of dislegomena to hapax legomena, $f(2)/f(1)$, is generally in the neighbourhood of $\frac{1}{3}$.

These are, according to Simon, the characteristics of word frequency distributions.

Remembering requirement (1) for the construction of satisfactory mathematical models, we ask: "does this picture of word counts correspond to the facts?" As will be now shown in detail for criteria (b) and (c), it does not.

I have not aimed at "random illustration" from the extensive literature in the field, but the following selection of instances from four different languages: Biblical Greek, Latin, English and Russian, is as far from any conceivable bias as I can make it.

In order to ascertain the extent to which Simon's characteristic (b) and, in particular, his dictum that in the case of word frequencies k is close to 2, correspond to the facts, we shall now apply formula (2) to five different word counts (See Table 6).

It is evident from Table 6 that Simon's characterisation of word count distributions under (b) does not correspond to the facts. The products $i^2 f(i)$ are far from being constant for a given word count; in fact, the quantity increases systematically in the first term of the series and the tail values are altogether greatly in excess of the other terms, which, in addition, is at variance with Simon's statement that for word frequencies function (1) also fits the extended tails.

Regarding criterion (c), it may be seen from Table 6a that although the values given by Simon for $f(1)/V$ and $f(2)/f(1)$, viz. $\frac{1}{2}$ and $\frac{1}{3}$ respectively, are not closely reflected in the empirical results, yet, by and large,—and with the exception of the New Testament—$f(1)/V$ appears to lie between .4 and .5 and $f(2)/f(1)$ between .3 and .4. I shall return to this point in Sects 7.2 and 7.4.

TABLE 6

Referring to criterion (b)

In this table, $i^2 f(i)$ is calculated for the first ten and the last five items of certain word frequency distributions.

i	New Testament (Greek)[2]	Imitatio[3]	Macaulay's Essay on Bacon[3]	Pushkin "The Captain's Daughter"[4,5]
1	$1 \times 1934 = 1934$	$1 \times 520 = 520$	$1 \times 990 = 990$	$1 \times 2384 = 2384$
2	$4 \times 842 = 3368$	$4 \times 174 = 696$	$4 \times 367 = 1468$	$4 \times 847 = 3388$
3	$9 \times 470 = 4230$	$9 \times 111 = 999$	$9 \times 173 = 1557$	$9 \times 433 = 3897$
4	$16 \times 322 = 5152$	$16 \times 70 = 1120$	$16 \times 112 = 1792$	$16 \times 238 = 3808$
5	$25 \times 221 = 5525$	$25 \times 37 = 925$	$25 \times 72 = 1800$	$25 \times 146 = 3650$
6	$36 \times 173 = 6228$	$36 \times 33 = 1188$	$36 \times 47 = 1692$	$36 \times 114 = 4104$
7	$49 \times 123 = 6027$	$49 \times 20 = 980$	$49 \times 41 = 2009$	$49 \times 82 = 4018$
8	$64 \times 110 = 7040$	$64 \times 28 = 1792$	$64 \times 31 = 1984$	$64 \times 79 = 5056$
9	$81 \times 107 = 8667$	$81 \times 11 = 891$	$81 \times 34 = 2754$	$81 \times 41 = 3321$
10	$100 \times 79 = 7900$	$100 \times 14 = 1400$	$100 \times 17 = 1700$	$100 \times 39 = 3900$
Last	$2713^2 \times 1$	$172^2 \times 1$	$65^2 \times 1 = 4225$	$479^2 \times 1$
five	$2771^2 \times 1$	$196^2 \times 1$	$76^2 \times 1 = 5776$	$528^2 \times 1$
items	$5534^2 \times 1$	$210^2 \times 1$	$81^2 \times 1 = 6561$	$724^2 \times 1$
	$8947^2 \times 1$	$242^2 \times 1$	$89^2 \times 1 = 7921$	$777^2 \times 1$
	$19734^2 \times 1$	$418^2 \times 1$	$255^2 \times 1 = 65025$	$1160^2 \times 1$

TABLE 6a

Referring to criterion (c)

This table gives the ratios $f(1)/V$ and $f(2)/f(1)$ for the 4 works used in Table 6.

	New Testament (Greek)	Imitatio	Macaulay's Essay on Bacon	Pushkin: "The Captain's Daughter"
$f(1)/V$	$1934/5436 = .36$	$520/1168 = .45$	$990/2048 = .48$	$2384/4783 = .50$
$f(2)/f(1)$	$842/1934 = .44$	$174/520 = .33$	$367/990 = .37$	$847/2384 = .36$

7.2   SIMON'S MODEL OF CERTAIN SKEW DISTRIBUTION FUNCTIONS
TESTED ON LINGUISTIC DATA

On the basis of his assumptions about word frequency distributions, Simon arrives at the expression

---

[2]   R. Morgenthaler, *Statistik des Neutestamentlichen Wortschatzes* (Zürich-Frankfurt am Main, 1958).

[3]   G. Udny Yule, *The Statistical Study of Literary Vocabulary* (Cambridge University Press, 1944).

[4]   H. H. Josselson, *The Russian Word Count* (para. 5 by B. Epstein) (Detroit, 1953).

[5]   *LCC*, Sect. 3.3.

$$f(i) = AB(i, \rho + 1) \tag{3}$$

where A and ρ are constants and $B(i, \rho + 1)$ is the Beta function of $i, \rho + 1$:

$$B(i, \rho + 1) = \int_1^0 \lambda^{i-1}(1-\lambda)\,d\lambda = \frac{\Gamma(i)\Gamma(\rho+1)}{\Gamma(i+\rho+1)}(0 < i; 0 < \rho < \infty) \tag{4}$$

Since for large i, and for any constant c

$$\frac{\Gamma(i)}{\Gamma(i+c)} \simeq i^{-c}, \tag{5}$$

we have from (4), as $i \to \infty$

$$f(i) \simeq A\,\Gamma(\rho+1)i^{-(\varrho+1)} \tag{6}$$

Therefore, Simon says, the distribution (3) approximates the distribution (4), through the range in which b of (1) is close to 1, which he regards as empirically true for word distributions. Further, if ρ is positive, k will be greater than 1, as required by (b), and if ρ is equal to 1, k will be equal to 2. In the latter case we will have

$$f(i) = \frac{1}{i(i+1)}, \text{ when } \sum_{i=1}^{\infty} f(i) = 1, \tag{7}$$

so that since $f(1) = \frac{1}{2}$ and $f(2) = \frac{1}{6}, f(2)/f(1) = \frac{1}{3}$, and $f(1)/\sum_1^{\infty} f(i) = \frac{1}{2}$, as required by (c).

We shall now test what may be regarded as the most important result of Simon's derivation, indeed as the embodiment of his "model". From formula (7) we have

$$i^2 f(i) + if(i) = 1 \tag{8}$$

Since the sum on the left of formula (8) is identically the same for every i, summing over all i will give on the right n, if n is the number of word classes according to occurrence frequency i.

In order to express (8) in terms of the absolute frequencies of words with particular occurrence i, we multiply by the total of vocabulary items in the sample, $\sum_{i=1}^{n} f(i) = V$, and obtain

$$i^2 f(i) + if(i) = V, \tag{9}$$

where $f(i)$ now stands for the *number* of words with occurrence frequency i.

Summing over all i, we get

$$\Sigma\, i^2 f(i) + \Sigma\, if(i) = nV \tag{10}$$

But the terms on the left constitute the nominator plus $2\,\Sigma f(i)$ in the formula for the quantity K defined by Yule

$$K = \frac{\Sigma i^2 f(i) - \Sigma if(i)}{[\Sigma if(i)]^2}, \tag{11}$$

and are, therefore, equal to $K\,[\Sigma\ if(i)]^2 + 2\Sigma\ if(i)$ or $KS_1^2 + 2\,S_1$, if by S_1 we denote the first moment of the word count distribution. We can therefore test nV against the value which is equal to the left-hand side of Simon's equation (10). If Simon's equation (8) were true for the whole range of i, then nV must be equal to $KS_1^2 + 2S_1$ which is, in fact, calculated from the whole range of i (see Table 7).

TABLE 7

Test of Simon's Equation

	K	nV	$K S_1^2 + 2 S_1$
Nouns in Imitatio	.008 42	$68 \times 1168 = 79\ 424$	586 068.3
Nouns in Macaulay's Essay on Bacon	.002 72	$50 \times 2048 = 102\ 400$	701.833.9
Nouns in St. John's Gospel. A.V.	.016 15	$35 \times 353 = 12\ 355$	86 112.6
All words in Pushkin's "The Captain's Daughter"	.006 03	$84 \times 4783 = 401\ 772$	4 986 270.4

The discrepancy between theory (Simon's formula) and observation is such as to invalidate Simon's claim that his model really fitted word frequency distributions in the whole range of the variable.

In order to see whether Simon's formula, in spite of being unsuitable for describing the whole word count distribution, may yet have some restricted validity for certain values of i, we list in Table 8 the quantities calculated by formula (3) in the range $i = 1$ to $i = 10$. These values may be regarded as the theoretical values corresponding to the empirical ones of Table 6. Each value listed there in lines 1-10 has been "corrected" by adding $if(i)$ to give Table 8. The order of magnitude of the five last values in each series is such that the correction can have no appreciable effect and they are, therefore, not listed. Inspection of Table 8 shows that the theoretical series of V-values can hardly be regarded as constant. The sum of the $i^2 f(i)$ and $if(i)$ does not for every i equal the number of vocabulary items, as suggested by Simon's formula. However, for a small range of i, say between $i = 1$ and $i = 5$, there is some degree of stability in the theoretical values of V, which here also appear to be more or less close to the observed vocabulary size.

This makes it quite clear where the fault of Simon's model lies. It was conceived on the basis of a superficial picture of what word counts are like by fixing the attention mostly upon the small values of i.

The fact that the ratios $f(2)/f(1)$ and $f(1)/V$ are not too far from the theoretical values of $\frac{1}{2}$ and $\frac{1}{3}$ as expected by Simon's formula, and the fact that for some of the word counts (e.g. from Pushkin's novel) Simon's formula gives a fairly constant value of V for a small range of i, which value is close to the observed number of vocabulary items, seems to indicate that Simon's formula has some degree of validity for the start of the curve from $i = 1$ to, say, $i = 5$, or thereabout, but not, as it is

TABLE 8

Listing the theoretical values of V calculated by formula (75)

i	New Testament (Greek)	Imitatio	Macaulay's Essay on Bacon	Pushkin, "The Captain's Daughter"
1	3868	1040	1980	4768
2	5052	1044	2202	5082
3	5640	1332	2076	5196
4	6440	1400	2240	4760
5	6630	1110	2160	4380
6	7266	1386	1974	4788
7	6888	1120	2296	4592
8	7920	2016	2232	5688
9	9630	990	3060	3690
10	8690	1540	1870	4290

claimed, for the whole curve and for the extended tail. This is typical for many attempts at fitting word count distributions by a comparatively simple formula: each such formula may be moderately suitable for a particular comparatively small range of the variable, but fails to describe the curve along the whole range of the occurrence frequency as its variable.

From all this the conclusion may be drawn that the whole of the extended distribution which, moreover, changes its shape with time or text length—a fact completely forgotten by Simon—is evidently not a homogenous curve obeying one simple function, but the result of the superimposition of a number of functions.

7.3   THE CONCEPTUAL ASSUMPTIONS UNDERLYING SIMON'S MODEL

In order to set up a mathematical model, the mathematician has to make certain assumptions which, if not obvious, must at least be sensible for the phenomenon in question. Since, as we have seen in Section 7.1, Simon's ideas as to word distributions do not really correspond to the facts, we can hardly expect that the particular assumptions he is going to use for setting up his model will be appropriate to the phenomenon in question. That this is so will now be shown in detail.

Simon makes two assumptions for the construction of his stochastic model:

Assumption 1. The probability that the $(r+1)$-st word is a word that has already appeared exactly i times is proportional to $if(i,r)$—that is, to the total number of occurrences of all the words that have appeared exactly i times.

Assumption 2. There is a constant probability, α, that the $(r+1)$-st word be a new word—a word that has not occurred in the first r words.

Assumptions 1 and 2 describe a stochastic process in which the probability that a particular word will be the next one written depends on what words have been written previously. Simon's assumptions clearly presuppose not only a continuous text, but a piece from the beginning up to a certain point. Otherwise, it would make no sense to speak of the "probability of the $(r+1)$-st word having appeared exactly i times", and of the "constant probability α that the $(r+1)$-st word be a new word—a word that has not occurred in the *first r* words".

However, the word frequency distributions which Simon mentions—and many others which he did not consider—are not from continuous text samples; for instance, the word frequency lists of English by E. L. Thorndike and I. Lorge (1937) and Eldridge (1911) and for French by Van der Beke (1929) are composite distributions of samples from quite different texts, and for such distributions Simon's assumptions make no sense, since we cannot speak of the "$(r+1)$-st word" in the whole distribution if for each particular text sample that word is a different one. Moreover, even when the sample is from one text only, the method of stratified sampling which is here generally used in order to spread the sample evenly over the whole text—for which purpose it is culled from a number of disconnected pages—implies that Simon's assumptions do not fit.

Moreover, the sample may even be selective in the sense that only nouns are considered (Yule, 1944) or verbs or other grammatical categories.

7.4   A NEW MODEL BASED UPON VOCABULARY CONNECTIVITY

It is now a remarkable fact that neither the compounded mass of the word frequency distribution, nor its selectivity as regards grammatical categories, has any disturbing influence upon the characteristic properties of such distributions. More precisely, we may compound different word frequency distributions from the same language at the same time of its development into one overall distribution, or we may split an overall frequency distribution characteristic for a given language into parts, i.e. into partial word frequency distributions, without altering the mathematical characteristics of the distribution function.

There is only one distribution function which has this property, and this fact can be used for identifying the mathematical structure of word frequency distributions. As Feller (1957) has shown, it is the compound Poisson distribution which has this property. The compound Poisson distribution:

$$\left\{h_j\right\} = e^{-\lambda t} \sum \frac{(\lambda t)^n}{n!} \left\{ f_j \right\}^{n*} \tag{12}$$

where $n*$ denotes the n-fold convolution of f_j, has the generating function:

$$(s,t) = e^{-\lambda t + \lambda t \, f(s)}, \tag{13}$$

which has the remarkable property that

$$h(s;t_1 + t_2) = h(s;t_1)h(s;t_2). \tag{14}$$

In an intuitive way we may describe this as follows. With each period of duration t there is associated a random variable with generating function $h(s,t)$ which we call the contribution of that period. The contributions of two non-overlapping periods are independent, which means that a partitioning $t = t_1 + t_2$ of a period into two parts induces a decomposition $\mathbf{X}(t) = \mathbf{X}(t_1) + \mathbf{X}(t_2)$ of the total variable into a sum of two independent variables. This assertion is contained in the following theorem (which is a special case of an important general theorem by P. Levy concerning arbitrary probability distributions):

If $\{h\}$ is infinitely divisible, its generating function can be written in the form (13), and it can be shown that *only the compound Poisson* distribution has this property.

Illustrations

In order to demonstrate the divisibility of word frequency distributions with retention of the essential characteristics of the total, we turn our attention to the characteristic ratios $f(1)/V$ and $f(2)/f(1)$ for such distributions (Table 9).

TABLE 9 [6]

Divisibility of Word Distribution in New Testament

	New Testament	Matthew	Mark	Luke
$2f(1)/V$	$\dfrac{3868}{5436} = 0.712$	$\dfrac{1340}{1691} = 0.792$	$\dfrac{1268}{1345} = 0.942$	$\dfrac{1942}{2055} = 0.945$

	John	Acts	Paul	Hebrews	Revelation
	$\dfrac{751}{1101} = 0.681$	$\dfrac{1886}{2038} = 0.925$	$\dfrac{2280}{2648} = 0.861$	$\dfrac{1150}{1038} = 1.108$	$\dfrac{620}{916} = 0.676$

For the whole *New Testament*, it is advisable to calculate the ratio $6f(2)/V$ not only from the *dislegomena*, but also from the *trislegomena*, according to formula (15) and take the average. We then have $6f(2) = 5052$ and $12 f(3) = 5640$, with a mean of 5346.

	New Testament	Matthew	Mark	Luke
$6f(2)/V$	$\dfrac{5346}{5436} = 0.983$	$\dfrac{1656}{1691} = 0.979$	$\dfrac{1314}{1345} = 0.976$	$\dfrac{2112}{2055} = 1.027$

[6] R. Morgenthaler, *Statistik des Neutestamentlichen Wortschatzes* (Zürich-Frankfurt a/M., 1958).

John	Acts	Paul	Hebrews	Revelation
$\dfrac{718}{1101} = 0.652$	$\dfrac{2010}{2038} = 0.986$	$\dfrac{2632}{2648} = 0.995$	$\dfrac{996}{1038} = 0.960$	$\dfrac{990}{916} = 1.080$

We see that the characteristic ratios are roughly the same for the whole *New Testament* and for any of the eight parts considered. If we continue the process of sub-division, for instance, for Paul's letters, we have

TABLE 10

Subdivision of word frequency distribution for two of Paul's Letters

	Romans	Corinthians
$2f(1)/V$	$\dfrac{1158}{1068} = 1.084$	$\dfrac{878}{967} = 0.908$
$6f(2)/V$	$\dfrac{942}{1068} = 0.882$	$\dfrac{1044}{967} = 1.078$

Since we thus find the word frequency distribution function characterised by the property of (a) combinability and (b) divisibility without altering the essential mathematical characteristics of the distribution function, and since it is only the compound Poisson distribution which has this property, we must conclude that the mathematical structure of the word frequency distributions is of the compound Poisson type, and that Yule's hypothesis to that effect, which Simon thinks is not suitable, was correct.

7.5 VOCABULARY PARTITION AS THE STRUCTURE OF MEANING UNDERLYING THE WORD FREQUENCY DISTRIBUTION

But Yule's accident hypothesis is a solution a posteriori. It was from the word frequency distribution as given that he constructed his hypothesis. It is, therefore, only a statistical solution which will hardly satisfy the linguist. Yule's λ's standing for the basic occurrence frequencies in groups of words are not easy to interpret linguistically, and the frequency hypothesis of word occurrence has, therefore, its opponents among linguists.[7] Even when the fact of statistical stability of such distributions is admitted, it is argued that they are not linguistically relevant, but are only the outcome of general statistical properties of the material or physical features of language, not of language itself. To counteract this argument, we must keep in mind

---

[7] M. Halle, *Kratylos*, III, 20 (1958).

that although the samples from one text or from different texts combined into one overall distribution are statistically independent, they yet have a common underlying structure: the word code of the given language, which is the counterpart in the plane of *expression*, to the concatenation of concepts, in the plane of *content*. And this would seem to be the reason why distributions with different origin could combine into one homogeneous distribution of essentially the same type. Briefly, we may express this by saying that word frequency distributions are *statistically independent, but semiologically connected.*

We shall now show that the pattern of word connectivity in different samples of one text or in samples from different texts provides a truly linguistic interpretation of the peculiarity of the word distribution function, and the mechanism by which it arises. The full explanation would involve an exposition of the *Random Partitioning Function* of vocabulary among samples or texts. However, so that this Section shall not be made inordinately long, the argument will here only be developed in outline and the reader is referred for greater detail to Chpts. XVI-XVIII and *TTM*, Chpts. III and XVII.

It is a characteristic property of the word code that if a text is divided into $2, 3 \ldots n$ equal parts, or if equal-sized samples from $2, 3 \ldots n$ different texts are analysed with regard to vocabulary, the number of words peculiar to one part or sample, common to $2, 3 \ldots n$ parts can be calculated from the frequency distribution function resulting from the combination of all parts or samples by a chance procedure called the "random partitioning function". This is the statistical way of arriving at those numbers. However, the dynamic process for the numbers of words to accumulate takes place, of course, during the composition of the text, and the accumulated word frequency distribution is only the statistical end result. We must always keep these two aspects, the statistical and the dynamical, well in mind.

The general pattern of the vocabulary connectivity between parts is as follows. The classes of one-sample and all-sample words are the most numerous classes, the former being the larger of the two; the average number of words peculiar to a combination of samples decreases as the number of samples included in the combination increases until a minimum in class frequency is reached for words of the middlemost class; from then on, the class frequencies rise again but in such a way that the classes have slightly greater frequencies than the symmetrically corresponding classes on the other side of the distribution.

In particular, there are characteristic constants for certain classes or groups of classes. The ratio of the sum of one-sample words plus all-sample words, i.e. of words peculiar to a sample and common to all of them, to the sample vocabulary, is a constant for a given number of divisions. In other words, it depends only upon that number. For instance, for division of a word frequency distribution into three parts, the ratio referred to is about 70%, for division into four parts it is between 55% and 60%, for five parts about 50%, for nine parts somewhat over 30%, and so on.

Furthermore, whereas the one-sample words in the total distribution are about one-half of the total vocabulary (provided that the number of parts is not too small), indicating a one-to-one balance between one-sample and two-or-more sample words together, there is a similar balance between two-sample words and the rest, i.e. three-or-more sample words, the ratio again approaching $\frac{1}{2}$ as the number increases. In terms of the total vocabulary V, the two groups are about $\frac{1}{6}$ and $\frac{1}{3}$.

Illustrations

The relationships between one-sample words, two-sample words, and the total vocabulary are exemplified by Tables 11 and 12. The basic data for Table 11 are in reference *TTM*, Chapter XVII and for Table 12 in reference footnote 3.

TABLE 11

Partition of Greek New Testament, or of portions of it

	3 Parts	5 Parts	9 Parts (Paul)		9 Books (Whole New Testament)	
$\dfrac{V}{\text{one-sample words}}$	$\dfrac{901}{610}=1.477$	$\dfrac{1271}{858}=1.481$	$\dfrac{2648}{1415}=1.871$		$\dfrac{5436}{2626}=2.070$	
			Obs.	Theor.*	Obs.	Theor.*
$\dfrac{V}{\text{two-sample words}}$	$\dfrac{901}{181}=4.978$	$\dfrac{1271}{217}=5.857$	$\dfrac{2648}{460.8}=5.747$	$\dfrac{2648}{475.2}=5.572$	$\dfrac{5436}{978.5}=5.555$	$\dfrac{5436}{918}=5.922$

* Calculated by the Random Partitioning Function.

TABLE 12

Partition into four parts

	Sampling experiment on Macaulay's essay on Bacon	Four of Macaulay's Essays	Four Works by Bunyan
$\dfrac{V}{\text{one-sample words}}$	$\dfrac{2048}{1138}=1.800$	$\dfrac{3543}{1698}=2.087$	$\dfrac{2246}{1250}=1.797$
$\dfrac{V}{\text{two-sample words}}$	$\dfrac{2048}{405}=5.057$	$\dfrac{3543}{772}=4.589$	$\dfrac{2246}{446}=5.036$

This shows the corresponding relations for the word frequency distribution to be, by and large, the reflection of vocabulary connectivity between the parts of a text as a consequence of the properties of the word code.

The value of the ratios in question are reasonably close to the theoretical values for the word frequency distribution, namely 2 and 6 respectively, considering that they cannot be expected to equal these values exactly. Although the relation between the word frequency distribution and the vocabulary partition as given by the random partitioning function is such that the *hapax legomena* are the statistical source for most of the one-sample words and the *dislegomena* the source for most of the two-sample words (though not quite to that extent as in the first case), yet it is only when the division is continued into smaller and smaller parts, that a very close approach of the corresponding classes of words in both the frequency distribution and the random partitioning function can be expected, and even then only for very small values of i only.

In the limit, when the parts are so small as to comprise only the words peculiar to a part and the words in the next group, i.e. the words common to two parts, these words will, by and large, correspond to the *hapax legomena* and the *dislegomena* of the word frequency distribution, respectively, the former correspondence being closer than the latter because, as observed above, the *hapax legomena* have the one-sample words as their main and only source, whereas the *dislegomena*, although having the two-sample words as their main source may yet also derive from words with frequency 3 and more. This is, of course, how the relation can be described in a dynamical way, that is during the accumulation of the word frequency distribution. Statistically, when we start from the word frequency distribution, we should have to describe the hapax legomena and dislegomena as the respective sources for the one-sample and two-sample words.

This replaces Simon's idea of an abstract probability mechanism as accounting for the characteristic ratios for small values of i in the word frequency distribution by *vocabulary connectivity* as the result of the concatenation of concepts or, as we say today, the structure of meaning, which is in full agreement with de Saussure's idea of language as "un système où tout se tient".

The essence of this way of accounting for the peculiar features of word frequency distribution is that in place of Simon's stochastic model, we have used the theorem that word frequency distributions, though statistically independent, are yet semiologically connected.

VIII

POETRY AND STRUCTURAL LINGUISTICS

8.1 A CRITIC REFUTED

The role which structural linguistics has to play in poetics is still underrated and often grossly misunderstood by literary scholars. In a review of "Style in Language" by Thomas A. Sebeok (Editor), in *The Times Literary Supplement*, Friday June 30th, 1961, the reviewer quotes Roman Jakobson as saying: "Poetics deals with problems of verbal structure ... Since linguistics is the global science of verbal structure, poetics may be regarded as an integral part of linguistics", and adds: "Professor Jakobson may think he has proved a point here: in fact he has merely moved his language around in a slightly confusing way," and "One piece of equivocation, one sleight of hand, and the whole question of the place of values in art has gone into the waste paper basket." According to the reviewer, the transition from linguistic structure to poetry is nothing but "a piece of verbal jugglery."

Rightly understood, it is nothing of the kind. It is an attempt to trace the integral effect, which we call "style", in the use of words as the elements of the language code at any moment of composition. In other words, one tries to see "style" as the integral effect of a particular linguistic behaviour in the use of the smaller and smallest elements of the linguistic code as its differentials. This is far from "verbal jugglery". It is indeed the very principle of what mathematicians call the Calculus, by means of which the phenomena of nature are conceived to be the integral effect of certain changes in the last elements of the process in question as differentials, e.g. the temperature of a gas as the macroscopic effect of the average velocity of its molecules.

So much about the formal side of the misconception. In the matter itself, the reviewer inclines to the opinion that "style can be intelligently talked about only as one aspect of a complete discourse or group of discourse", by which he evidently means particular authors and groups of authors according to time of linguistic development. Since the reviewer agrees that authors can be distinguished with regard to style, and that similarities in that respect justify their grouping into style categories, it is at once evident that it is arbitrary to stop here, and refuse to inquire whether such "groups of discourse" have not something in common, and thus arrive at style characteristics of still greater generality. This does not mean, as the reviewer believes, establishing an abstract "style in language", but only the greatest possible empirical generalisation of the concept of style as an important part of the tactics of language. It is only through tracing the literary phenomenon to our behaviour in using the smaller and smallest linguistic elements, that generalisation is achieved. This leads to the distinction between style- and language-conditioned elements in what we usually call "style".

8.2 VARIATION IN SHAKESPEARE'S METRICAL STYLE SUBJECTED TO STYLO-STATISTICAL ANALYSIS

For substantiating R. Jakobson's dictum that "Poetics deals with problems of verbal structure", and that "Since linguistics is the global science of verbal structure, poetics may be regarded as an integral part of linguistics",[1] I have chosen certain characteristic changes of Shakespeare's metrical style between different types of play, and with time.

Shakespeare's metrical style has been studied to a tremendous extent. To utilise the whole body of collected data is not possible. Most of it has to be rejected either as not being reliable enough, or as having no chronological value. Of the available metrical data the variation of stress and pause and any redundant final syllables seemed the most promising for the purpose of chronology, that is of change of metrical style with time. The most easily distinguishable type of stress variation are the redundant final syllables. The figures (col. 1, Table 13) for these are taken from an investigation by Fleay.[2] As regards pausation, it is almost certain that Shakespeare's language became less and less formal with the growing complexity of his thoughts, which has its structural counterpart in a marked tendency to end a speech in mid line, and this may result either in unsplit lines with pauses and fully split lines. The data in col. 2 and 3 of Table 13 are taken from E. K. Chambers "William Shakespeare".[3] Since all these counts will obviously vary with the total number of speech lines in a play, this is taken as a fourth variable (col. 4, Table 13, After Fleay).

Before tackling the question of chronology, let us first examine in detail the figures of Table 13. Since, as remarked above, the figures will be dependent upon the length of play in terms of the number of lines, the percentages of variables x, y, z, are also entered. Fixing our attention upon variable y, fully split lines, mere inspection of the table reveals a remarkable phenomenon. The plays themselves are arranged according to the supposed time of production as established by methods of literary criticism. The percentage figures for full split lines show, on the whole, a trend with time increasing, by and large, with the chronological sequence of the plays. But there are distinct exceptions to that rule where the percentage leaps up significantly above the neighbouring values. This is the case for Richard III, Romeo and Juliet, Merchant

---

[1]   Roman Jakobson, "Linguistics and Poetics", in *Style in Language*, quoted above.
[2]   F. G. Fleay, "On Metrical Tests as applied to Dramatic Poetry", *New Shakespeare Society*, Vol. I (1874).
[3]   E. K. Chambers, *William Shakespeare* (Oxford, 1930), Appendix II: Metrical Tables.

of Venice, Julius Caesar, Hamlet, Othello, Anthony and Cleopatra. What all these plays have in common is that they are tragedies and, as such, stand apart from both the comedies and the historical plays. It is true that tragedies like King Lear, Macbeth, Antony and Cleopatra, should also show such peak values, but they are not so clearly marked, for the simple reason that they are all chronologically later plays and, as such, have higher percentages of the variable in question which partly obscures their particular peak value as tragedies.

TABLE 13

	(1)		(2)		(3)		(4)	
	x	%	y	%	z	%	w	%
1. Henry VI 2	332	10.49	13	.41	270	8.54	3162	.66
2. Henry VI 3	366	12.60	8	.28	340	11.71	2904	.49
3. Henry VI 1	191	7.13	17	.64	233	8.70	2677	.81
4. *Richard III*	638	*17.62*	66	*1.82*	423	*11.69*	3619	1.38
5. Comedy of Errors	198	11.14	8	.45	171	9.62	1777	.65
6. Titus Andronicus	200	7.93	17	.67	303	12.01	2523	.83
7. Taming of the Shrew	208	14.41	21	1.46	194	13.44	1443	1.12
8. Two Gentlemen of Verona	269	11.73	43	1.88	174	7.59	2292	1.32
9. Love's Labour's Lost	26	.93	11	.39	79	2.83	2785	.57
10. *Romeo and Juliet*	168	*5.50*	71	*2.33*	496	*15.38*	3050	1.31
11. Richard II	258	9.35	34	1.23	293	10.62	2757	1.11
12. Midsummer Night's Dream	59	2.71	28	1.29	131	6.02	2174	1.08
13. King John	151	5.88	64	2.49	357	13.89	2570	1.37
14. *Merchant of Venice*	325	*12.23*	79	*2.97*	369	*13.88*	2658	1.51
15. Henry IV, 1	92	2.90	43	1.35	235	7.39	3176	1.09
16. Henry IV, 2	221	6.41	43	1.25	208	6.03	3446	1.10
17. Much Ado about Nothing	145	5.13	35	1.24	126	4.46	2825	1.10
18. Henry V	363	10.73	31	.92	219	6.47	3381	1.02
19. *Julius Caesar*	410	*16.55*	129	*5.21*	437	*17.64*	2477	1.77
20. As You Like It	23	.81	34	1.19	177	6.19	2856	1.11
21. Twelfth Night	167	6.21	44	1.64	161	5.98	2690	1.23
22. *Hamlet*	528	*13.43*	194	*4.94*	552	*14.04*	3929	1.73
23. Merry Wives of Windsor	54	1.79	9	.30	41	1.36	3018	.46
24. Troilus and Cressida	463	13.24	133	3.8	439	12.56	3496	1.64
25. All's Well that Ends Well	349	11.76	138	4.65	316	10.65	2966	1.72
26. Measure for Measure	377	13.37	148	5.23	398	14.11	2820	1.77
27. *Othello*	679	*20.47*	268	*8.08*	694	*20.92*	3316	2.00
28. *King Lear*	580	*17.42*	243	*7.30*	691	*20.76*	3328	1.92
29. *Macbeth*	420	*19.94*	246	*11.68*	494	*23.45*	2106	2.11
30. *Antony and Cleopatra*	666	*21.77*	470	*15.36*	935	*30.59*	3059	2.24
31. Coriolanus	710	20.84	394	11.57	749	21.99	3406	2.16
32. Timon of Athens	334	14.07	145	6.11	404	17.02	2374	1.82
33. Cymbeline	799	23.93	393	11.76	1027	30.75	3339	2.15
34. Winter's Tale	675	21.96	330	10.73	699	22.73	3074	2.13
35. The Tempest	472	22.89	227	11.01	481	23.32	2062	2.10
36. Henry VIII	374	32.05	179	15.34	437	15.53	1167	2.12

x = redundant final syllables   z = unsplit lines with pauses
y = fully split lines   w = total number of speech lines

Inspection of the percentage series of the variable z (unsplit lines with pauses) provides, by and large, good support for these findings and so does, though to a lesser extent, the percentage series of variable x (redundant final syllable). It may therefore be concluded that the metrical characteristics considered here, and especially those of fully split lines (y) and unsplit lines with pauses (z) may be regarded as prominent characteristics of Shakespeare's *tragedy* style. This shows how valuable even the simple inspection of a percentage series of metrical characteristics can be.

8.3 THE CHRONOLOGY OF SHAKESPEARE'S PLAYS AND DISCRIMINANT ANALYSIS

For the purpose of chronology, the Indian statistician M. R. Yardi[4] has combined the numerical data in series 1-3, Table 13, by the method of discriminant analysis (R. A. Fisher). The method is too complicated to be set forth here, and I will only give the results. According to discriminant analysis a parameter called the "discriminant score" can be calculated. Its essence is that if the 36 plays are divided into a number of groups according to the time of production, the discriminant score is calculated in such a way as to make differences between the groups as large as possible. Column 4 shows the scores for the 36 plays and the trend with time of production is quite unmistakable, but even here the tragedies are outstanding.

For the purpose of estimating the time of production of a given play from its score, it is first necessary to arrive at a decision as to the form of the relation between the discriminant score and time. As it turns out, the relation can be taken to be linear. From the linear regression equation estimates can be made as to the chronology of the different plays.

Valuable though this is, it should not be forgotten that the linear trend between the different metrical characteristics, and also the discriminant score, on the one hand, and time on the other, is only an overall trend on which are superimposed the significant fluctuations due to the different type of play—troughs for the comedies and also for the historical plays, and peaks for the tragedies proper.

8.4 THE RECURRENCE OF INITIAL PHONEMES

In order to show phoneme recurrence to be of importance in literary work, we shall develop the argument in connection with the well-known feature of alliteration in verse.

Alliteration through repetition of the initial letter of verse lines is a well-known prosodic device. E.g. it is part of Welsh poetic technique (of Dafydd ap Gwilym etc.)[5] to begin verses with the same letter. They are known in Welsh as the "Cymeriadau",

[4] M. R. Yardi, "A Statistical Approach to the Problem of Chronology of Shakespeare's Plays", *Sankhya, The Indian Journal of Statistics*, Vol. VII, pp. 263-8 (1945/46).
[5] An eminent Welsh poet of the 14th century. See T. Parry, *The History of Welsh Lit.* (Engl.trans.), Chapter V.

and are a very ancient characteristic of traditional poetic composition. According to the Red Book of Hergest,[6] they are as old as the concatenation and the rhyme in Welsh. Sir J. Morris-Jones says that the old bards wished to mark the beginning of a line with certain letters as well as the end of it with rhyme, and this device was employed mnemonically, as it were, carrying the beginning of one line to the next, etc.[7] The same letter may be kept throughout the poem.

A similar phenomenon is known to occur in Hebrew poetry, both ancient and medieval cf. the alphabetic schemes in Lamentations i-iv. The Old Testament contains several acrostic poems and the general law of these acrostics is that the initial letter of each section must follow the order of the alphabet and that the sections devoted to each letter should be of approximately the same length, viz. Lamentations c iii, where each of the three lines of each section begins with the same letter; cf. Eccles. i 13-30.[8] On reading the Georgics of Vergil, one is struck by the extremely common occurrence of couplets (triplets) of verses beginning with the same letter.

Before, however, jumping to conclusions about such repetitions of initial letters being a deliberate product and thus being a characteristic device of the poet's style, one must make certain that the repetitions are not due to chance. It goes without saying that there must be repetitions of initial letters and that by mere chance the gaps between them may be so small as to give the impression of a deliberate pattern. What is, therefore, required, is to separate the part chance plays in such repetitions, from that played by deliberation.

Moreover, it is one thing to have the impression, or even to know, that the poet has used alliteration of the initial sounds of verse lines as the means of his poetic style, and quite another to establish a definite *pattern* of such repetition of initials. By "pattern" we mean that he had a preference for gaps of specified length between the repetitions of initial sounds.

It is with this problem in mind that the repetitions of line initials in Vergil's Georgics were examined. For both suggestion and material I am indebted to Mr. E. Wyn Roberts, Cambridge.

8.5   A METHOD FOR ESTABLISHING THE PATTERN OF REPETITION
OF INITIAL LINE PHONEMES

It was observed in Section 8.4 that the initial letters of the hexameters of Vergil's Georgics seem to occur in systematic combinations which do not seem likely to be

---

[6] The Red Book of Hergest is an early corpus of Welsh poetry from c. 6th Cent. to c. 1450. The Cymeriadau are seen everywhere in the poetry, e.g. E throughout in "Eiry mynyd gwynt a berth..."; G in "Gorwyn blaen onn...". There seems to be a "Virgilian" type of alternation in Taliesin's (Cent. 6th) "Grogy gogyfercheis..." e.g. lines II ff. KJKVK, DSD... DYD... etc., etc., cf. Dafydd ap Gwilym, "Cyngor y Biogen" AMADAABACAAC.

[7] Viz. Sir J. Morris-Jones' Cerdd Dafod (Welsh Poetic Art) pp. 290 ff. This word according to the authorities on the subject derives from the Welsh "cymeryd" = to take, i.e. the letter is taken (by the memory) from one verse to the next.

[8] G. B. Gray, *The Forms of Hebrew Poetry*, pp. 8, 24, 88, 244 ff., 267 ff.

accidental. To establish whether these combinations were accidental or whether they were due to an intention on the part of the poet, the following method was adopted.

We consider the intervals or gaps between repetitions of a particular linguistic unit along the line. The gaps themselves may be in terms of any sort of linguistic unit. They may be in terms of letter-, phoneme-, word-number, or in terms of larger units.

TABLE 13a

Gap frequencies in Vergil's Georgics

Gaps	Book	A	B	C	D	E	F	G	H	IJ	L	M	N	O	P	Q	R	S	T	UV	CQ
XX	1	11	0	3	0	3	0	0	0	6	1	1	3	0	0	2	0	3	2	1	8
	2	11	0	0	0	2	0	0	2	4	0	0	8	0	3	2	0	3	0	1	4
	3	3	0	4	1	2	0	0	0	9	0	0	3	0	3	1	0	5	2	2	8
	4	7	0	3	1	7	1	0	0	7	0	3	0	3	3	3	0	5	5	2	11
X1X	1	10	0	0	0	7	1	0	1	5	0	1	5	0	1	4	0	6	4	4	8
	2	11	0	1	0	6	2	0	2	4	0	0	2	1	3	2	0	7	1	0	8
	3	8	0	1	0	4	1	0	4	6	0	0	3	1	5	1	0	11	4	1	1
	4	3	0	4	1	5	0	0	1	10	0	0	2	0	4	3	0	4	0	3	11
X2X	1	8	0	2	0	2	0	0	0	4	0	0	2	0	1	1	0	5	2	3	4
	2	1	0	4	0	1	4	0	0	7	0	1	3	0	5	0	0	4	0	0	5
	3	7	0	6	0	2	0	0	0	3	0	0	4	0	2	0	0	1	1	1	8
	4	4	0	0	1	6	3	0	0	8	0	0	0	0	2	1	0	7	3	0	1
X3X	1	2	0	2	0	1	0	0	0	7	0	1	2	0	2	0	0	6	1	2	3
	2	6	0	2	0	7	1	0	0	2	0	0	3	0	2	0	0	4	2	0	3
	3	4	0	4	0	1	0	0	1	5	0	0	0	0	1	2	0	3	1	0	9
	4	7	0	3	3	2	0	0	3	2	0	0	3	2	1	0	2	2	1	2	6
X4X	1	3	0	2	1	4	0	0	1	1	0	1	1	0	1	1	0	2	2	1	6
	2	1	0	4	0	3	0	0	1	4	1	1	5	0	2	5	1	1	1	0	9
	3	12	0	5	0	2	0	0	0	3	0	0	2	0	1	2	0	3	2	0	8
	4	4	0	2	0	1	1	0	2	3	0	1	2	0	0	2	0	2	0	2	6
X5X	1	2	0	1	0	2	2	0	0	3	0	0	1	0	0	3	0	3	0	0	2
	2	5	1	2	1	3	1	0	2	1	0	0	3	0	2	1	0	6	1	0	3
	3	5	0	1	0	0	1	0	0	4	0	0	2	0	1	1	0	3	1	1	3
	4	4	0	1	0	1	0	0	2	4	0	0	0	1	4	3	0	1	2	1	5
X6X	1	3	0	2	1	4	1	0	0	0	0	0	3	1	0	2	0	2	1	0	3
	2	5	0	3	0	1	3	0	0	2	0	0	3	0	1	5	0	3	0	0	10
	3	4	0	1	0	1	0	0	1	3	0	3	4	0	8	2	0	5	0	0	5
	4	4	0	4	1	2	0	0	0	1	0	1	0	1	3	2	0	2	1	2	9
X7X	1	3	0	0	0	2	2	0	1	3	0	1	0	0	1	0	0	2	0	1	2
	2	5	0	1	2	2	0	0	2	2	0	1	2	0	2	0	0	1	2	1	0
	3	1	0	0	1	3	0	0	1	4	0	0	0	0	1	1	0	4	2	0	1
	4	4	0	1	0	2	0	0	1	7	6	0	1	1	2	2	0	3	1	0	5
X8X	1	3	0	0	2	4	1	0	1	3	0	1	5	0	1	0	0	3	2	0	0
	2	0	0	0	0	2	0	0	0	3	0	0	2	0	2	0	0	4	2	1	0
	3	3	0	4	1	1	0	0	0	2	0	1	1	0	0	1	0	0	1	1	8
	4	6	0	1	1	4	0	0	0	3	0	1	3	0	0	3	0	2	2	3	1

such as lines or even pages, all depending upon the frequency of repetition of the unit in question. However, in order to apply the method with precision, it is advisable to measure gap length, that is the length of the interval, in terms of the sites occupied by the unit in question.

The site to be occupied by the linguistic unit in whose repetition we are interested is here that of the initial letter. Successive initials, though actually separated by a whole line minus the initial letter, are considered to be in neighbouring sites. This is not only in accordance with the definition of "site" as that of the initial letter, but also because the line length is simply constant throughout and thus without influence upon the "gap lengths" in which we are interested.

In the analysis of intervals, the text must be regarded as a continuous sequence of places, sites, to be occupied by the unit in terms of which the length of interval is expressed. For two successive occurrences of the unit, we say that the interval is zero, if they are separated by one site we say that the interval length is 1, and so on. We shall symbolise the gap lengths $0, 1, 2, \ldots$ by XX, X1X, X2X $\ldots$, respectively, where X stands for a specified letter. Table 13a gives the frequency of gaps of different length between line initials in Vergil's Georgics.

We are interested in the numerical distribution of intervals with respect to length in terms of the number of sites. In order to decide whether the distribution of gap length for a particular unit in a certain text is the result of intention on the part of the writer, or better, due to his particular style, or whether it is the result of chance only, we require the chance distribution as a standard of comparison.[9]

We consider the occurrence of a particular unit whose probability is p. The probability then of its non-occurrence is $1-p$. By taking the unit's occurrence as the starting point of the distribution, we actually start with a definite point on the line of discourse. The "probability" of its occurrence in this point is tantamount to certainty, and thus equals unity. The probability of the next site to be occupied again by the same type of unit is p, and the probability thus of two neighbouring sites being occupied by the same unit is, according to the multiplication theorem of probability,

$$p_o = 1.p = p \tag{15}$$

The probability that the two following sites will be occupied by the unit in question and another unit—implying a gap of length 1—, is

$$p_1 = p_o(1-p) = p(1-p) \tag{16}$$

For three successive sites—implying a gap of length 2—we have

$$p_2 = p(1-p)^2 \tag{17}$$

and the probability of r empty sites between two successive occurrences—or gaps of length r—of the unit in question, is

$$p_r = p(1-p)^r \tag{18}$$

TTM, Sect. 11.1.

The probabilities of gaps of different length between the line initials are calculated according to formulae (15)-(18) using the probability p for the different letters of the alphabet, as shown in Table 14 (in percent).

8.6   APPLICATION TO VERGIL'S GEORGICS

TABLE 14

Relative frequencies for all initial phonemes in the four books of Vergil's Georgics

	Book				Av.	Probabilities (in %)
	I	II	III	IV		
A	67	68	68	65	67.00	12.25
B	2	5	6	1	3.50	.64
C	32	32	47	37	37.00	6.76
D	21	16	21	22	20.00	3.67
E	51	49	42	58	50.00	9.14
F	21	27	15	20	20.75	3.79
G	5	1	3	4	3.25	.59
H	20	31	22	24	24.25	4.43
IJ	52	48	64	66	57.50	10.51
L	11	7	14	6	9.50	1.74
M	18	15	16	17	16.50	3.02
N	39	52	42	28	40.25	7.36
O	9	13	7	22	12.75	2.33
P	26	38	53	40	39.25	7.18
Q	27	31	26	36	30.00	5.50
R	5	10	7	6	7.00	1.28
S	48	52	58	47	51.25	9.37
T	31	27	32	35	31.25	5.71
UV	29	20	23	32	26.00	4.75
CQ	59	63	73	73	67.00	12.25
Total	514	542	566	566	547	
Grand total			2188			

TABLE 14a

Gap frequencies for selected initials (in %)

	A	E	IJ	Q	S	T
XX	17.8	13.8	17.9	15.3	12.5	17.3
X1X	17.8	21.5	17.3	16.9	21.8	17.3
X2X	11.1	10.8	15.1	3.4	13.4	11.5
X3X	10.6	10.8	10.9	3.4	11.7	9.6
X4X	11.1	9.8	7.6	16.9	6.2	9.6
X5X	8.9	5.8	8.2	13.6	10.1	7.6
X6X	8.9	7.9	4.2	18.6	9.5	3.8
X7X	7.2	8.8	11.0	5.1	7.8	9.6
X8X	6.7	10.8	7.6	6.8	7.0	13.5

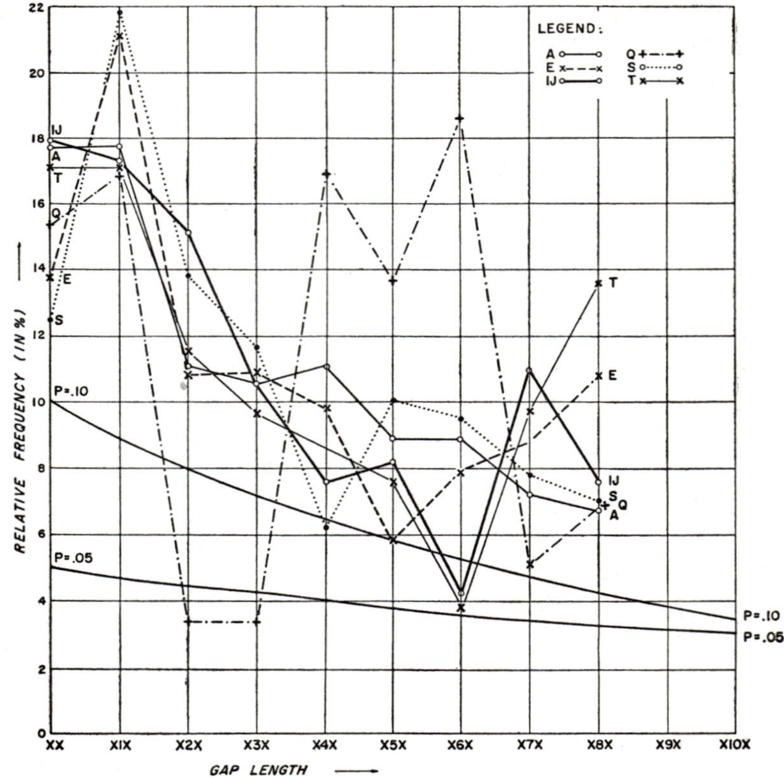

Fig. 1.

The comparison between observed and expected gap frequencies is best shown in graphical form (Figure 1). The expected frequencies as calculated by formulae (1)-(4) are represented as continuous curves in a co-ordinate system with gap length as the abscissa and frequency as the ordinate. Such curves are the continuous lines in Figure 1 for $p = .10$ and $p = .05$ respectively. Against these lines are plotted the observed relative frequencies of gap length for selected line initials (Table 14a).

The curves for $p = .10$ and $p = .05$, that is the curves for the probability distribution of gaps between letter occurrences if the letters have exactly the probability $p = .10$ and $p = .05$ respectively, could be used, strictly speaking, as standards of comparison for actual gap occurrence only if the initials in question had the same probabilities $p = .10$ and $p = .05$. The completely correct method would therefore be to construct a line of comparison for the precise probability which each letter has in the whole text, but that would make the graph anything but easy to read. An approximate method was therefore adopted. Since the letters IJ have a combined probability of $p_{IJ} = .1051$ (last col., Table 14), the chance distribution of $p = .10$ may serve as an approximate standard of comparison. This applies also to the letters A with probability

$p_A = .1225$, E with probability $p_E = .0914$ and S with probability $p_S = .0937$. Similarly, for the letters Q and T which are close to .05, with probabilities $p_Q = .0550$ and $p_T = .0571$, we can use the continuous line for $p = .05$ for purposes of comparison.

Even so, the graph gives the information we require. It can be seen that for the letters mentioned above, it is mainly the patterns XX, X1X, X2X in which the observed figures exceed by far, and significantly so, the chance frequencies. The remaining patterns are, by and large, also in excess of the chance distribution, but not very much so.

This leads to the conclusion that the attention of the poet and, of course, the reader, was fixed upon the initials of successive lines and the lines distant by one or two spaces. It also shows that it is the X1X pattern, that is the frequency of gaps of length 1, which for E is preferred by the poet to any other pattern, since it exceeds by far even the otherwise preferred patterns XX (gap length 0) and X1X (gap length 2). Not so for A and IJ, which show no striking difference between X1X on the one hand and XX and X2X on the other.

Conclusions

A mathematical method has been devised for deciding whether the repetitions of initial line phonemes in a given poet are accidental or in conformity with a definite pattern.

On the basis of the theory developed in Sect. 8.5 it may be regarded as established that the repetitions of initial verse line phonemes in Vergil's Georgics cannot only be regarded as a deliberate use of the device of alliteration, but as revealing a definite *pattern* through preference for repetition of line initials in gaps of a specified length, We may now enquire about other possibilities which this knowledge holds for us, firstly in our study of Vergil's poetry other than the Georgics; secondly, over a wider range of the study of Latin poetry in general. Regularity in the repetition of initial phonemes seems to occur also in Lucretius, Tibullus, etc., but so far no statistical investigation has been made. Perfunctory examination of the Bucolics and the Aeneid seems to show that the frequency of occurrence of specified gaps between repetitions of the same initial letter is here not so pronounced as in the Georgics. But it still remains to be verified to what extent they have been used. A further statistical analysis of Vergil's work along these lines may yield valuable evidence and enable us to study Vergil's style from a new angle, and perhaps the differences in his poetic style at various stages of his literary career. The characteristic of the frequency of specified gaps between repetitions of the same inital letter, if established for Vergil's poetry in general, may also be used as a style characteristic and may help us in establishing, for instance, whether Vergil is the author of the Culex, Ciris etc. In other words, the method may provide a new tool for decision in cases of disputed authorship.

IX

GENEALOGICAL RELATIONSHIP BETWEEN LANGUAGES—
VOCABULARY CORRELATION

9.1 PREVIOUS ATTEMPTS AT DETERMINATION OF NEARNESS
OF LINGUISTIC RELATIONSHIP

In his paper on Philological Probability Problems (1950), Ross has described certain attempts at mathematical formulation of linguistic relationship. He mentions briefly the method of Kroeber and Chrétien (1937, 1939) on the relationship of Indo-Germanic languages which he criticises without, however, offering an alternative solution.

Kroeber and Chrétien constructed four-cell tables for each language pair and calculated the product-moment correlation coefficient, with values 1 and 0 for each language according to whether a word is found in it or not, and consequently with classes 11, 10, 01, 00 according to whether a word occurs in both languages, in one only, in the other only, in neither. The product-moment correlation coefficient, which for a table of this kind is also known as the Bernoullian correlation coefficient (see *LCC*, pp. 344-352) reduces then to

$$r = \frac{ad-bc}{\sqrt{(a+b)(a+c)(c+d)(b+d)}} \tag{19}$$

where a stands for the class 11, b for 10, c for 01, and d for 00. The value of r varies between the values of -1 and $+1$, with 0 for lack of correlation. When ad is greater than bc, the correlation is said to be positive (between 0 and $+1$), when bc is greater than ad it is said to be negative (between 0 and -1).

However, it was found that when relationship was measured in this way, the results sometimes contradicted what had been established previously by philological considerations: some such established genealogical relationships appeared in terms of r to be not significant.

This induced Ellegård (1959) to use another formula for the correlation coefficient, viz.,

$$r_n = \frac{a}{\sqrt{(a+b)(a+c)}} \tag{20}$$

where, as before, a is the overlap in words between two languages, b the words peculiar to one language, and c the words peculiar to the other. Ellegård was not the first to use that formula. In *LCC*, Sect. 4.2, it was used for the determination of vocabulary correlation, and it had been used before, e.g. by Kroeber (1932). This measure of relationship is always positive, and can vary from 0 to $+1$. It has the intelligible meaning that the values of a, b and c stand for all features which are positively recorded in one or both of the languages.

Ellegård regards r_n as a measure of similarity, and r as one of interdependence or interinfluence. A more unambiguous definition and one which will prove helpful in arriving at a more satisfactory treatment of the problem is this. The relationship measured by r is based not only upon the words common to both languages, and those peculiar to one or the other, but also upon the words belonging to a larger whole and not appearing in either language. The larger whole is what I call the Universe of Discourse (Sect. 18.1) which, in the case under consideration, is the total of indogermanic roots established so far. The coefficient r_n, on the other hand, is based only upon what is positively recorded of the two languages, i.e. the words in common and those peculiar to either, the negative class, and with it the universe of discourse, being taken as infinite.

Ellegård is right in regarding r_n as a more suitable measure of linguistic relationship. However, in spite of this, it cannot by itself be regarded as a full substitute of r, because it just leaves out the important feature of the common parentage of all roots, which is the basis of the IE theory of linguistic relationship. This may account for the great dialectical difficulties in which Ellegård gets involved when trying to supplement the information given by r_n, in order to bring the results of the mathematical method into harmony with the philologically established facts of the genealogical relationship of Indo-European languages. So vast an amount of argument on top of a mathematical method detracts very much from the value of the latter, one of the great advantages of using mathematics being that it makes additional argument largely superfluous. This can be achieved by choosing a more suitable mathematical procedure, and as such a procedure I propose to use the method of Factor Analysis for the determination of linguistic relationship. It enables us to work with r_n without abandoning the basic fact of a common ancestor of all the languages under consideration. The interpretation of results is straightforward, and does not require to be supplemented by extensive argument.

9.2 FACTOR ANALYSIS AS THE APPROPRIATE METHOD FOR THE PROBLEM— APPLICATION TO INDO-EUROPEAN LANGUAGES

The suitability of factor analysis for the problem in question follows from these features:

1. It considers not only particular pairs of languages with regard to the number of Proto-Indoeuropean (PIE) roots they have in common, but every language in its relation to all the other languages in the group.

2. It enables us to determine the "saturation" of a given language with PIE as the factor common to all languages, the influence of what may be called secondary factors, such as geographical position, and finally the amount of "specificity" as that which distinguishes a given language from all others in the group.

As is well known, the relationship between Indo-Germanic languages is usually based upon the number of roots they have in common. The following table of Indo-European roots as given in the paper by Ross was compiled from the standard work by Walde and Pokorny (1926-32). The first column gives selected pairs of Indo-European languages, the second and third columns give the numbers of Indo-European roots in the first language of the pair and in the second language, respectively, and the third gives the overlap, i.e. the number of roots they have in common.

TABLE 15

Number of Roots Common to Certain Indo-European Branches

	n_1	n_2	R		n_1	n_2	R
Ce It-Gr	1,184	1,165	783	Ar-Ir Sk	442	1,016	305
-Ar	1,184	442	333	-Sl Ba	442	1,213	312
-Ir Sk	1,184	1,016	694	-Ge	442	1,256	329
-Sl Ba	1,184	1,213	777	-Al	442	290	130
-Ge	1,184	1,256	865	Ir Sk-Sl Ba	1,016	1,213	657
-Al	1,184	290	236	-Ge	1,016	1,256	693
Gr-Ar	1,165	442	333	-Al	1,016	290	223
-Ir Sk	1,165	1,016	694	Sl Ba-Ge	1,213	1,256	876
-Sl Ba	1,165	1,213	753	-Al	1,213	290	220
-Ge	1,165	1,256	763	Ge-Al	1,256	290	228
-Al	1,165	290	242				

The abbreviations are as follows:

$$\begin{aligned}
\text{Ce It} &= \text{Italo-Celtic} \\
\text{Ar} &= \text{Armenian} \\
\text{Ir Sk} &= \text{Indo-Iranian} \\
\text{Sl Ba} &= \text{Balto-Slavonic} \\
\text{Ge} &= \text{Germanic} \\
\text{Al} &= \text{Albanian}
\end{aligned}$$

The data of the above table enable us to calculate the correlation coefficient by formula (20)

$$r_n = R/(n_1 \times n_2)^{\frac{1}{2}}$$

where R is the overlap in Indo-European roots in the given pair of languages and n_1, n_2 are the numbers of Indo-European roots in the two languages concerned. The use of that formula for correlation is discussed in detail in *LCC*, p. 49 ff., and, as mentioned above, more recently by Ellegård (1959). We then obtain the following table of correlation coefficients (Table 16). The decimal point has been left out in the body of the table. Table 17 has the same elements, but re-arranged according to magnitude of column size.

TABLE 16

	Ce It	Gr	Ar	Ir Sk	Sl Ba	Ge	Al
Ce it	—	665	459	633	648	709	403
Gr	665	—	464	636	633	631	416
Ar	459	464	—	455	426	442	363
Ir Sk	633	636	455	—	592	613	411
Sl Ba	648	633	426	592	—	710	371
Ge	709	631	442	613	710	—	378
Al	403	416	364	411	371	378	—
Sum	3.517	3.445	2.609	3.340	3.380	3.483	2.342

TABLE 17

	Ce It	Ge	Gr	Sl Ba	Ir Sk	Ar	Al
Ce It	—	709	665	648	633	459	403
Ge	709 (669)	—	631	710	613	442	378
Gr	665 (661)	631 (654)	—	633	636	464	416
Sl Ba	648 (645)	710 (637)	633 (630)	—	592	426	371
Ir Sk	633 (637)	613 (629)	636 (622)	592 (607)	—	455	411
Ar	459 (477)	442 (471)	464 (466)	426 (454)	455 (448)	—	363
Al	403 (421)	378 (416)	416 (412)	371 (401)	411 (396)	363 (297)	—
Sum	3.517	3.483	3.445	3.380	3.340	2.609	2.342

TABLE 18

	A^2	A^1	A^2-A^0	$2A$	T-$2A$	$\dfrac{A^2-A^1}{T-2A}$	Saturation g	Specific sj
Ce It	12.370	2.139	10.231	7.034	15.082	.678	.823	.568
Ge	12.131	2.118	10.013	6.966	15.150	.661	.813	.582
Gr	11.869	2.033	9.836	6.890	15.226	.646	.804	.595
Sl Ba	11.424	1.995	9.429	6.760	15.356	.614	.784	.622
Ir Sk	11.156	1.908	9.248	6.680	15.436	.599	.774	.633
Ar	6.807	1.142	5.665	5.218	16.898	.335	.579	.816
Al	5.485	0.918	4.567	4.684	17.432	.262	.512	.859

Using factor analysis in its simplest form as devised by Spearman and assuming, as a first approximation, one general factor to be responsible for the correlation, and thus a matrix of rank 1, the saturations of the variables by the general factor are calculated according to the formula

$$\text{Saturation} = \frac{A^2 - A'}{T - 2A} \qquad (21)$$

where the A's are the sums of the rows (or columns) of the correlation matrix without entries in the diagonal cells, T the sum of all A's, and the A''s are the sums of rows (or columns) of the matrix whose elements are the squared correlation coefficients of Table 16. The calculation is exhibited in Table 18.

The last two columns give the saturation with the general factor which, in this case, is, of course, PIE as the common parent language, and the specific factor for each language. For specifying the composition of language with regard to general factor and specific factors, assuming the order to be hierarchical, that is assuming only one general factor and also excluding specific correlations between the languages we have the equations:

$$
\begin{aligned}
\text{Italo-Celtic} \quad & z_1 = .823\,g + .568\,s_1 \\
\text{Germanic} \quad & z_2 = .813\,g + .582\,s_2 \\
\text{Greek} \quad & z_3 = .804\,g + .595\,s_3 \\
\text{Balto-Slavonic} \quad & z_4 = .784\,g + .622\,s_4 \\
\text{Indo-Iranian} \quad & z_5 = .774\,g + .633\,s_5 \\
\text{Armenian} \quad & z_6 = .579\,g + .816\,s_6 \\
\text{Albanian} \quad & z_7 = .512\,g + .859\,s_7
\end{aligned}
$$

9.3   INTERPRETATION OF RESULTS

We see that by the token of common roots the saturation with PIE as a common factor ranges in our 7 languages from .823 for Italo-Celtic to .512 for Albanian, the "specific" rising in the opposite direction from .568 for Italo-Celtic to .859 for Albanian. Under the assumption that one general factor only was responsible for the relationship between our 7 languages, the observed correlations of Table 16 should be obtainable from the saturations as the correlations of each language with the general factor. Since the languages are conceived to be correlated among themselves only through a third factor, g, their correlations r_{ij}, should be sensibly equal to the product of two saturations,

$$
r_{ij} = r_{ig} \cdot r_{jg} \tag{22}
$$

These correlations were calculated and are entered in brackets next to the corresponding observed correlation in Table 17. On the whole, there is very good agreement which shows how powerful the PIE factor is for the relationship between any two of our languages. However, there are certain discrepancies, for instance, the estimated correlation between Ge and Sl Ba (.637) is considerably less than the observed correlation (.710); on the other hand, the estimated correlation between Ge and Ar (.476) is greater than the observed correlation (.442) and the same applies to the correlation between Ge and Al (.416 calculated as against .378 observed). This might point to another factor common to some of the languages but not to all. It may be that the nearness in geographical location between Ge and Sl Ba, on the one hand,

and another secondary factor for the differences between Ge and Ar, and Ge and Al, on the other hand, could account for the discrepancy between the correlations calculated under the assumption of one common factor only and the observed correlations.

It should be emphasized that in establishing these relations between languages only one language characteristic was used, viz. vocabulary. It follows that to the extent to which vocabulary is independent of grammar and phonemic system, it is by no means certain that the same series of relationships between our languages would hold if other characteristics than vocabulary were taken into consideration.

A perhaps obvious criticism of the results might conceivably be that the numerical estimate of nearness of relationship did not add much to our previous knowledge in the matter arrived at without mathematics.

But even if this were true—it is not altogether true because the merely subjective impression of nearness of relationship is always open to criticism, and can never really claim general acceptance—, so much must be conceded that the *method* used is remarkable for its clarity and for the suitability of its conceptual structure for establishing genealogical relationship between languages. That the method enables one to say to what extent a language is "saturated" with PIE as the common factor of all the languages in the group, and to what extent a language is to be regarded as specific or individual, and insofar different from the other languages,—quite apart from the possibility of accounting for special correlations between languages by secondary factors, such as geographical location etc.—and to do all this in terms of strictly defined concepts which are moreover capable of quantitative expression, shows clearly how superior factor analysis is for our purpose to other methods which have been tried so far, e.g. the method used by Kroeber in a more recent paper on "Statistics, Indo-European and Taxonomy' (Language, 1960) with its mixture of legitimate statistical method, arbitrariness and fanciful geometrical construction.

E. Pulgram's views in the matter of establishing linguistic relationship, and his critical attitude to the methods so far used, are of great interest (*Language*, 1959, and *Lingua*, 1961). Although he seems to accept the mathematical argument involved, he makes no secret of his distrust of statistical methods in linguistics. Factor Analysis as an additional instrument for establishing linguistic relationship enables one to avoid some of the pitfalls in this respect to which he has drawn attention.

Pulgram's method of criticism may be briefly characterised like this. His argument rests mostly upon the assumption that the investigator does not know at the outset whether the two blocks of linguistic units he is comparing are different languages, or different stages of development of one language, or languages belonging to different families, and that therefore his conclusion about the parent-offspring relation between the two blocks of linguistic units may be fallacious. In other words, he assumes that the investigator acts blindly as regards both language history and language geography. It is difficult to believe that a linguist will really embark on an investigation in this way, but for the sake of argument we will assume that the investigator, while regarding his material as homogeneous in the sense of the above assumption, is actually comparing the vocabulary of a number of Indogermanic languages with that of two chronologically different stages of, say, German, and with two non-related languages, say, French and Arabic. The difference in magnitude of the correlation coefficient of r would show him at once that he had not compared like with like. Whereas the different Indogermanic languages among themselves would have correlation coefficients between, say, .4 and .7, the two stages of German among themselves would have a correlation coefficient close to unity, and French and Arabic a non-significant correlation coefficient. Furthermore, such inhomogeneousness of the correlation coefficients would violently disturb the so-called hierarchical order of the correlation matrix *which is indicative of one general factor only*, as being responsible for all the correlations. From this the conclusion could be drawn that what was responsible for the association of the two stages of development of German, is not the general factor, nor was it active in such spurious connection as could perhaps be found between French and Arabic.

Thus, it is the mathematical method which will reveal the nature of the relationship: whether it is one between different stages of one language, or one between different genealogically related languages, or one between linguistically unrelated languages.

Factor analysis has developed into a very complete and complex method of which I have given here only the very first stage. But I fear that if I were to develop its application to language and use all the refinements of the method to help the linguistic research worker, the very first objection to be encountered on the part of the linguist would be that the linguistic research worker does not start ab ovo, or double-blind with regard to language history and geography, but with a sound knowledge of what he is about, and the mathematician ought to be aware of this and should not include a lot of heterogeneous word masses in his design, but adjust his methods accordingly. Paraphrasing the well-known couplet in one of Gilbert and Sullivan's operas about the "Policeman's Lot", it would appear that "The Linguistic Statistician's Lot is not **a Happy One**".

SPECTROGRAPHY
OF SPEECH ON THE MORPHEMIC LEVEL

X

THE PARALLELISM BETWEEN
PHONOLOGY AND VOCABULARY STATISTICS

10.1   PHONOLOGY AND VOCABULARY STATISTICS: A PARALLEL

In the Introduction to his "Anleitung zu phonologischen Beschreibungen" (1935), Trubetzkoy speaks about the methodological differences between phonetics in its physical and physiological and also, perhaps, psychological aspects, and the other part of linguistics (Sprachlehre) and then makes the following statement (translated):

> "This state of affairs is altered abruptly if, from the fact of the distinctive property of the sounds of speech, the logical conclusion is drawn that it is just their symbolic values which must be made a subject of research as being linguistically the most essential feature, *for the world behind the empirical sounds of human speech appears to be an ordered system which, through its fundamentally regular structure, is comparable to the grammatical values,* so that *between phonetics studied from this angle and grammar there exists no longer a fundamental difference.*"

This is today accepted wisdom. But the attitude of some linguists to mathematics and, in particular, to statistics as a branch of linguistics is quite parallel to that which was entertained in Trubetzkoy's time by linguists towards phonetics. Even when the results of statistical linguistics are accepted as being true, i.e. corresponding to facts, it is often argued that the applicability of statistics to language rests upon only such properties of language which that field shares with all the rest of the material world, and that therefore the results of statistical linguistics are linguistically not relevant (Chomsky, 1958). In particular, they maintain that the neglect of grammar when compiling frequency lists of words makes the results of statistics irrelevant to language as they understand it (Halle, 1957). Be it said at once that none of these critics has, to my knowledge, defined in this connection what he regards as linguistically relevant. But since my purpose here is to exhibit the parallelism between the former attitude of linguists to scientific phonetics and their present one to statistical linguistics, I shall not go into the question of the exact definition of the term "linguistically relevant". As a working definition I propose to regard all properties of the linguistic code which are specific to that code, as linguistically relevant.

I shall show that the concept of statistical frequency which underlies all applications of statistics to language is such that if both lexicon (vocabulary) and grammar are studied from this angle, there exists no longer a fundamental difference between them. Whereas phonology has abolished the distinction—as a fundamental one—between phonetic changes of a paradigmatic nature (bound grammar forms) and the changes or differences in sound between lexicon items, or between grammar and morphology, *statistical linguistics abolishes the distinction between grammar words, in the widest sense of the term, and lexicon.* My claim for statistical linguistics is, therefore, perfectly parallel to Trubetzkoy's claim for phonology.

10.2 PREVIOUS ATTEMPTS AT MORPHEME ANALYSIS

The parallelism to which I am drawing attention has had its forerunner in what is known as "morpheme analysis". To quote Dwight L. Bolinger (1950):

"Analysts returning from their impressive conquest of phonology, bring with them the weapon that stood them in good stead: the principle of oppositions, of absolute identity vs. absolute difference. It is only natural that a weapon which proved itself in one field should be favoured by those who used it there when they pass to another field... In the little that has been done with morpheme analysis up to now, linguists have displayed their bias for identity-difference... The phonologist regards any two phonemes qua phonemes as absolutely distinct... This procedure of absolute oppositions (whether reified, as by some linguists, or regarded as expedient, as by some others) has worked very well with phonemes which may number a dozen, or forty, or a hundred. It even works with morphemes when one addresses only a few phonemes as analysts have done so far in English..., but the exploring analyst must face up to the multiple and pluralistic stock of English with its 20- or 30-thousand discrete—or not so discrete?—forms popularly used. Are absolute identity and opposition any longer practical, and is the area not too crowded for compartment-alisation?"

Bolinger's doubts, which made him arrive at essentially negative conclusions about the feasibility of morpheme analysis if extended beyond a comparatively narrow zone, suggest that with a wider zone, that is for morpheme analysis of such generality as is intrinsic to its conception, we must choose a characteristic of greater generality.

Thus, the attempts at modifying the phoneme-variant distinction, with all that belongs to it, so as to make it equally useful on the morphemic level have, so far, not been successful. The reason is not far to seek. It lies in the discrepancy of the numbers of phonemes and morphemes in a language. Of phonemes there are comparatively few in a given language, say, between 20 and 40 in most languages. Even if somebody were not prepared to accept these limits, he could not go much beyond them on either side, so let us say that 50 is the upper limit of the number of phonemes in a language. The number of morphemes, on the other hand, is very much greater—and so are the differences between languages in this respect. An upper limit of 50,000 may be appropriate if highly developed languages are considered.

This has the consequence that whereas the different kinds of opposition between phonemes, and with them the system of phonological oppositions in a language, can easily be kept present in the mind, this is quite impossible with the oppositions in form or meaning between morphemes. Even though it might be feasible to some extent for the grammatical oppositions, it will be out of question for the oppositions between lexicon items. If there exists a device in language on the morphemic level, comparable to that on the phonemic level, it must be one using a number of oppositions of a similar order of magnitude.

When it comes to dealing with great masses of data, the linguist must learn from the statistician, and the statistician suggests that due to the great area, the only characteristic which will admit using the tool of phonology, i.e. that of absolute identity vs. absolute difference, and of significant element vs. variant, must be a quantitative one, namely, frequency of occurrence. This is also a morpheme characteristic which, like the phoneme, is independent of meaning.

The phonemic device is a qualitative one: we distinguish phonemes according to certain qualitative features of sound forms: according to place of articulation as labials, dentals, palatals, velars, and to manner of articulation as plosives, affricates, fricatives, nasals and liquids. That spectography of speech claims to have succeeded in expressing the phonemic oppositions quantitatively, is quite true, but for our using and understanding language as a live instrument of communication of thought, the oppositions remain qualitative ones.

On the morphemic level, the qualitative oppositions are those between meanings, and they are of such number, and their system of such complexity, that all the books that have been written are only just enough to display that system of oppositions. A device on that level comparable to that we found on the phonemic level, must be such as to reduce the possibility of error in that manifold of meanings. It must, therefore, be something different from "meaning" itself, something non-qualitative, and thus a quantitative feature. This is quite in accordance with how in empirical science the need for quantitative treatment arises: when the masses of observation become too great for individual or qualitative classification, then it is time to have recourse to quantitative classification by number and measurement, and, in general, to statistics.

The quantitative feature which appears to come to our rescue here, on the morphemic level, is the frequency of occurrence of morphemes. I avoid speaking of the "principle of frequency" or, still worse, the "principle of relative frequency" (Zipf). It is not a principle, but just a characteristic feature in the use of words, which enables us to express the difference in the use of words quantitatively.

As will be shown, the isomorphy between phonology and morphology (vocabulary) appears to be three-fold. To the independence between phoneme and meaning of words in phonology there corresponds that between word occurrence and meaning (content) of texts (Sect. 10.3). To the opposition of phoneme vs. variant in phonology, corresponds that between population probabilities vs. statistical relative frequencies in vocabulary statistics (Sect. 10.4). What corresponds to the phonological opposition is in the sphere of morpheme analysis the vocabulary partition (Sect. 10.5).

10.3   INDEPENDENCE OF THE FORM OF THE OCCURRENCE DISTRIBUTION FROM CONTENT

The distinction between grammar and lexicon of language is, as a rule, regarded as essential for a language. Grammar is said (Jespersen, 1924, Sweet 1898) to deal with the general facts of language, and lexicology with special facts. The distinction is not always easy and unequivocal.

What is meant by "general facts" is clearly such facts as occur in practically every part of the universe of discourse, no matter how small we take them. As such minimum we may regard the sentence or a specified number of word occurrences, say 50 or 100, and show that grammar facts are such as occur in every small part of the universe of discourse, taking as a lower limit of size, the sentence. This is, of course, to be understood cum grano salis: not every grammar fact must occur in every sentence, but the more fundamental grammar facts do.

Lexicon items, on the other hand, may be unique (hapax legomena) in a text, or they may occur repeatedly but with different frequency. We therefore define lexicon items as linguistic events which do not, as a rule, recur in the smallest meaningful segments of speech, the sentence, but in parts which vary in size according to the usefulness of the vocabulary items. The nearer the word stands in frequency to the grammar words, the smaller may the parts be; the more particular its use, the larger, until for a true hapax legomenon there is no recurrence at all in different parts.

Redefining grammar and lexicon in this way, we have replaced their qualitative distinction in terms of "generality" and "speciality" by a quantitative one, and thus by one of degree only.

We have now the following picture of the frequency distribution of words in a given text. Taking any literary text and arranging the vocabulary items according to whether they are used once, twice ... n times, we invariably get the distribution pattern in which the largest class is that of words used only once, the next largest comprising words used twice, and so on, the class sizes falling off rather quickly at first and slower as we come to the higher and highest occurrence frequencies. Starting from the other end, i.e. the very extended distribution tail, we have here as the forms used most often, the grammar words, which are immediately preceded by vocabulary items of such general use as to have frequencies not radically differing from the rarer grammar words, which vocabulary items are again preceded by vocabulary items of less general and less frequent use, and so forth, the individual words within frequency classes becoming more and more different from text to text, until we reach the hapax legomena of the text in question, which will overlap only to a very small extent between texts. This is the general pattern no matter what the content of the text and we must, therefore, regard it as the analogon in the vocabulary domain of the axiom of independence of sound and content in the phonetic domain.

For a statistical parameter to be suitable for linguistics, there must exist a certain degree of independence between the linguistic symbols to which it applies, and the semantic content of the message. Such independence has been established by de Saussure between the linguistic unit symbols, the sounds or phonemes, and the meaning of the words composed of the phonemes. In his review of *TTM* (1960), Ross calls this the axiom that there is no causal connection between sound and meaning. We shall adhere to that term, though strictly speaking an axiom cannot suffer exceptions, as this axiom does, e.g. in imitative words. But Ross denies (in the last paragraph of his review) in accordance with his deep-seated antipathy to statistics, the working of an analogous axiom in the domain of vocabulary, which makes him antagonistic to Yule's Characteristic and similar measures. In this he is by no means alone among linguists. But as shown above, what in the domain of vocabulary corresponds to the axiom of the independence of sound and meaning, is the axiom of the independence of the distribution pattern of vocabulary according to occurrence frequency and the content of the message or text.

From this it follows that statistical parameters are just as suitable in the domain of vocabulary as in that of phonetics and phonemics, and that statistics applied correctly in the domain of vocabulary must, just as in that of phonemics, lead to linguistically relevant results. For if de Saussure's statement is regarded as an axiom and if, as I have shown, there exists a perfectly analogous axiom of independence in the domain of vocabulary, the statistical results based upon these independence axioms must clearly be linguistically relevant. Otherwise, we would come to the very paradoxical view that the basic axioms of the linguistic code are not linguistically relevant. As it is, they are eminently characteristic for language, since both are the outcome of fundamental properties of linguistic coding.

As will be shown in Chpt. 11, the frequency distribution is really the result of the ordered system of words, or the regular structure of meaning.

10.4 YULE'S MATHEMATICAL MODEL FOR THE USE OF WORDS IN A TEXT

This will reveal, as another aspect of the parallelism between phonology and vocabulary statistics, that what corresponds on the vocabulary level to the distinction between phonemes and variants, is the distinction between vocabulary population probability and the actual relative frequencies of words in a literary text.

Yule (1944) maintains that to the word distribution according to occurrence frequency, there apply notions similar to those which are suitable for the distribution of persons according to the number of accidents they suffer. However, this need not imply that a particular word is used by accident, and we may avoid the term "accident" altogether, if we wish, since the theory of accidents is only an application of the statistical theory of rare events. Rarity as a quantitative eoncept, i.e. one admitting of degrees, is not different from "frequency" as used in statistics and, in particular, in statistical linguistics.

Yule was led to that view by comparing the empirical numerical relations in both distributions. The development of the theory of accident necessarily involves some, if not very serious, mathematical work, but it is possible to explain to the non-mathematical reader the general lines which the theory of personal accident has followed.[1]

If a number of persons exposed to the risk of accident all have exactly the same liability to accident, theory suggests that the resulting frequency distribution should be of a particularly simple type—Poisson's distribution—which is characterised by the remarkable relation

$$\sigma^2 = M \tag{1}$$

i.e. the square of the standard deviation σ, which is a measure of spread around the mean, M, is equal to the mean. Actual investigation of many accident distributions show, on the contrary, that in the vast majority of instances we have

$$\sigma^2 \gg M, \tag{2}$$

the squared standard deviation, or variance as it is sometimes termed, often greatly exceeding the mean. This is also a characteristic feature of word distributions according to frequency.

What is the explanation of this? The simplest explanation that suggests itself is that the liabilities of different individuals to accident are not the same, that they vary in "liability" to accident, just as they vary in intelligence or in stature. The "liability" of an individual might be ideally defined as the mean number of accidents he would tend to meet with in the time of exposure to risk, say unit time. We call this liability λ. Let us suppose the liabilities of the persons at risk to be known and grouped into a frequency distribution—just as we may group their statures or weights—,and that this distribution has mean $\bar{\lambda}$ and standard deviation σ_λ. Then from the mean and standard deviation of the accident distribution, M and σ, we can calculate $\bar{\lambda}$ and σ_λ.

Translated into language terms, we assume that the frequency distribution of words, all with the same liability to be used by the writer, follows the simple Poisson law. The characteristic excess, however, of σ^2 over M for the whole distribution of vocabulary in the text sample suggests that words differ with respect to their liability

---

[1] It should be noted that a relation between two variables observed in a given body of numerical data may conceivably be fitted by more than one mathematical function. Applied to our case, the distribution of vocabulary items according to occurrence frequency may be fitted by Yule's law or by a lognormal distribution (*TTM*, Chpt. II). The "goodness of fit" can be ascertained by statistical methods of testing. If both mathematical functions comply with the requirements for curve fitting, one may be more suitable for theoretical reasons and the other from a practical point of view. It is very likely that one distribution function will not fit all possible linguistic distributions.

to be used which is in accordance with common sense. The words of a homogenous word group have the same liability of use, λ, this being also, by and large, the mean occurrence frequency of words within such a group, with σ_i as a measure of dispersion of the actual frequencies around the mean λ_i. The mean of all λ_i, and therefore of the whole distribution of λ in the sample is $\bar{\lambda}$, and thus M, with σ_λ as the measure of dispersion between the λ's.

Observe the parallelism between the phonemes and the λ's. The phoneme is to be understood—at least Trubetzkoy insisted that it should be—as distinct from its phonetical manifestation as "something behind the empirical sounds" (translated—Trubetzkoy 1938). Quite parallel to this is the distinction between the hypothetical frequencies λ as belonging to what is called the statistical population of vocabulary probabilities, and their manifestation in actual writing as the observed word frequencies, i.e. as samples of the population probabilities. The *variants* of a phoneme have their exact counterpart in the "*variance*" (this is the term for σ^2, the squared standard deviation as a measure of dispersion) of the frequencies of words belonging to a group with a given λ, that is, of words having basically the same probability of occurrence, just as the variants of a given phoneme have basically the same sound.

Now if we extend the period of exposure to risk from one unit to two units, and all individuals retain their relative liability, $\bar{\lambda}$ becomes $2\bar{\lambda}$ and σ_λ becomes $2\sigma_\lambda$. It follows that the coefficient of variation of $\bar{\lambda}$, $v_\lambda = \sigma_\lambda/\bar{\lambda}$, remains the same and is independent of the period of exposure to risk; we say it is a *time invariant* for the distribution in question. Expressing the hypothetical quantities $\bar{\lambda}$ and σ_λ in v_λ in terms of the observed statistics M and σ, we then have a characteristic of the accident distribution which, under the circumstances, is independent of the period of exposure to risk.

These considerations are now applied to the word distribution.

The entire distribution is supposed to be compounded of a number of components, i.e. homogenous word groups with different values of λ. Let the mean of the λ-distribution be $\bar{\lambda}$, and its standard deviation σ_λ, and let the mean of the complete word distribution be M and its standard deviation σ. Since, as observed above, the liability of a word to occur might be ideally defined as its mean number of occurrences, we have, at once,

$$M = \bar{\lambda} \tag{3}$$

In words: the mean of the complete word distribution equals the mean of the liabilities of word occurrence.

Since the total variance equals the mean variance of the component distributions—which by the Poisson law equals the mean—$\bar{\lambda}$—plus the variance of the means themselves, which is σ_λ^2, we have

$$\sigma^2 = \bar{\lambda} + \sigma_\lambda^2 = M + \sigma_\lambda^2 \tag{4}$$

Now, since all λ's are directly proportional to the number of occurrences, doubling, say, the number of occurrences will double $\bar{\lambda}$ and also double σ_λ. Hence the coefficient of variation of λ, or $v_\lambda = \sigma_\lambda/\bar{\lambda}$, is independent of the number of occurrences. But

$$v_\lambda{}^2 = \sigma_\lambda{}^2/\bar{\lambda}^2 = \frac{\sigma^2 - M}{M^2}, \tag{5}$$

and hence the last term of this equation is independent of the number of occurrences, that is of size of sample. It is a "characteristic" of the complete distribution independent of size of sample.

Yule's Characteristic is usually given, not in terms of the mean and the standard deviation, but in terms of the so-called first and second moments of the distribution, S_1 and S_2, as

$$\frac{S_2 - S_1}{S_1^2} \tag{6}$$

where $S_1 = \Sigma f_x X$
$\quad\;\; S_2 = \Sigma f_x X^2,$

Σ being the sign of summation, and f_x the number of vocabulary items with frequency X.

The essential identity of (5) and (6) is easily demonstrated. Writing (5) in terms of S_1, S_2 and N as the total number of vocabulary items in the sample, we have, since $M = S_1/N$ and $\sigma^2 = S_2/N - (S_1/N)^2$,

$$v_\lambda{}^2 = \frac{N^2}{S_1^2} \left(\frac{S_2}{N} \frac{S_1^2}{N^2} \frac{S_1}{N} \right) = \frac{N S_2}{S_1^2} - 1 - \frac{N}{S_1} = N \left(\frac{S_2}{S_2^1} - \frac{1}{S_1} \right) - 1 \tag{7}$$

$$\text{and } v_\lambda{}^2/N = \frac{S_2 - S_1}{S_1^2} - \frac{1}{N}. \tag{8}$$

But $v_\lambda{}^2/N$ is the coefficient of variation of the mean, $\dfrac{\sigma_\lambda{}^2/N}{M^2}$, and Yule's Characteristic $K - 1/N$ thus appears as the coefficient of variation of the $\bar{\lambda}$'s. It has, therefore, the property of the coefficient of variation, namely, that it is independent of the sample size or of text length, which can also be expressed by saying that it is a *time invariant*, time being here measured by the number of word occurrences in the sample.

10.4.1   *The quantification of de Saussure's 'valeur'*

The gulf between the language of the linguist and the symbolism of the mathematician shows itself in de Saussure's description of the essential features of the word codes and the mathematical hypothesis of the structure of the frequency distribution of words.

The central concept in de Saussure's description is that of "valeur". Words differ in value according to the type and frequency of their associations, both lexical and syntagmatic. This is a consequence of de Saussure's conception of language as a "système où tout se tient". The "valeur" of a particular word means its importance as a part of that system. In terms of Bloomfield's frequency map of language, the words of a language differ in "valeur" just like towns, villages, settlements in a country according to their importance for communication, some being key points of the communication system, others just stops. So far, the term "valeur" is fairly clear, but how such a concept fits into de Saussure's basic idea of language as a code and as just another branch of semiology, this is not apparent. Since "valeur" is mainly considered as having reference to meaning, lexical or grammatical, it is difficult to see its role in a branch of semiology, where, as in any code, quantity is important.

The mathematical hypothesis, on the other hand, of the word frequency distribution function, uses certain hypothetical quantities, the λ's, denoting the "basic" frequencies for words belonging to different frequency groups.

If we wish to go a little deeper, we cannot but ask what the λ's really are, and where they ought to be imagined as existing. To say that to a certain group of words there belongs a particular λ cannot really satisfy us. What are the λ's by themselves and how are they attached to the words, considering that "frequencies" do not exist by themselves? In a word, it is one thing to stand by a mathematical hypothesis or model and to derive from it a function which can be satisfactorily fitted to the observed distribution, and another to make sure that to the hypothetical entities used for that purpose there corresponds something real in the field of observation. Thus here, on the mathematical side, we have a hypothetical quantity—the basic or population occurrence frequency of words—, for which we must find a linguistic interpretation that would give it life.

It was the great physicist, Schrödinger, of wave equation fame, who said that "one of the fascinating features of statistical thermodynamics is that quantities and functions introduced primarily by mathematical devices almost invariably acquire a fundamental meaning". This also applies to statistical linguistics, and as a beautiful instance of that "fascinating feature" in our field of investigation, we shall now demonstrate that the fundamental linguistic meaning of the λ's is nothing but de Saussure's "valeur".

Let us recall (Sect. 10.4) that the symbols λ stand for the hypothetical basic occurrence frequencies of different word groups, and that "word occurrence" is considered a rare event and, consequently, words with the same λ are distributed with regard to occurrence frequency according to the law of rare events, called after the mathematician who first described it as the Poisson law. The total word frequency distribution is conceived as the superimposition of such distributions, one for each λ, and is called the compound Poisson law.

So far, we have not troubled much about the justification of speaking of a word occurrence as a rare event. Clearly, this does not go without saying, and the applicability of the law of rare events to the word frequency distribution stands and falls with whether word occurrence *is* a rare event.

Let us imagine both the world of thought in the "plane of content" and the world of words in the "plane of expression". Paraphrasing *Einstein's dictum about the world being finite but unbounded,* we say that the world of expression is finite, but the world of thought is unbounded. Language, like any other code, has a finite number of symbols, i.e. words, if we think in terms of the word code, whereas there is no limit to the number of concepts and relations between them or, briefly, there are no bounds to thought.

This means a comparative scarcity of linguistic material for the expression of thought, and we can, in this sense, speak of the occurrence of linguistic forms—words—as a rare event. When seen against the background of the world of thought requiring expression, the actual expression of a particular thought is a rare event. But, thoughts or concepts will differ in that respect. For some the "waiting queue" may be very long, for others it may be short with all possible variants between these extremes. It all depends upon their "valeur" as the term for their richness in lexical and syntagmatic associations. If the "valeur" is high, the quest of the concept for materialisation, i.e. expression in words, will be great and result in a high frequency of use; if the "valeur" is small, that quest will also be small, and the word denoting the concept or relation in question will occur only rarely.

The magnitude of the quest for a particular word is like that of its "valeur" inversely related to the size of interval between successive occurrences of that word, and inversely related to the size of text parts having that particular word in common. The concatenation of concepts which we call "structure of meaning" is such that if a very large text is divided into equal parts—non-continuous preferably—, λ for a particular word would be determined by the size of interval between successive occurrences of the word. If the word recurs in any other part no matter how small the parts, then λ is very great; the larger the interval between successive occurrences of the word, the greater can the parts be to which that word is common, with λ getting smaller and smaller as the parts increase in size; if the word occurs only once in the whole text, we have a true hapax legomenon, $\lambda = 1$, as the other extreme.

This then, the differential quest of concepts for finding expression in words according to their "valeur", is the linguistic interpretation of the mathematical device λ, or rather the series of λ's of different magnitude. Due to the "structure of meaning" different words have quests for materialisation (expression) of different intensity. This explains the compound Poisson law as the distribution law of word frequency with λ corresponding to "valeur" (associative and syntagmatic).

It should be observed that this interpretation of the term "valeur" is in full accordance with its quantitative meaning, namely, as being a variable quantity responsible for various occurrence frequencies of words, whereas de Saussure used the term for denoting only qualitative properties of words. This shows our interpretation as the complement of de Saussure's, and as being in agreement with the meaning of "valeur".

10.5   ERROR-REDUCING DEVICE ON THE MORPHEMIC LEVEL

The *alphabet* can be regarded as an error-reducing device of language of the first magnitude. Having one symbol for all the non-significant variations of a sound reduces the risk of misunderstanding the sound, the picture of the written language acting as a sort of corroborative version of the spoken word.

The conception of the *phoneme* has considerably clarified the idea of an error-reducing feature of language on the phonemic level by substituting for the alphabet the system of phonemes or, still better, that of phonological oppositions. Through it, the somewhat ill-defined distinction between the written letter and the spoken sound has been replaced by that of the phoneme as the prototype of the sound in question and its variants, all of which are regarded as manifestations of a particular phoneme. This has led to regarding phonemes as a distinctive feature of words, and the system of oppositions between phonemes of a language as characteristic for that language. The more we know about that system of oppositions and about the rules for the association of its phonemes, their "likes and dislikes" of one another, the greater will be the redundancy of the language in that respect, i.e. on the sound level, and the smaller the risk of misunderstanding.

The error-reducing properties of the phoneme as the significant phonetic element in contradistinction to the allophones as the non-significant variants, can be said to bring linguistic theory in this respect into line with statistical theory. We shall now show that there exists a similar device on the morphemic level.

The distinction between grammar and lexicon is given by Jespersen as that between the general versus special facts of language. As shown in Sect. 10.3, the qualitative distinction could be replaced by a quantitative one.

Dividing a text into smaller and smaller parts down to sentence size, there will still be words common to the parts: grammar words, such as article, conjunction, auxiliary verbs. Going in the other direction and increasing the size of the parts, words which the parts have in common will be—apart from grammar words, of course,—lexical items. There may be such items common to all parts, but words of less general use will be common only to fewer parts: all but one, all but two, etc., until the rarest words will be peculiar to one part only.

The qualitative criterion for distinguishing grammar and lexicon words is thus replaced by the quantitative one of a word being common to all parts or to fewer than all parts, but so that the distinction is now a gradual one, without watertight compartments of grammar and lexicon. There are grammar words which do not occur in any sentence and, on the other hand, there are lexicon items of such generality as to occur in all parts. But, by and large, the distribution between grammar and lexicon is quantitative in terms of morpheme occurrence in all or fewer parts, depending also on the size of the parts.

This unity of grammar and lexicon when characterised in terms of occurrence frequency, affords the explanation why in lexicon word counts or stylostatistics the grammatical connection is apparently left out, without, however, detracting from the validity of the count.

That such word counts should provide—as they do—valid information about style and the use of vocabulary in general, in spite of not having taken the particular grammatical connection of the words into account, looks as if the frequency characteristic were a sufficient substitute for grammar. And this turns out to be quite true in the light of our quantitative distinction between grammar and lexicon, since the frequency range embraces high and highest frequencies (grammar words) and low and lowest frequencies (lexicon words). Even if the count is selective and grammar words are not included, there would still be the gradient of frequencies which is characteristic of the difference between lexicon items and grammar words in this respect, and it is this gradient which serves for the characterisation of word masses, regardless of the type of words comprised in the count, provided always that the selection is not such as to defeat the idea of a representative gradient of frequencies.

Using the quantitative definition of grammar and lexicon, the oppositions between words can be conceived in terms of the number of parts to which they belong. This criterion takes the place of the qualitative difference—in meaning or form—between the morphemes. Words are distinguished according to whether they belong to one part exclusively, to two parts, three … all parts. Having established this, we can inquire after the particular part, pairs, triplets etc. of parts, to which the word belongs, any such enquiry being best conducted in the manner of binary coding as the optimum way of enquiry according to the principles of information theory.

As we assume—and with good reason—that it is in this way, by using the binary phonological oppositions, that we distinguish between morphemes, so we can assume that by using the method of binary opposition between the various combinations of the parts of a text we also distinguish between groups of morphemes. It goes without saying that this leads immediately only to the particular part or parts to which a morpheme belongs, not to the morpheme itself.

Now anything that connects linguistic forms in speech will contribute to "structure" and, with it, will increase redundancy, or reduce error. Having, through use of the language, learned whether a particular morpheme is likely to be more inclined to be solitary—a hapax legomenon—or sociable—a good mixer—, we by and by get a good idea of its "valeur", in the concatenation of morphemes, and this helps the understanding of a given content. If the word were missing somewhere, it would be an easy matter to guess it.

Thus, just as the grammar morphemes are the easier replaced or guessed, the oftener they occur, and in terms of the size of segments or parts, the smaller the segments in which there is a good chance of finding them, so does the different sociability of lexical items in the universe of discourse, which accounts for their belonging to a greater or smaller number of parts, enable us to make intelligent guesses at missing lexical items. What is of greater practical value, it gives advance information of the structure of meaning in a given universe of discourse by making us anticipate morphemes through having a good sense of their "valeur" in the universe of discourse. This is what underlies the characteristic gift of a good writer: to have the correct word ready at the right moment and in the right place.

10.5.1   Frequency and vocabulary partition

We cannot assume to have with every word its probability plus transition probability to other words fixed in our minds. The mind simply would not be big enough for that, nor could we distinguish between these probabilities—which after all, can only vary between 0 and 1—as quickly as is required for their use in speech and writing. What is needed, therefore, is a stereotyped version of the morpheme differences in this respect, and this is provided by our attention being fixed upon the number and size of the segments to which a morpheme belongs in a given universe of discourse.

Instead of considering each individual word with regard to meaning, and trying to classify the whole vocabulary by meaning, we make use of the fact that the words differ in their degree of association with other words in the language, and form word groups accordingly. That is, we work with the conception of *solidarity* among the words of a language (de Saussure). This leads to groups of vocabulary items with the same or similar degree of association with other items. The degree of association is epitomised by the frequency of use, and we then arrive at word groups characterised by similar frequency of use, or a basic frequency λ.

But even though this has the effect of reducing the number of points in a structure of meaning, there is no way of determining how many such frequency groups there are in a text, or in the language, because the basic differences as regards frequency between the groups is obscured by accidental variation in frequency of a vocabulary item with a given basic frequency. If we are to arrive at a system of oppositions on the morphemic level comparable to that on the phonemic level, there must be a possibility of quick assessment of the occurrence frequency—not in exact numbers, of course, but only as to order of magnitude—and with it of the association richness of a vocabulary item. Such a possibility is actually given through the feature of what is known as the vocabulary connectivity between the parts of a text, or the partitioning of vocabulary.

This is what is stored in the memory. The number of segments of a given size to which a morpheme is likely to belong, is a rough and ready version of what de Saussure has called "valeur" and what I call the *sociability* of a morpheme.

The probability that a given word is to appear in a specified number of segments if the whole is divided into *n* such segments, this is what is stored in the mind, not in terms of figures, of course, but as *an expectation of a certain strength for the word to appear*. For a rare word in a given universe of discourse, that expectation would be small, if not negligible, for all combinations of segments, and the more so, the greater the number of segments comprised in the combination, but it would be appreciable for single segments; for very frequent words, it would be appreciable for the higher combinations of segments, and for words of medium frequency for combinations of medium numbers of segments. The size of segments in relation to the total universe must also be taken into account.

The essence of the explanation as given here of the global word frequencies is that it traces these frequencies back to the deployment of concepts, and words, in the writer's head before he begins to write or while he is writing. More formally expressed, the deployment of concepts in two or three dimensions must precede the linear sequence of the corresponding words in speech or writing. Taking this into account constitutes the main difference between my explanation and that given by Simon who considers exclusively the linear sequence of words as such, as can be seen from his assumptions 1 and 2 (Sect. 7.3).

10.6   COMMON CHARACTERISTICS OF THE SYSTEM OF PHONEMIC AND MORPHEMIC OPPOSITIONS

When studying the phonological opposition in operation, we must consider the phonemes, not by themselves or in isolation, but with their surroundings in the morphemes of the language. Analogously, when studying the morphemic opposition in operation we must consider the morphemes not in isolation, but with their surroundings in segments of the line of discourse.

The length of such segments is a matter of arbitrary decision. In other words, it is left to us to decide into how many parts we wish to divide the text. If the segments are small, the connectivity between them will be given mainly through grammar words and the more frequently used lexical items; the longer we make the segments, i.e. the fewer the parts into which the text is divided, the more complex will the vocabulary concatenation be through certain vocabulary items of smaller frequency connecting some, and others other parts. In this way the global frequency distribution of words is reduced to a network of connecting links between the segments of a text— not only neighbouring segments but also distant ones—, and the confusing mass of morphemic relations to a few points characterising that network, whose number will be equal to the number of parts into which the text was divided.

As an illustration, I reproduce below a table of vocabulary connectivity between the *Five Catholic Letters* in the New Testament (Greek text).

The first 4 lines give the number of words peculiar to each Letter, the next 10 lines the words common to any two, but not occurring in the other three Letters; the next 10 lines, similarly the words common to any three of the Letters; the next 5 lines the words common to any four Letters, and the next line the number of words common to all Letters. The last line gives the total of different vocabulary items in each of the five Letters with a grand total of 1271 different words.

	Jacob	1 Pt.	2 Pt.	1-3 Jo.	Judas
1	277				
		263			
			165		
				87	
					66
2	59	59			
	23		23		
	26			26	
	15				15
		23	23		
		20		20	
		12			12
			12	12	
			21		21
				6	6
3	16	16	16		
	22	22		22	
	9	9			9
	11		11	11	
	3		3		3
	3			3	3
		13	13	13	
		9	9		9
		1		1	1
			6	6	6
4	27	27	27	27	
	8	8	8		8
	4	4		4	4
	5		5	5	5
		7	7	7	7
5	52	52	52	52	52
	560	545	401	302	227

Total vocabulary 1271

In general, a table of this sort has the following characteristic features: the word group to which a vocabulary item occurring in the text belongs can be ascertained by a finite number of questions. By the method of binary coding, Sect. 12.1, we first ascertain to which of the 5 word groups in our case it belongs; whether it is peculiar to a Letter, or common to two Letters, etc., or common to all Letters; having determined the overall group, we then establish by the same procedure to which of the 5 groups of the same denomination our word belongs. Observe how, in locating the group to which a word belongs, the variable "occurrence frequency" is replaced by the binary opposition of presence vs. absence.

This shows *binary* opposition to be a characteristic of the substitution of occurrence frequency for the qualitative features of morphemes. Another characteristic is *symmetry*, since the combinations of text parts in which a word appears are perfectly democratic in the sense that what applies to one such combination applies to all of the same type: according to the random partitioning function a word has the same

chance of appearing in any of a specified combination of parts. The third characteristic is the *parsimony* in the partition of vocabulary which was described in *TTM*,
Sect. 21.5, and was there compared to the statistical design known as "incompletely
balanced randomised blocks". The concatenation of vocabulary between the text
parts is briefly such as to ensure the consideration of all words needed for the content
in question with the least amount of repetition of vocabulary items in different parts
compatible with completeness.

The three characteristics of binarity, symmetry and parsimony were shown by
R. B. Lees (Language 1959) to be the characteristic features of the system of phonological oppositions according to Trubetzkoy. We thus find vocabulary connectivity
to be an error-reducing device of language on the morphemic level characterised by
precisely the same features as the system of phonological oppositions as an error-
reducing device on the phonemic level.

XI

SPECTROGRAPHY OF SPEECH (WRITING) ON THE MORPHEMIC LEVEL

11.1 THE CONCEPT OF MORPHEME SPECTROGRAPHY

The theorem of the isomorphy between phonology and the frequency theory of vocabulary use has its strongest support in what I call "spectrography of speech on the morphemic level", this being the analogue, even the isomorph, of the spectrography of speech on the phonemic level.

The latter is a variety of Spectrum Analysis. Ordinary "white" light such as that from an electric glow lamp, when analysed by the apparatus called the Spectroscope, is found to contain all the colours of the visible spectrum in form of a continuous band of colour varying gradually from red at one end, through orange, yellow, green, blue, indigo, to violet, at the other. This is known as a *continuous spectrum*, and it is obtainable from any brightly glowing solid or liquid. Glowing gases, however, give a number of isolated colours, each appearing as an image of the slit of the spectroscope through which the light falls on a screen: they are called *spectrum lines* on that account. No two gases, of different chemical composition, give the same spectrum. This is the basis of *spectrum analysis*, which consists in vaporising the substance to be analysed, making it luminous by heat or by an electric current or otherwise, and examining its radiation by the spectroscope. The resulting spectrum is always characteristic of the materials present.

Extension of the principle of the spectrum analysis of light to sound has led to the variety known as spectrography of speech. It is the decomposition of a given sound phenomenon into its constituent sound waves of different length. In both cases, the term "frequency" refers to vibrations, more exactly, the number of waves passing a point in unit time. But the waves of light are transverse waves, i.e. waves formed through the vibrating particles being displaced, not along the direction in which the wave moves, but at right angles to it. Conversely, if they are displaced in the direction of the wave's progress, as in the case of sound, they are called "longitudinal" waves. I mention this important difference between the two types of spectrum analysis in order to make the transition from sound spectrography to morphemic spectrography appear less startling.

On the morphemic level, the term "frequency" means "frequency of occurrence" of a morpheme in passages of substantial length of continued speech, written or otherwise. That a new variety of spectrum analysis should use a new conception of frequency is not surprising. The meanings of frequency in the sense of vibration of molecules of air and of repetition of morphemes are not so far distant as might appear at first. We know that recurrence of certain grammar forms along the line of discourse approaches periodicity, and recurrence of lexicon items of great frequency along the line of discourse may be said to be quasi-periodical. But be it understood, that the substitution of occurrence frequency for physical periodicity for the purpose of morphemic spectrography does not require any true identity of the two phenomena. There are intrinsic reasons for using occurrence frequency as a morpheme variable (Chpt. 10). It is the *isomorphy of function* which is essential for speaking of spectrum analysis on the morphemic level.

The relation between global frequency of vocabulary items and vocabulary connectivity in terms of the number of text parts to which a word belongs is such that spectral analysis could be performed both ways: as the analysis of the global frequencies according to the contributions from the possible combinations of text parts, or as the analysis of the frequency of words appearing in the various combinations of text parts according to the contributions by the different frequency classes. In either case a morphemic frequency phenomenon is analysed into its constituent frequencies, just as in other forms of spectrum analysis.

The two-sidedness of the relation between global frequency distribution and vocabulary partitioning is a perfect example of what I have called Type-Token Duality. In the vocabulary distribution according to frequency, the vocabulary item is the *type* and its repeated occurrences the *token*; in the vocabulary partitioning it is the word groups peculiar to a segment, common to 2 segments, ... all segments which are the *type*, and the vocabulary items belonging to such groups which are the *token*.

Having arrived at the conclusion that it is the vocabulary connectivity in terms of the number of words common to the various combinations of text segments which is vital for the redundancy or the reduction of error in transmitting and receiving a message, or briefly for the quick understanding of a message, we shall concentrate upon the spectrum analysis of these word groups. The method is as follows. Empirically, i.e. by counting and sorting, we arrive at the global frequency distribution of vocabulary according to occurrence frequency of the individual items, and also at the numbers for vocabulary connectivity, i.e. the words peculiar to one part, common to two, ... all parts. The analysis consists in accounting for the numbers of vocabulary items belonging to specified combinations of text parts by the contributions to these numbers from the various frequency classes of the global frequency distribution.

11.2   THE TECHNIQUE OF MORPHEME SPECTROGRAPHY

The mathematical model used for calculating the contributions is the Random Partitioning Function, *TTM*, Chpt. III, XVII. The numerical table of the function,

TABLE 19

showing the number f_x of nouns occurring X times in samples from four of Macaulay's essays: Milton, Hampden, Frederick the Great and Bacon, the samples of the first three being of about 4,000 occurrences each, that from the fourth of about 8,000 occurrences corresponding to two samples of 4,000 each.

X	f_x	X	f_x	X	f_x	X	f_x
1	1460	22	11	44	2	74	2
2	605	23	5	46	1	82	2
3	315	24	7	47	3	86	1
4	212	25	4	48	2	88	2
5	159	26	4	49	3	90	1
6	122	27	6	50	2	94	1
7	84	28	5	51	4	95	1
8	68	29	9	52	3	100	1
9	58	30	6	54	3	104	1
10	46	31	7	55	3	106	1
11	40	32	1	56	2	128	1
12	25	33	5	57	2	134	1
13	30	34	5	58	1	139	1
14	24	35	2	59	2	141	1
15	23	36	7	60	4	143	1
16	19	37	5	62	1	193	1
17	24	38	4	64	3	239	1
18	25	39	5	65	1	459	1
19	11	40	3	68	1		
20	9	42	3	72	1	Total 3543	
21	12	43	2	73	1		

TTM, pp. 341-412, makes it possible to calculate the contributions with the least possible arithmetical labour. For a specified combination of K segments, if the whole text has been divided into R parts, or if R parts or samples are combined into one total, we read in the table the probability of a vocabulary item of specified occurrence frequency X to appear in such a combination K. Multiplying the global frequency X with the corresponding probability, we get the number of words of that frequency class as its contribution to the words appearing in specified combinations of segments.

The illustration of Table 19 utilises some of the material of Yule's word count in samples from Macaulay's essays, combining, however, that material in a way more suitable for our purpose. Five samples of about 4,000 occurrences each were taken from four of Macaulay's essays, namely one from each of the essays on

Milton   with   3923 occurrences and 1537 different words
Hampden   with   4149 occurrences and 1333 different words
Frederick the Great with   4061 occurrences and 1545 different words

and two samples from the essay on

Bacon   with   4021 occurrences and 1413 different words
                   and   4022 occurrences and 1413 different words

Total occurrences   20,178

For the mathematics of the random partitioning function of vocabulary, it is immaterial whether the samples are from different works or from the same work. We regard, therefore, the combined frequency distribution of these counts as the result of com-

TABLE 20

Numerical spectrum of the expected class frequencies (ABCDE) (ABCDε), (ABCδε), (ABγδε), (Aβγδε) by random partitioning from the data of the word count from samples of Macaulay's essays, Table 19. Col. 7 gives the "check total" which should reproduce f_x of that table within the limits of errors of rounding off. In cols. 2-6 a dash signifies zero or a contribution of less than 0.1 words.

X	$(ABCDE)$	$(ABCDε)$	$(ABCδε)$	$(ABγδε)$	$(Aβγδε)$	"Check Total"
1	—	—	—	—	292	1460
2	—	—	—	48.4	24.2	605
3	—	—	15.12	15.12	2.52	315
4	—	8.14	12.21	4.75	.34	212
5	6.11	12.21	7.63	1.53	—	158.8
6	14.05	12.18	4.21	.49	—	122
7	18.06	9.03	1.94	.13	—	83.9
8	21.93	7.11	1.01	—	—	67.6
9	24.77	5.54	.54	—	—	57.9
10	24.04	3.86	.26	—	—	45.9
11	24.25	2.87	.14	—	—	40
12	16.95	1.50	—	—	—	24.5
13	22.14	1.49	—	—	—	29.6
14	18.91	.98	—	—	—	23.8
15	19.06	.77	—	—	—	22.9
16	16.38	.51	—	—	—	18.9
17	21.34	.52	—	—	—	23.9
18	22.77	.44	—	—	—	25
19	10.21	.16	—	—	—	11
20	8.48	.10	—	—	—	9
21	11.45	.11	—	—	—	12
22	10.60	.10	—	—	—	11
23	4.85	—	—	—	—	4.9
24	6.84	—	—	—	—	6.8
25	3.93	—	—	—	—	3.9
26	3.94	—	—	—	—	3.9
27	5.93	—	—	—	—	5.9
28⎰ 459⎱	135	—	—	—	—	135
Total	472	67.62	43.06	70.42	319.06	3540

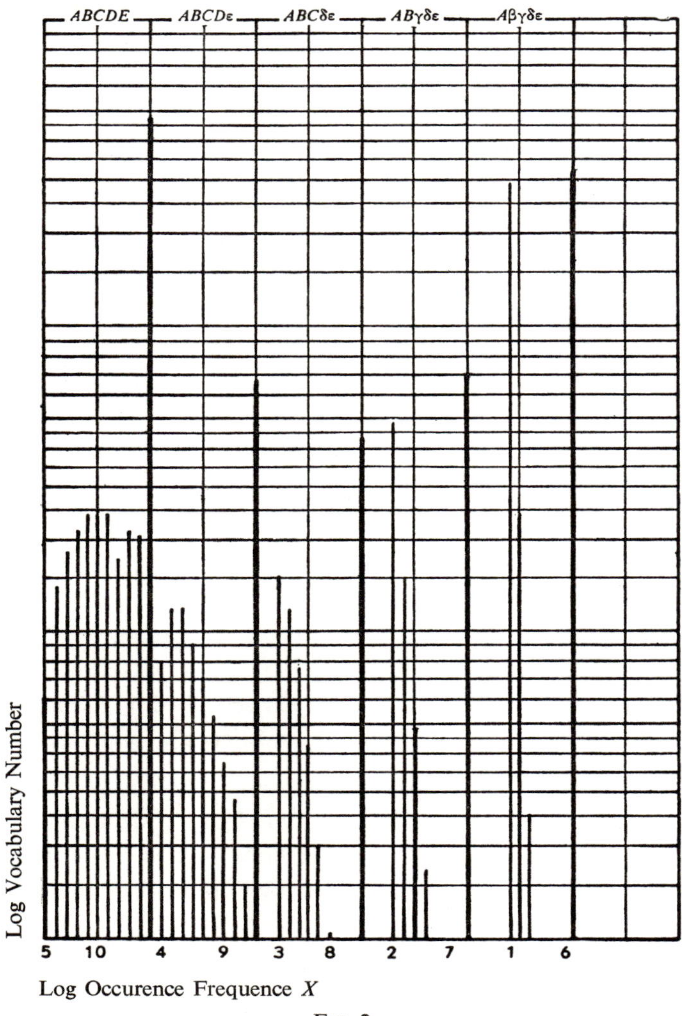

Fig. 2.

pounding five samples of 4,000 occurrences each into one overall distribution of 20,178 occurrences. The total vocabulary distribution is given in Table 19.

Table 20 gives the number of words in specified combinations of parts calculated by the random partitioning function.

The possible number of combinations of five parts, denoting these parts by the letters A, B, C, D, E, and the absence in a given part by the corresponding small letters of the Greek alphabet α, β, γ, δ, ε, are calculated by the formula $n!/(n-r)!\,r!$, n being 5 in our case, and r varying from 1 to 5. The numbers of combinations of each type calculated by this formula are shown below

$$
\begin{aligned}
ABCDE&... \quad 1\\
ABCD\varepsilon&... \quad 5\\
ABC\delta\varepsilon&.... \quad 10\\
AB\gamma\delta\varepsilon&.... \quad 10\\
A\beta\gamma\delta\varepsilon&.... \quad 5
\end{aligned}
$$

Multiplying the number of words common to a specified combination of parts by the number of such combinations, that is, in the order of the columns, by 1, 5, 10, 10, 5, respectively, and summing over all combinations belonging to a specified X, gives the global frequency of vocabulary items, column 7.

Figure 2 is the Spectrogram of vocabulary partitioning based upon Table 20. The ordinates (thin lines) represent the contribution by individual X to a class of combination. For the first two classes of combinations, only the contribution from the first five values of X are plotted; contributions of less than unity are not plotted. The strong lines represent the sums of the contributions for any class of combination.

11.3   THE METHOD OF SELECTIVE OPERATORS

In mathematical language, what we are doing in sorting the words according to the number of parts of the text in which they appear, is to use the method of *selective operators*. The action of such operators has been described by Eddington in a rather amusing way (A. Eddington, "New Pathways in Science", Cambridge, 1935):

"In my schooldays a foolish riddle was current—'How do you catch lions in the desert?' Answer:'In the desert you have lots of sand and a few lions; so you take a sieve and sieve out the sand, and the lions remain'. I recall it because it describes one of the most usual methods used in quantum theory for obtaining anything that we wish to study.

Let Z denote the zoo, and S_l the operation of sieving out or selecting lions; then $S_l Z = L$, where L denotes lions—or, as we might more formally say, L denotes a pure ensemble having the leonine characteristic. These pure selective operators have a rather curious mathematical property, viz.

$$
S_{l_2} = S_l \tag{A}
$$

For S_l^2 (an abbreviation for $S_l S_l$) indicates that having selected all the lions, you repeat the operation, selecting all the lions from what you have obtained. Putting through the sieve a second time makes no difference; and in fact, repeating it n times you have $S_l^n = S_l$. The property expressed by equation (A) *is called idempotency*."

Observe the identity in form of the property expressed by equation (A) with Boole's law of duality $x^2 = x$.

Now let S_t be the operation of selecting tigers. We have

$$S_t\, S_l = 0 \tag{B}$$

For if you have first selected all the lions, and go on to select from these all the tigers, you obtain nothing.

"Now suppose that the different kinds of animals in the zoo are numbered in a catalogue from 1 to n and we introduce a selective operator for each; then

$$S_1 + S_2 + S_3 + \ldots + S_n = I \tag{C}$$

where I is the stay-as-you-were operator. For if you sieve out each constituent in turn and add together the results, you get the mixture you started with."

Let us now formulate the sorting of words according to the number of parts to which they belong in terms of a sieving operation of particulate material, i.e. material consisting of discrete units: if we let the words peculiar to a part, and therefore having the fewest associations, correspond to the particles passing the sieve with the smallest sieve opening, the words common to two parts correspond to the particles passing the sieve with the next largest sieve opening and so on, until we come to the words common to all parts, and thus the words having the greatest number of linkages with other words, as corresponding to the largest particles, i.e. those passing only the sieve with the largest sieve openings in the series, the results of a word count according to the number of segments to which a word belongs is completely comparable to a sieving operation of particulate matter using a number of sieves with graduated differences in the size of the sieve openings.

The formula at which we arrive is precisely that for selecting the different animals from the zoo. Denoting the various word groups by V_1, V_2, etc. and the total by V, we have

$$V_1 + V_2 + \ldots + V_n = V$$

A set of operators which satisfies (A), (B) and (C) is called a *spectral set,* because it analyses any aggregation into pure constituents in the same way that light is analysed by a prism or grating into the different pure colours which form the spectrum. The three equations respectively secure that the operators of a spectral set are idempotent, non-overlapping and exhaustive.

It is precisely such a spectral set which our diagram, Fig. 2 represents, but it does so in a two-fold way: it gives the spectrum of the total vocabulary according to the different combinations, K, of segments, and of such word groups according to the contribution by the global frequencies X. Since a particular sieving operation, i.e. for a specified combination of segments, need not exhaust a particular frequency X, but let only a fraction of it through, we speak here of a *fractioning operator.*

It should be emphasized that the method of selective operators, or in terms of the principal operating instrument, of sieving, is of fundamental importance in Quantum theory where the sieve is replaced by a grating. As Eddington puts it: "In Einstein's theory of relativity the observer is a man who sets out in quest of truth armed with a measuring-rod. In quantum theory he sets out armed with a sieve."

As on anther occasion, Chpts. XVII-XIX, we find that the appropriate mathematical procedures to be used when taking into account the content value of words—in this case more particularly their association values—are those of quantum theory.

BOOK TWO

THE RELATION BETWEEN LANGUAGE IN THE MASS AND LANGUAGE IN THE LINE

PART IV

THE STATISTICAL THEORY OF
LINGUISTIC CODING – INFORMATION THEORY

XII

FUNDAMENTAL CONCEPTS—INFORMATION AS A
STATISTICAL CONCEPT

The study of language as a code as different from the historical study of language is a prerequisite for establishing non-genealogical relationships and, in particular, isomorphy between languages. If it is a case of structure rather than genealogy, the appropriate methodological instrument is the mathematical theory of information, because it can be regarded as the quantification of de Saussure's conception of language as a branch of semiology. It enables us to exhibit in unequivocal terms what different languages have in common through being only different coding systems of sensibly the same manifold of experience.

12.1   THE STRATEGY OF INQUIRY

It would be rash to assume that all readers of this book are familiar with the mathematical theory of information as put forward by C. E. Shannon in 1948, and I shall therefore give in this Section an outline of the basic concepts and ideas of that theory, in particular with a view to their use in structural linguistics. For a more general exposition, the reader is referred to Meyer-Eppler (1959) and *LCC*, Chpts. 9, 10; *TTM*, Chpts. 12, 13.

We start with what may be called the "strategy of inquiry". Let us suppose we were engaged in the well-known game of having to guess an object by asking questions which may only be answered by "yes" and "no". The strategy of inquiry may consist in dividing the whole inventory of objects into two parts, A and B, say, and asking whether the object was in A or B; having ascertained that it was in B, say, the process of approximative identification is continued by division of B into two parts, and so on until the part in which the object has been located is reduced in size to one item only which provides the required answer.

There exists, however, what may be called an "optimum strategy of inquiry" by division and subdivision, whose operating characteristic is to put the questions in such a way that the positive or negative answer may be expected with sensibly the same probability. This will be the case if the inventory is divided into as nearly as possible equal parts, the half in which the object is located to be divided again into equal parts, and so on. For this case, the number of questions required for identification of the object equals the dyadic logarithm, i.e. the logarithm to the base 2, rounded off to the next whole number, of the number of objects in the inventory. This quantity is considered to be a measure of information—better, of the effort needed for obtaining the information in question. It is usually denoted by the symbol I or H (we shall use the latter) and called the Entropy because of the similarity of its mathematical structure with that of the Entropy of statistical physics.

12.2   DERIVATION OF THE ENTROPY AS A MEASURE OF INFORMATION

We assume that for the transmission of a message there are different signs at our disposal, and that the message requires N signs altogether. The relative frequency of one of the r different signs is p_i and their sum, of course, unity:

$$\Sigma\, p_i = 1$$

For the number of different messages of length N which can be formed out of r different signs with relative frequencies p_i, we obtain by the combinatorial calculus:

$$Z = N!\,/\,(p_1N)!\,(p_2N)!\,\ldots\,(p_rN)! \tag{1}$$

This number becomes a maximum for $p_1 = p_2 = \ldots p_r = p = 1/r$:

$$Z \;= N!\,/\left(\frac{N}{r}!\right) \tag{1a}$$

The application of Sterling's formula $N! = r \log N - N\ (N \gg 1)$ gives

$$\log Z = -N\,\Sigma\, p_i \log p_i \tag{2}$$

$$\log Z' = N \log r = -N \log p \tag{2a}$$

If the logarithm is that to the base 2 (ld), these quantities represent the total information in N symbols. Dividing by N gives the average information per symbol·

$$H = -\ \Sigma\, p_i\, \mathrm{ld}\, p_i \tag{3}$$

$$H' = -\mathrm{ld}\, p \tag{3a}$$

where ld denotes the dyadic logarithm. For unequal p_i, $\bar{p}$ takes the place of p.

Their quotient

$$h = \Sigma\, p_i\, \mathrm{ld}\, p_i/\mathrm{ld}\, p \tag{4}$$

shows the influence of weighting the symbols by their actual probabilities, or roughly, the influence of the statistical distribution of the signs.

Because of their formal similarity with the expression for the Entropy of statistical mechanics, H and H' are called Entropies, and their quotient h the Relative Entropy. Its complement to unity

$$R = 1 - h \tag{5}$$

is a measure of the redundancy of the code, that is the property which enables us to use the stability of the relative frequency for making guesses as to the missing parts of the message with a reasonable degree of expectation to be correct.

It is peculiar to information theory to use logarithms to the base 2 implying a binary code for purposes of regarding H as the "information". As an example of how H is used in that respect may serve the following illustration.

From the probability of occurrence p for the letters of English in a large sample of the written language, the entropy H was calculated according to formula (3) and resulted as 4.76 binary units ("bits") per letter. The reason for calling H the information is that it represents the number of binary choices required for guessing or identifying a particular letter. In our case of printed English it means that a missing letter could be effectively guessed and restored by not more than five guesses.

In this way, "information" is easily recognised as being derived from the *combinatorial coefficient* of the probability according to the multinomial theorem, Sect. 2.2. The reason is that information theory, though mainly concerned with arrangements of symbols along the line of discourse, is so only for transmission purposes, not for reasons of working with linguistic structure. Distribution in the linguistic sense is not its subject.

The fact that H is not a probability but only the combinatorial coefficient of a probability is not always understood and appreciated in information theory, where the sample relative frequencies p' of a given language sample are often not distinguished from the population probabilities p, though it is a matter well understood by physicists, who in statistical mechanics are often faced with the problem of having to determine the probability of a joint occurrence of particle numbers $n_1, n_2 \ldots n_r$ if the probability for the r categories are $p_1, p_2 \ldots p_r$. It is indeed a question of whether the communication engineer is ever aware of that distinction and of the role it plays in using the entropy. For very great samples, the sample relative frequencies can be regarded as satisfactory estimates of the population probabilities, but this does not change the fact that in principle the entropy as calculated corresponds only to the combinatorial factor of the probability, formula (4), Part I. In this respect we must not be misled by the second part of the probability using p apparently as the first uses p'. It does so only in $\log p$, but not in the statistical weights of $\log p$, which are the p'. The fact that H represents the 1st term of $\log P$ by the multinomial theorem brings out the mathematical unity of language statistics and information theory.

12.3 BINARY CODING AS OPTIMUM STRATEGY OF INQUIRY

The process of the optimum strategy of inquiry can be used with great advantage for coding a given inventory of items. Such items may be only qualitatively distinguishable from each other, or they may be quantitatively distinguishable, their conventional order, however, not being throughout one according to magnitude of probability of occurrence. Instances of this are the series of English word frequencies from a dictionary count or from running texts according to phoneme or letter number per word, and the series of Chinese ideograms in the order of the dictionary, where the increase in the stroke number of radicals is not concomitant with the increase of the frequency of derivatives per radical. The possibility of reducing the information-theoretical effort—for instance, in terms of costs—, through suitable codification was, as a practical method, known long before Shannon formulated his mathematical theory of information. A case in question is the Morse alphabet as used in telegraphy. The Morse Code was originally such that the most frequent letters in English (e, t, a, i, n, o, s ...) were given the shortest, and the rarest letters (z, x, j, q, k ...) the longest, and therefore most expensive, signals. In today's Morse alphabet this principle is still clearly recognizable; the codification is adapted to the frequency distribution of the letters of the alphabet in English. It follows, however, that the advantage which this codification provides could, to a large extent, disappear, or even become a disadvantage, if the telegraphic communication is in languages which have an essentially different frequency distribution of letters than English. For most of the European languages this risk is not great; however, for a telegram in Russian or Serbo-Croatian, where the letter "o" is the most frequent one, and where also the other letters have a different ranking order for frequency than in English, the conventional Morse Code would not be the most suitable.

In order to describe the process of binary codification in mathematical symbols, we shall use the symbols

N = text length in terms of number of symbols

f_i = number of occurrences of symbol i

$p_i = f_i/N$ relative frequency of symbol i

b_i = number of binary units ("bits") for the symbol i

Then, the entropy after coding

$$H_{\text{cod}} = \Sigma \, b_i \, p_i \tag{6}$$

The relative entropy h changes correspondingly to

$$h^* = \frac{H}{H_{\text{cod}}} = \frac{\Sigma \, p_i \, \text{ld} \, p_i}{\Sigma \, b_i \, p_i} \tag{7}$$

Binary coding has reduced the information-theoretical effort if h^* exceeds the original relative entropy h, i.e. if $H_{\text{cod}} = \Sigma \, b_i \, p_i < -\text{ld} \, \bar{p}$.

For every distribution there exists an optimal case, i.e. a coding procedure which makes H_{cod} a minimum and, consequently, h^* a maximum. This is achieved if we succeed in making the relative entropy h^* equal to unity. The condition for this is

$$H_{\text{cod}} = H$$

or

$$b_i = \operatorname{ld} \frac{1}{p_i}, \tag{8}$$

which means that the best coding is one which leaves the entropy of the source unchanged.

If the probabilities p_i of symbols are not integral powers of $\frac{1}{2}$, the best approximation to ideal coding, i.e. minimum redundancy, is achieved as follows.

We arrange the symbols of the alphabet according to their frequency of occurrence, starting with the symbol occurring most often. The series is then divided into two as nearly as possible equal parts. The first part is given the binary symbol 0, the second the binary symbol 1. With the partial masses of symbols obtained in this way, we proceed in the same way, until no further sub-division is possible, adding always for the first part of a sub-division the symbol 0 and for the second part the symbol 1. The number of binary units obtained in this way for an alphabetic symbol is then equal to the number of dichotomies which were necessary for its isolation.

12.4 BINARY CODING OF THE ENGLISH ALPHABETIC SYSTEM

The following is an illustration of the method applied to the letters of the English alphabet. The letters are listed in Table 21 according to frequency of occurrence in terms of percent:

TABLE 21 (after Dewey, 1923)

Letters	Percentage frequency	Letters	Percentage frequency
e	12.68	f	2.56
t	9.78	m	2.44
a	7.88	w	2.14
o	7.76	y	2.02
i	7.07	g	1.87
n	7.06	p	1.86
s	6.34	b	1.56
r	5.94	v	1.02
h	5.73	k	.60
l	3.94	x	.16
d	3.89	j	.10
u	2.80	q	.09
c	2.68	z	.06

The first dichotomy gives the partial masses

0 ~ e, t, a, o, i, n, with a combined frequency of 52,23% and

1 ~ s, r, h, l, d, u, c, f, m, w, y, g, p, b, v, k, x, j, q, z, with a combined frequency of 47.7%.

No symbol has been isolated by the first dichotomy, and a further dichotomy is therefore necessary. In the case of 0, it leads to the partial masses

$$00\ (22.46\%) \quad \text{and} \quad 01\ (29.78\%)$$

Through the third dichotomy symbols are isolated

$$
\begin{array}{lll}
000 & e & (12.68\%) \\
001 & t & (9.78\%)
\end{array}
$$

A fourth dichotomy gives

$$
\begin{array}{lll}
0100 & a & (7.88\%) \\
0101 & o & (7.76\%) \\
0110 & i & (7.07\%) \\
0111 & n & (7.06\%)
\end{array}
$$

These binary symbols represent one of the possible codings. We thus obtain the following series

Letter	e	t	a	o	i	n
Symbol	000	001	0100	0101	0110	0111

In the same way we dichotomise the partial mass having in the first dichotomy the symbol 1, and obtain

s	1000	u	11000	y	11100	k	1111100
r	1001	c	11001	g	111010	x	1111101
h	1010	f	11010	p	111011	j	1111110
l	10110	m	110110	b	111100	q	11111110
d	10111	w	110111	v	111101	z	11111111

The structure of the binary code is exhibited in figure 3, which shows the successive dichotomies in graphical form.

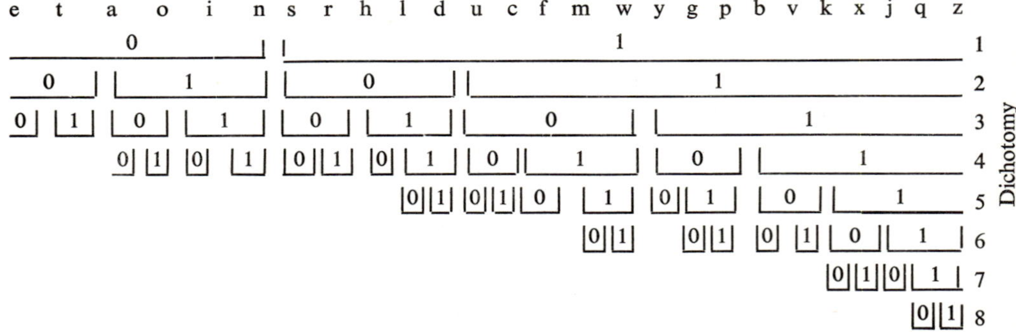

FIG. 3.

The extent of approximation of this binary coding to the idea of coding as defined by equation

$$b_i = \operatorname{ld} \frac{1}{p_i} \tag{9}$$

is shown in figure 4. The entropy H_{cod} calculated by equation (6) gives

$$H_{\text{cod}} = \Sigma \, b_i \, p_i = 4.14$$

as against the observed entropy

$$H = -\Sigma \, p_i \operatorname{ld} p_i = 3.98.$$

The relative entropy is

$$h^* = H/H_{\text{cod}} = .946 \tag{9a}$$

and the redundancy R^*

$$R^* = 1 - .946 = .054, \tag{10}$$

which is reduced against the redundancy

$$R = H/H' = 1 - 3.928/4.701 = .164 \tag{11}$$

This shows the binary coding to be of advantage from a non-theoretical point of view.

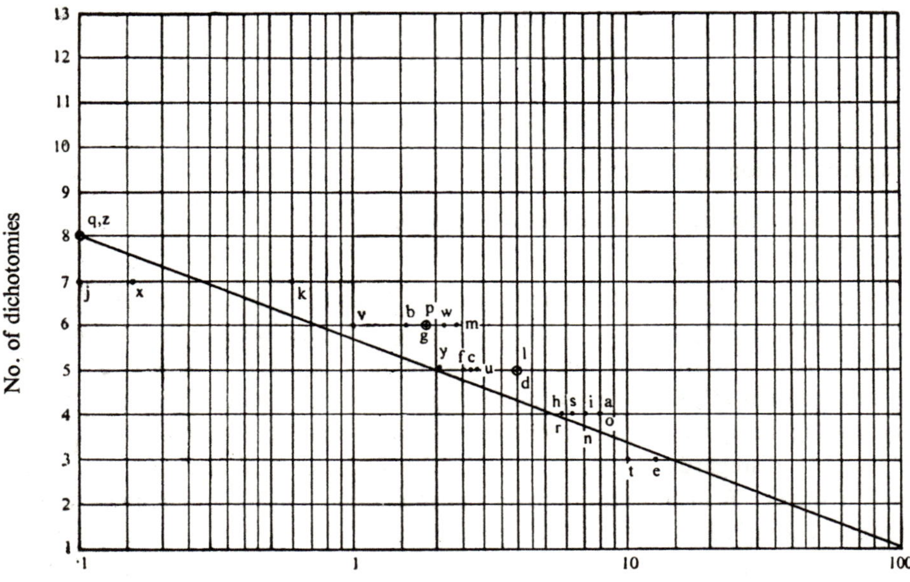

FIG. 4.   Binary coding of English alphabet.

12.5 BINARY CODING OF THE CYRILLIC ALPHABETIC SYSTEM

As another illustration, we give the *binary coding of the Russian alphabet:*

TABLE 22

Letters	Percentage Frequency	Binary Coding	Letters	Percentage Frequency	Binary Coding
O	10.8	000	Ы	1.8	110111
E	9.3	001	З	1.5	111000
И	8.0	0100	Г	1.5	111001
A	7.3	0101	У	1.5	111010
H	6.6	0110	Б	1.3	111011
T	6.4	0111	X	1.3	1111000
C	5.5	1000	Ъ	1.2	1111001
P	5.3	1001	Й	1.0	1111010
B	4.2	10100	Ж	.8	1111011
Λ	4.0	10101	Ю	.7	1111100
M	3.5	10110	Ц	.6	1111101
П	3.4	10111	Щ	.6	11111100
K	3.0	11000	Ф	.4	11111101
Д	2.7	11001	Ш	.4	11111110
Я	2.5	11010	Э	.3	111111110
У	2.0	110110	Ь	.1	111111111

$$H_{\text{cod}} = 4.478$$
$$H \quad = 4.328$$
$$R^* \quad = 1 - H/H_{\text{cod}} = .035$$
$$H' \quad = 5$$
$$R \quad = 1 - H/H' = .134$$

The approximation of binary coding according to Figure 3 to the ideal code, $b_i = \operatorname{ld} \dfrac{1}{p_i}$ is, graphically represented in Figure 5.

Any increase or reduction of the redundancy, R and R^*, must be carefully interpreted. Neither can by itself be regarded as a sign of deterioration or improvement of coding. In our illustration, the reduction of R^* against R is only due to H_{cod} being smaller than H', the entropy for equi-distribution; in other words, it is due to binary coding being an improvement on the most uneconomical kind of coding which simply disregards the differences in the frequency of alphabetic symbols. Insofar, a smaller R means an improvement in coding. On the other hand, a truly economical coding will result in H being smaller than H', and the more so, the better the coding, i.e. the more the numbers of bits per coding symbol stand in inverse relation to the frequency of the alphabetic symbols. Insofar, great economy in coding through the coding symbols being in better conformity with the ideal binary

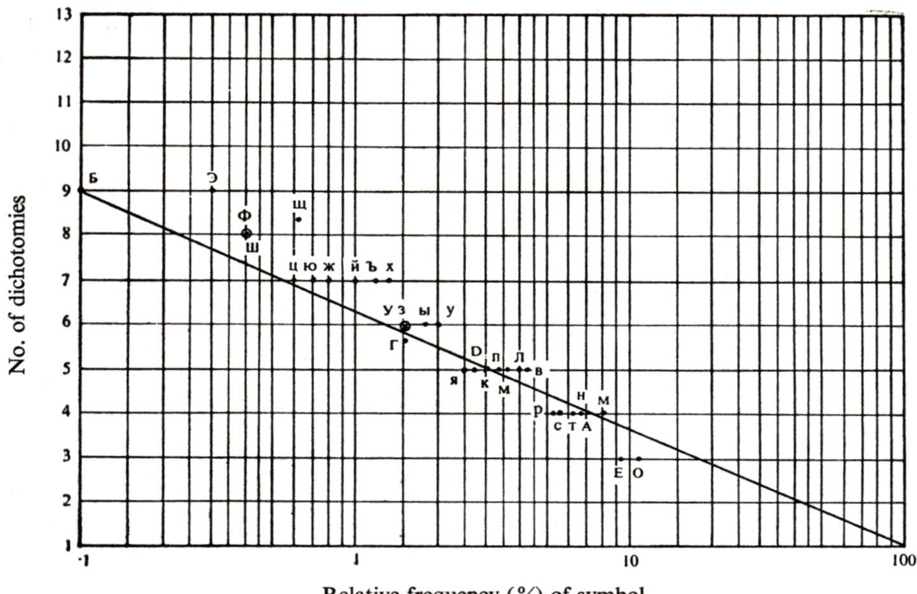

FIG. 5.   Binary coding of Cyrillian alphabet.

coding (represented by the straight line in our Figures 2 and 3) will, for a given alphabet, and thus for a constant H, result in an increase in R.

Conclusions

The values of H_{cod} and h^* by themselves, and in comparison with the corresponding values of H and h, show a high degree of similarity for the two alphabetic distributions, i.e. of English and Russian, in spite of the ranking of individual letters (phonemes) being rather different in the two languages. Thus, what the method of binary coding has brought out very neatly is the high degree of isomorphy between the languages in respect of the alphabetic distribution, in spite of different ranking of the individual phonemes. Mathematically, this is expressed by the high coefficient of linear regression between letter frequency and the number of dichotomies. It is a safe guess that such isomorphies are not restricted to this particular pair of languages, but can be regarded as expressing a general characteristic of all alphabetic languages.

The importance of isomorphy for the study of languages has been stressed by R. Jakobson (R. Jakobson, "Typological Studies and their Contribution to Historical Comparative Linguistics", *Proceedings of the VIIIth International Congress of Linguists, Oslo, 1957*). Jakobson starts his paper with a very apt quotation from Alf Sommerfelt: "Il n'y a pas de différence de principe entre les systèmes phonétiques du monde." As Jakobson has pointed out, instead of lightening the linguist's burden of constructive thinking, by taking the standpoint that each language has its unique history, and therefore its unique structure, isomorphism tends to unite different states of one language, or two states, whether simultaneous or temporarily distant, of two different languages, whether contiguous or remote and whether cognate or not. Briefly, thus, whereas the genetical method operates with kinship and the areal with affinity, the typological method must work with isomorphism. Rightly understood, the discovery of isomorphy with respect to certain aspects of genetically unrelated languages, is only a consequence of de Saussure's treatment of language as a code for the expression of thought and, consequently, as a branch of semiology.

Typology discloses laws which underlie the phonological and the morphological structure of languages. In this way, we detect in genetically unrelated languages of the world uniformities or near-uniformities. "Exceptions in cases of some near-uniformities will call for a more supple formulation of the general law, and do not compel us to abandon the idea of isomorphy." (Jakobson, *l.c.*).

Moreover, the binary principle introduced in our illustrations primarily as a mathematical device, may acquire linguistic meaning. It was said by E. Schrödinger of wave-equation fame in his *Statistical Thermodynamics* (1946) that it is "one of the fascinating features of statistical thermodynamics (which provided the prototype of statistical information theory) that quantities and functions, introduced primarily as mathematical features, almost invariably acquire a fundamental physical meaning". The same may be said of statistical linguistics.

It would be well worth ascertaining whether the quantities b_i do not correspond to what Jakobson has called the number of distinctive features of phonemes. As is well known, Jakobson has formulated a theory according to which every phoneme is to be regarded as a bundle of distinctive features determinable by 12 binary choices. If isomorphy between the b_i, the symbol length according to binary coding, and the number of distinctive features of phonemes could be established, it would show Jakobson's principle of binary choices as being isomorph, or near-isomorph, with binary coding.

XIII A

EFFICIENCY OF CODING—THE LAW OF OPTIMAL REDUNDANCY

13.1   THE CONDITION FOR OPTIMAL CODING

A characteristic feature of information theory as communication theory, and thus in its application to language, is the reciprocal relation between symbol length and symbol probability (Hartley, 1928). It is on this that the efficiency of the code depends.

But although the need for this relation was known, nothing specific had emerged about the particular form the descending series of probabilities assumes according to the efficiency of the code until it was shown (*TTM*, Chpt. XIII) that the condition for optimum coding, that is for coding with the best possible discrimination between symbol length was that the probabilities of symbols of different length should form a geometric series descending from the probability of the smallest symbol.

The general formula for the optimum entropy, the mean symbol length M being given, is

$$\max (H|M) = M \log M - (M-1) \log (M-1) \tag{12}$$

Proof:

Definitions:

$$-\Sigma p_n \log_e p_n = H, \ \Sigma np_n = M, \ \Sigma p_n = 1 \tag{13}$$

if M is given, to maximise H.

We differentiate the three equations (13) partially with respect to p_n, and introduce Lagrange undetermined multipliers and μ. We get for all n,

$$1 + \log_e p_n + \lambda + n\mu = 0 \tag{14}$$

from which we deduce equ. (12) as follows:

$$p_n = e^{-n\mu - \lambda - 1} \tag{15}$$

Thus, the p_n form a geometrical series with $e^{-\mu}$ as common factor, and

$$p_1 = e^{-\mu - \lambda - 1}$$

Since for a geometric series $p_1 = 1/M$, and common factor $e^{-\mu} = 1 - p_1$

$$e^{-\mu - \lambda - 1} = 1 - e^{-\mu} \tag{16}$$

Furthermore, since

$$p_1 = e^{\mu-\lambda-1} = 1/M$$

and

$$e^{-\mu} = 1-1/M,$$

we have

$$e^{-\lambda-1} = (M-1)^{-1}$$

and

$$p_n = 1/M\,(1-1/M)^{n-1}$$

$H_{\max}$ as the negative arithmetic mean of $\log_2 p_n$ is then calculated as

$$H_{\max} = - \Sigma\, p_n \log_2 p_n = \sum \frac{1}{M}\left(1-\frac{1}{N}\right)^{n-1}\left\{ -\log_2 M + (n-1)\log_2 \frac{M-1}{M} \right\}$$

which, after a little algebra, reduces to

$$M \log_2 M - (M-1)\log_2 (M-1) \tag{17}$$

If M is given and H maximised, the probabilities

$$p_n = 1/M\,(1-1/M)^{n-1} \tag{18}$$

form a geometric series with common ratio $(1-1/M)$.

    max. (H) can, therefore, be used as a standard of efficiency.

    This can be interpreted as a parallel to the suitability of the lognormal law in statistical linguistics.

13.2   THE LAW OF FACILITY FOR THE DISCRIMINATION OF PROBABILITIES OF LINGUISTIC UNITS

The lognormal law, when it was first introduced by Galton and MacAllister, was described by the latter as the *"law of facility"*, because it used the fact of experimental psychology according to which visual and other sense data were most easily discriminated by using as a criterion not their differences but their ratios. This is also the reason for the suitability of the lognormal law in statistical linguistics for variables like word length. Evidently, it is the *ratios* of word length which come more readily to our mind for purposes of discrimination than their *differences*.

The lognormal distribution can, therefore, be described as the law of facility for discrimination between different values of the *variable*. In information theory we encounter the curious fact that it is not the variable which is used in logarithmic form but the probabilities of the different categories of the variable, and as a consequence of formula (17) it was found that for optimum discrimination between the linguistic symbols these probabilities should form a geometric series. But this implies a constant ratio between successive probabilities belonging to different categories of the linguistic variable and, therefore, shows discrimination between probabilities according to that law as following the same principle as the discrimination between variables according to the lognormal law, namely, that instead of working with differences for the purpose of discrimination we work here with ratios.

So far, the Hartley relation was only one of the differences in the use of symbols according to symbol length. The importance of (17) lies in this, that it shows the appropriateness of discrimination not by differences but by ratios for optimum discrimination. It seems, therefore, appropriate to call formula (17) *the law of facility for the discrimination of probabilities of linguistic units*, and regard it as the parallel of the lognormal law as that of facility in discriminating between different values of variables occurring in nature.

To test the new law of facility we shall apply formula (17) to the distribution of species according to the number of individuals. This type of distribution was shown to be fitted satisfactorily by the logarithmic series (Fisher et al., 1943).

13.3   THE LOGARITHMIC SERIES IN ITS RELATION TO THE 'LAW OF FACILITY'
(HERDAN, 1959)

Writing ln for $\log_e$, the logarithmic series yields, for $x < 1$,

$$-(1/x) \ln (1-x) = 1 + x/2 + x^2/3 + x^3/4 + \ldots \tag{19}$$

We denote the frequencies of species containing one individual, two individuals etc. by $n_1, n_2 \ldots$ Since the first term in the series is n_1, the number of species with single individuals, the logarithmic series becomes

$$n_1 + \frac{n_1 x}{2} + \frac{n_1 x^2}{3} + \frac{n_1 x^3}{4} + \ldots \tag{20}$$

The sum of all terms to infinity, which is the total number of species, is given by

$$N = \frac{n_1}{x} \left\{ - \ln (1-x) \right\} \tag{21}$$

which is finite for $x < 1$; that is to say the series is convergent.

The $r + 1$st term is obtained from the rth by multiplying by $rx/(r+1)$; the second term is thus less than $\frac{1}{2} n_1$, the third term less than $\frac{1}{3} n_1$, and so on. In general

$$n_{r+1} = n_r \frac{rx}{r+1}$$

$$(r+1) n_{r+1} = rn_r x \tag{22}$$

which, incidentally, enables one to verify Dr. Turing's smoothing formula, as used by Good (1953), as a parameter-free distribution which tacitly implies the logarithmic distribution. Since as n approaches infinity, x approaches unity, formula (22) goes over into Turing's formula

$$r^* \simeq (r+1) n_{r+1} / n_r$$

$$r^* n_r \simeq (r+1) n_{r+1} \tag{23}$$

If the frequencies of species are plotted against the number of specimens, we obtain a graph similar to a hyperbola. The nearer x approaches unity, the closer the resemblance; when $x = 1$ the graph becomes a hyperbola.

The successive terms of the series are the number of species containing 1, 2, 3 ... specimens; it follows that the numbers of specimens in each successive term are,

$$n_1, \, 2\frac{n_1 x}{2}, \, 3\frac{n_1 x^2}{3}, \, 4\frac{n_1 x^3}{4} \text{ etc.}$$

or

$$n_1, \, n_1 x, \, n_1 x^2, \, n_1 x^3 \text{ etc.} \tag{24}$$

This is a geometric series, and its sum to infinity which is the total number of units in the sample or, in terms of the distribution of species according to no. of specimens, the total number of specimens is the first moment about zero:

$$S_1 = \frac{n}{1-x} \tag{25}$$

This is finite if x is less than unity.

From (21) and (25) we obtain the average number of units per group as

$$\frac{S_1}{N} = \frac{x}{(1-x)(-\log_e \overline{1-x})} \tag{26}$$

The second moment about zero, $S_2 = \Sigma f_x x^2$ equals for the logarithmic series

$$\frac{N}{1-x} = \frac{n_1}{(1-x)^2} \tag{27}$$

The ratio of the two quantities of the distribution n_1 and x is a constant which Williams has called α, that is

$$\frac{n_1}{x} = \alpha \ \text{ or } \ n_1 = \alpha x \tag{28}$$

The logarithmic series can therefore be written as

$$\alpha x, \, \alpha\frac{x^2}{2}, \, \alpha\frac{x^3}{3}, \, \alpha\frac{x^4}{4} \ldots \tag{29}$$

In this case the total number of groups is

$$N = -\alpha \log_e (1-x) \tag{30}$$

and the total number of units

$$S_1 = \alpha\frac{x}{1-x} \tag{31}$$

Attention is called to certain differences in notation as used in this Chapter and by Yule, and in the paper by Fisher et al. (1943);

	Fisher et al.	Our notation
Total number of specimens	N	S_1
Total number of species	S	N
Average number of specimens per species	N/S	S_1/N

The Index of Diversity α has been shown by Williams to be nothing but the reciprocal of Yule's Characteristic, or rather to be reciprocal to $K/10^4$. Yule's Characteristic $K = 10^4\,(S_2 - S_1)/S_1^2$ where S_1 and S_2 are the first and second moments about zero. Since for the logarithmic series

$$S_1 = \frac{n_1}{1-x} \text{ and } S_2 = \frac{n_1}{(1-x)^2} \tag{32}$$

it follows that

$$\frac{S_2 - S_1}{S_1{}^2} = \frac{x}{(1-x)\,S_1} = \frac{x}{n_1} = \frac{1}{\alpha} \tag{33}$$

As an illustration, we use results obtained with Malayan butterflies.

TABLE 23 (after Fisher et al., 1943)

Calculated and observed distribution frequencies of butterflies collected in Malaya
The values in the second column are obtained from the logarithmic series (formula 20)) taking $x = 0.997$.

n	S (calc.)	S (found)	Deviations
1	135.05	118	17.05
2	67.33	74	−6.77
3	44.75	44	0.75
4	33.46	24	9.46
5	26.69	29	−2.31
6	22.17	22	0.17
7	18.95	20	−1.05
8	16.53	19	−2.47
9	14.65	20	−5.35
10	13.14	15	−1.86
11	11.91	12	−0.09
12	10.89	14	−3.11
13	10.02	6	4.02
14	9.28	12	−2.72
15	8.63	6	2.63
16	8.07	9	−0.93
17	7.57	9	−1.43
18	7.13	6	1.13
19	6.74	10	−3.26
20	6.38	10	−3.62
21	6.06	11	−4.94
22	5.77	5	0.77
23	5.50	3	2.50
24	5.25	3	2.25
			0.82

$H = 3.817$ Diff. $H = 3.885$ Diff.

$H_{\max} = 3.931$ .114 $H_{\max} = 4.050$ .165

For the observed series, the number of species with individuals between $n = 1$ and $n = 24$ is 501 and the total number of individuals in all these species was 3306; for the series calculated according to the logarithmic series, the corresponding figures were 501.92 and 3132.24 respectively.

For the series in Table 23, $\chi^2 = 19.270$ which for 23 degrees of freedom has a probability of between 0.90 and 0.80 of arising on random sampling, which shows the observed results as being satisfactorily fitted by the log series.

For both series the entropy was calculated according to formula (3) and according to formula (17), that is without any assumption about the distribution form and under the assumption of the series of probabilities being a geometric series and thus compatible with optimal coding. The values are shown at the bottom of the table.

Inspection of the values of H shows that H from the observed series, and still more so that from the theoretical series, approach closely to H_{max}. This throws an interesting light upon the matter and shows the good fit of the observed values by the logarithmic series to be in complete accordance with the law of facility (17). In the light of that law, the fact that the probabilities of the species of butterflies form a geometric series, appears now to be the consequence of the classification of the butterflies being one of maximum efficiency for the purpose of discrimination. We can, therefore, say that the species code is optimal. Moreover, since the law of facility for linguistic observations must be regarded as one applying primarily to the field of language as a human creation, the species code, or rather the optimality of the species code, must also be regarded as a *human* achievement rather than a law of *nature*.

However, attention must be drawn to the fact that the two series of Table 23, although conforming to the definition of the log series, are not geometrical series; it is only their first moment distribution which is a geometrical series.

BI-VARIATE ENTROPY

As bi-variate information parameters could be used the conventional correlation measures, such as the correlation coefficient, the regression coefficient. However, true to its character of working with a frequency only, not with the variable, information theory has its own bi-variate entropy for expressing correlation.

Suppose there are two variates, x and y, each of which has a frequency distribution, x with n and y with m class intervals, and suppose that for N individual events their belonging to a class of both x and y has been recorded, or as we say, their bivariate distribution with regard to x and y has been obtained. Let $P(i, j)$ be the probability of the joint occurrence of the event in the class intervals i of x and j of y. The entropy of the joint event is then

$$H(x,y) = - \sum_{ij} p(i,j) \log p(i,j) \tag{34}$$

while

$$H(x) = - \sum_{ij} p(i,j) \log \sum_{j} p(i,j) = - \sum_{i} p(i) \log p(i)$$

$$H(y) = - \sum_{ij} p(i,j) \log \sum_{i} p(i,j) = - \sum_{j} p(j) \log p(j) \tag{35}$$

The conditional entropy of y, $H_x(y)$ is defined as

$$H_x(y) = - \sum_{ij} p(i,j) \log p_i(j) \tag{35a}$$

similarly the conditional entropy of x:

$$H_y(x) = - \sum_{ij} p(i,j) \log p_j(i) \tag{35b}$$

It is also called the equivocation, or the ambiguity, and measures how uncertain we are of y, on an average, if we know x, and vice versa.

Substituting in (35a) for $p_i(j)$

$$p_i(j) = p(i,j) / \sum_{j} p(i,j),$$

we obtain

$$H_x(y) = -\sum_{ij} p(i,j) \log p(i,j) + \sum_{ij} p(i,j) \log \sum_j p(i,{}^i) = H(x,y) - H(x),$$

and
$$H(x,y) = H(x) + H_x(y). \tag{36}$$

In words, the uncertainty of the joint event is equal to the sum of the uncertainty of one separate event plus the relative uncertainty of the other. Since now the relative uncertainty as that within arrays can never exceed the uncertainty calculated without that restriction,

$$H(x) > H_y(x)$$
$$H(y) > H_x(y), \tag{37}$$

it follows that between the uncertainty of the joint event $H(x, y)$ and those of the separate events $H(x)$, $H(y)$ there must be the inequality relation

$$H(x,y) \leqslant H(x) + H(y) \tag{38}$$

where the equality sign applies only if the events are independent, i.e. $p(i,j) = p(i)\,p(j)$.

In words; the uncertainty of the joint event cannot exceed the sum of the uncertainties of the separate events.

The difference $H(y) - H_x(y)$ and $H(x) - H_y(x)$ measures the average amount of information received.

Insofar, this difference

$$R = H(y) - H_x(y) = H(x) - H_y(x) = H(x) + H(y) - H(x,y) \tag{39}$$

may serve as a measure of the intensity of dependence or correlation between x and y.

13.4 BI-VARIATE ENTROPY AND THE THEORY OF LANGUAGE TRANSLATION

We consider a linguistic text. For the purpose of this investigation we regard the words as units of which the text has been built up. The translation of the message into another language is a similar text whose units are equivalents of those in the original.

Let the units or elements of the original text be

$$a_1, a_2, a_3 \ldots$$

having respectively the properties

$$x_1, x_2, x_3 \ldots$$

the subscript denoting the order of occurrence in the text, and let the equivalent units of the translation be

$$\alpha_1, \alpha_2, \alpha_3 \ldots$$

having respectively the properties

$$y_1, y_2, y_3 \ldots$$

the subscript denoting here not the order in the translation, but the correspondence with the units of the original.

If the text represented a truly random sequence of the values x and y, then the combination of the elements in pairs, triplets, etc. should have no effect upon the randomness of their arrangement. If, on the other hand, the characteristic y of the translation was to some extent dependent upon the characteristic x of the original, a Markoff chain would result as the following consideration shows. We conceive of the original text in the translation as being brought into a one-to-one correspondence, a_i corresponding to α_1 which results in the following series of doublets:

$$a_1, \; \alpha_1/a_2, \; \alpha_2/a_3, \; \alpha_3 \ldots$$
$$x_1, \; y_1/x_2, \; y_2/x_3, \; y_3 \ldots$$

That is, we have conceived of the original and the translation as being combined into one linear sequence of units, in which translational equivalents follow immediately upon one another, with transition probabilities between particular values of x and y as given in the p_{ij} matrix, where the subscripts of p refer no longer to the order in the text but to the value of the variables x, y:

	x_1	x_2	x_3	
y_1	p_{11}	p_{12}	p_{13}	$\ldots$
y_2	p_{21}	p_{22}	p_{23}	$\ldots$
y_3	p_{31}	p_{32}	p_{33}	$\ldots$

If such transition probabilities exist, the occurrence of α_i having a particular y_i value will, to that extent, be dependent only upon the preceding a_i having a particular x_i value, but not upon the whole preceding array of units, and the sequence would thus fulfil the conditions for a Markoff process.

As the criterion of dependence between a and α with respect to the properties x and y we use the relation between the bi-variate entropy, as defined above. Let $p(i, j)$ be the probability of the joint occurrence of the events according to the above matrix. The entropy of the joint event is then calculated as

$$H(x,y) = - \Sigma p(i,j) \log_2 p(i,j) \tag{40}$$

while those of the single event are given by

$$H(x) = - \Sigma p(i) \log_2(i)$$

$$H(y) = - \Sigma p(i) \log_2(j) \tag{41}$$

In the case of the stochastic independence of x and y, the bi-variate entropy $H(x, y)$ equals the sum of the uni-variate entropies $H(x)$ and $H(y)$:

$$H(x, y) = H(x) + H(y) \tag{42}$$

This property of H suggests using the difference

$$R = H(x) + H(y) - H(x, y) \qquad (43)$$

as a criterion for the dependence or otherwise of the translation upon the original as regards the chosen characteristic. It measures the constraint which the original exerts upon the translation in that respect. The difference R may also be written in another way which shows it to be the result of both, probabilities and transition probabilities:

$$R = H(y) - H_x(y) = H(x) - H_y(x) \qquad (44)$$

where $H_x(y)$ is the transition probability of values of y for any given value of x, and $H_y(x)$ the transition probability of values of x for any given value of y. Since it is based upon the transition probabilities of x and y in immediate neighbourhood only, its mathematical structure is indicative of a Markoff chain between the two groups of events, i.e. word length in the original and in the translation.

13.5 APPLICATION

As a linguistically important and comparatively easily measurable property with regard to which to compare the original with the translation, the number of syllables per word was selected. As experimental material for the investigation were chosen translations into English from four languages: French, German, Czech and Russian. The bi-variate distributions required for the computation of the various entropies were obtained by recording for each word occurrence its length in terms of the number of syllables in the original and in the language of translation.

The results from 8 such bi-variate syllable counts are given in *LCC*, Tables 68-72. Table 24 is an example of the bi-variate distribution and calculation of the relevant quantities required for establishing a Markoff chain.

TABLE 24

Translation from Tolstoy (Childhood, Boyhood and Youth).
(N = 1,187, reduced to N = 1,000)
No. of syllables in Russian words.

No. of syllables in English words	1	2	3	4	5	6	7	Totals
1	294	187	72	15	2	1	1	572
2	32	99	88	35	8	1	1	264
3	4	23	41	36	12	5	2	123
4	1	1	12	14	7	1	—	36
5	—	1	1	—	2	1	—	5
Totals	331	311	214	100	31	9	4	1,000

$$\text{Russian} \qquad\qquad\qquad \text{English}$$

$$M_R = 2.200 \qquad\qquad\qquad M_E = 1.640$$

$$H(R) = 2.109 \qquad\qquad\qquad H(E) = 1.550$$

$$H(R,E) = 3.358$$

$$\text{and thus} \quad H(R,E) < H(R) + H(E) = 3.659$$

$$R = H(R) + H(E) - H(R,E) = .30$$

$$\mathbf{R'} = 1 - H_E(R)/H' = 1 - \frac{1.81}{2.71} = .33$$

From the fact that the bi-variate entropy is in each case less than the sum of the uni-variate entropies, we draw the conclusion that in translation from one language into another there exists a stochastic dependence of the Markoff process type between certain quantitative characteristics of the words in the original and in the translation.

The strength of the Markoff chain is measured by the difference (R) between the bi-variate entropy for the characteristic of "word length" and the sum of the uni-variate entropies for the same characteristic.

If χ^2 is calculated according to formula (6) Part I, as an approximation to the information statistic $2I$, it results for the German-English comparison as 516.6, and for the Russian-English translation as 397.8. The difference between these two values of χ^2 indicates a considerably higher correlation for the first pair of the languages, which is in accordance with linguistic facts.

XIV

THE ENTROPY AS A DISCRIMINATING PARAMETER—THE RELATION BETWEEN ENTROPY AND LOG-LIKELIHOOD

The log-likelihood ratio can be shown to be essentially of the form of a difference of two entropies. Apart from the theoretical interest of such an interpretation of the log-likelihood ratio, it is of practical interest since it suggests a way for calculating the log-likelihood ratio by machine operation only, without the use of a table of logarithms.

14.1 THE RELATION BETWEEN ENTROPY AND LOG-LIKELIHOOD

The definition of the log-likelihood ratio is as follows. If there are two populations P_1, P_2 of individuals, each individual falling into one of r types, the probabilities being $p_{11}, \ldots p_{1r}; p_{21}, \ldots p_{2r}$, which probabilities we assume to be known, and if we have a sample of $N = n_1 + \ldots + n_r$ individuals from the population P_1 or P_2, n_i being the frequency of individuals belonging to the i'th type, and we wish to decide which of the two populations has been sampled, then, as Welch (1939) has shown, we may use the likelihood ratio for obtaining optimum discrimination between the two populations. The probability of the observations in sampling from P_1, say, is of the multinomial form

$$\frac{N!}{n_1! \, n_2! \ldots n_r!} \, p_{11}{}^{n_1} p_{12}{}^{n_2} \ldots p_{1r}{}^{n_r} \tag{45}$$

so that the log-likelihood ratio is

$$\Sigma \, n_i \log \frac{p_{1i}}{p_{2i}} \tag{46}$$

Any system of logarithms can be used.

The method as proposed by Cox and Brandwood (1959) for using the log-likelihood ratio for purposes of discrimination consists in giving each relative frequency n_i/N a score

$$s_i = \log \frac{p_{1i}}{p_{2i}}$$

The log-likelihood ratio is then calculated as the sum of scores, each weighted by the relative frequencies n_i/N.

What is not too satisfactory in this derivation of the log-likelihood ratio for discrimination purposes is the conception of "giving a score". This in fact amounts to the abandoning of a theoretical justification and it looks as if it was only a sort of working method for arriving at optimum discrimination. It will be shown that there is more to it than this, and that we can arrive at a theoretical justification by the information-theoretical interpretation of the "score".

If we want to decide in favour of one of two hypotheses, H_1 or H_2, this must be on the basis of relevant information. Using the term "information" in the technical sense, i.e. according to its mathematical definition in information theory, we shall show that what the use of the logarithmic likelihood ratio as discriminatory function amounts to is that we are using the information from observation for discrimination in favour of H_1 against H_2. For this purpose we start from the fact that the essential element of the score, and therefore of the weighted sum of the scores, is that it uses only logarithms of probabilities or of numbers. This it has in common with the concept of information as defined in information theory according to which information is the logarithm of a number, or of a probability. This more than suggests that the "score s_i" and its weighted sum, the log-likelihood ratio, should be expressible in terms of the information which each item of the weighted sum of the information values contributes to the discrimination, and consequently the sum of scores by the entropy.

There is, however, a new element introduced by the log-likelihood ratio insofar as it deals with the difference of logarithmic probabilities which, for the weighted sum of s_i, that is for the log-likelihood ratio, becomes the difference of absolute values of entropies. That new element of dealing with differences of information instead of with information is quite natural considering that what we are out to construct is a discriminatory function, that is a function which enables us to discriminate between two distributions. Instead, therefore, of dealing with information as used hitherto in information theory, we are here concerned with differences of two values of information and, if these values are sums of all items, with the difference of entropies.

Moreover, the use of the entropy for discrimination purposes necessitates the following generalisation of the usual conception of the entropy. As Good (1953) has expressed it, the population parameters

$$c_{m,n} = \sum_{\mu=1}^{s} p_{\mu}^{m} \left(-\log p_{\mu}\right)^{n} \; (m,n = 0,1,2, \ldots) \tag{47}$$

can be regarded as measures of heterogeneity of the population and the sequence $c_{00} = 1$, $c_{10} = s$, c_{20}, c_{30} ... may be called the moment constants of the population, while c_{11} is called the entropy of the modern theory of communication. The general formula for $c_{m,n}$ as the basic formula for the entropy does not exclude the probability that the weight p should be of another power than $\log p$, and it is this possibility of which we are going to make use when interpreting the log-likelihood ratio as a measure of information about a difference. Moreover, there is no intrinsic reason for either

m or n to be constant throughout the summation. On the contrary, it would seem in accordance with Good's basic idea to let m and n vary. Good introduced formula (47) evidently only as a generalisation, for moments of any power, of the entropy with $m = n = 1$, his intention being evidently to let the entropy appear as a particular case of the more general formula. It is, therefore, in accordance with this device for generalisation if the powers m and n are not constant nor whole numbers, but vary with the value of i.

We write for the values of s_i

$$\log \frac{p_{1i}}{p_{2i}}, \text{ say,}$$

and calculate the log-likelihood ratio for each population P_1 and P_2, by forming the weighted sum of s_i. Thus, for P_1 we have for each type a term $p_{1i} \log p_{1i} - p_{1i} \log p_{2i}$, and summing over all the types we get the log-likelihood ratio (divided by N) as $\bar{s} = \dfrac{1}{N} \Sigma\, n_i\, s_i$, or since $n_i/N = p_i$

$$\Sigma\, p_{1i} \log \frac{p_{1i}}{p_{2i}}$$

or

$$\Sigma\, p_{1i} \log p_{1i} - \Sigma\, p_{1i} \log p_{2i} \tag{48a}$$

Similarly for P_2 we obtain

$$\Sigma\, p_{2i} \log \frac{p_{1i}}{p_{2i}}$$

or

$$\Sigma\, p_{2i} \log p_{1i} - \Sigma\, p_{2i} \log p_{2i} \tag{48b}$$

We now write formulae (48a) and (48b) as follows:

$$\Sigma\, p_{1i} \log p_{1i} - \sum \frac{p_{1i}}{p_{2i}} p_{2i} \log p_{2i} \tag{49a}$$

and

$$\sum \frac{p_{2i}}{p_{1i}} p_{1i} \log p_{1i} - \Sigma\, p_{2i} \log p_{2i} \tag{49b}$$

The first quantity in (49a) clearly is the entropy c_1; writing r_i for p_{i1}/p_{2i}, the second quantity is

$$\Sigma\, r_i\, p_2 \log p_2 \tag{50a}$$

If we write the r_i'th multiple of p_{2i} as a power of p_{2i}

$$r_i\, p_{2i} = p_{2i}^{\,1 + \log r_i/\log p_{2i}}$$

it is seen that the quantity (50a) is in complete accordance with the generalised population parameter $c_{m_i,\, n_i}$, the statistical weight of $\log p$ being of a different power than $\log p$ and a function of i. In the same way we transform the log-likelihood ratio for the second population (49b). The second term is clearly of the form c_2; the first term is

$$\sum \left(\frac{1}{r_i}\right) p_{1i} \log p_{11} \tag{50b}$$

which, since $\left(\dfrac{1}{r_i}\right) p_{1i} = p_{1i}{}^{1-\log r_i/\log p_{1i}}$ can be written as

$$\Sigma\, p_{1i}{}^{1-\log r_i/\log p_{1i}} \log p_{1i}$$

On the basis of the transformation described above, each log-likelihood ratio appears as the difference of two c-values taken absolutely:

$$\left|\Sigma\, p_{1i} \log p_{1i}\right| \text{ and } \left|\Sigma\,(r_i)\, p_{2i} \log p_{2i}\right| \tag{51a}$$

$$\left|\sum \left(\frac{1}{r_i}\right) p_{1i} \log p_{1i}\right| \quad \text{and} \quad \left|\Sigma\, p_{2i} \log p_{2i}\right| \tag{51b}$$

We, therefore, write for the two log-likelihood ratios in Good's notation

$$\left|c_1\left\{1,1\right\}\right| - \left|c_2\left\{1+\frac{\log r_i}{\log p_{1i}}, 1\right\}\right| \tag{52a}$$

and

$$\left|c_1\left\{1-\frac{\log r_i}{\log p_{1i}}, 1\right\}\right| - \left[c_2\left\{1,1\right\}\right] \tag{52b}$$

Since $s_i = \log r_i$, (52a) and (52b) can also be written as

$$\left|c_1\{1,1\}\right| - \left|c_2\{1+s_i/\log p_{1i}, 1\}\right| \tag{53a}$$

and

$$\left|c_1\{1-s_i/\log p_{1i}, 1\}\right| - \left|c_2\{1,1\}\right| \tag{53b}$$

Considering that $\log r_i = \log p_{1i} - \log p_{2i}$, we can now define the log-likelihood ratios by

$$\left|c_1\left\{1,1\right\}\right| - \left|c_2\left\{\frac{\log p_{1i}}{\log p_{2i}}, 1\right\}\right| \tag{54a}$$

and

$$\left|c_1\left\{\frac{\log p_{2i}}{\log p_{1i}}, 1\right\}\right| - \left|\left\{c_2\right\}1,1\right\}| \tag{54b}$$

The advantage of the information theoretical interpretation is not only that instead of regarding s_i as a "score" we conceive of it in terms of a difference of two values of information, but provided we have a table of information values, i.e. of $-p_1 \log_2 p_1 = -3.322\, p_1 \log_{10} p_1$ available, the calculation of the log-likelihood ratios can be carried out completely by machine without consulting a table of logarithms. The formulae to be used for this purpose are (49a) (49b). The values $-p_1 \log_2 p_1$ have been tabulated by W. Meyer-Eppler (1959) and G. Herdan (1960).

We shall work throughout with the dyadic logarithm as being appropriate to the information theoretical interpretation of the log-likelihood ratio.

14.2   APPLICATION TO ASSESSING THE GERMANIC AND ROMANCE COMPONENTS OF VOCABULARY IN ENGLISH WRITERS

In this section it will be shown how to establish by means of the log-likelihood ratio whether an English writer has a preference for either the Germanic or the Romance component of vocabulary, having nothing before us but a sample of the alphabetic distribution of nouns in a text by that writer.

English has two main etymological components: Germanic and Romance, or according to the source languages, Old English (O.E.) and Latin-Romance (L-R). In order to ascertain style differences between English writers in their use of Germanic and Romance vocabulary, there would seem to be no way but to look up each word in an etymological dictionary and ascertain its origin, which involves a very great amount of work if the text to be examined is of some appreciable length, and otherwise there would be little use in doing it. However, as Yule has found, much of the work could be saved by making use of the fact that each etymological component of English is characterised by a characteristic distribution of initials of nouns. If two writers differ significantly in the alphabetic distribution of nouns, this justifies the conclusion of the etymological components of English being used by them in different proportions. Since this is clearly a case of discrimination between writers with regard to their use of Romance and Germanic vocabulary by the token of the alphabetic distribution of nouns, we shall apply the theory developed in the previous section to this problem. The two writers examined in this respect by Yule (1944) were Macaulay and Bunyan. Table 25 shows the alphabetic distribution in samples from these two writers, Table 26 gives the alphabetic distribution of nouns according to whether they are of Germanic or of Romance origin. In addition, both tables give also the distribution relative to 10,000 words, and thus the relative frequencies.

1.   The two populations corresponding to P_1, P_2, are here the Germanic vocabulary and the Romance vocabulary of nouns in English. Since complete counts of these two parts of the English vocabulary are not available in the form in which we would require them, we shall use the relative frequencies in the samples from the two writers in question instead of the population probabilities. The justification for this procedure lies in this: not only are the samples fairly large, 2,246 different vocabulary items in a sample of ca. 16,000 occurrences from Bunyan and 3,543 different vocabulary items in a sample of ca. 16,000 occurrences from Macaulay, but the distribution of the relative frequencies for each component is, by and large, the same in both writers, which indicates that the samples taken are big enough to render the relative frequencies stable and thus suitable for being used in place of the population probabilities.

As will be shown below, the correctness of this conclusion is supported by the values of the logarithmic likelihood ratio for the comparison of the same etymological component in both writers. Consequently, we could regard the alphabetic distribution for each etymological component in either (Bunyan or Macaulay) as corresponding

TABLE 25 (Yule, 1944)

Alphabetical distribution of nouns in the vocabularies of samples from Bunyan and Macaulay. Cols. 2 and 3 give the actual numbers of nouns with each initial letter, cols. 4 and 5 the distribution per 10,000 nouns.*

1	2	3	4	5
Initial letter of noun	Number of nouns		Per 10,000	
	Bunyan	Macaulay	Bunyan	Macaulay
A	111	249	494	703
B	147	169	654	477
C	210	391	935	1104
D	153	237	681	669
E	69	162	307	457
F	112	150	499	423
G	72	107	321	302
H	110	112	490	316
I	72	172	321	485
J	22	27	98	76
K	18	22	80	62
L	84	122	374	344
M	124	209	552	590
N	40	52	178	147
O	41	73	183	206
P	188	338	837	954
Q	7	14	31	40
R	133	191	592	539
S	256	380	1140	1073
T	112	179	499	505
U	16	22	71	62
V	43	64	191	181
W	100	89	445	251
X	—	—	—	—
Y	5	8	22	23
Z	1	4	4	11
Total	2246	3543	9999	10,000

* In samples of ca. 16,000 words.

to P_1 and P_2. However, since Macaulay might, in a way, be regarded as the exponent of a style which prefers Romance, and Bunyan of a style which prefers Germanic vocabulary, we have for the purpose of our calculation taken the Germanic component in Bunyan to correspond to P_1 and the Romance component in Macaulay to correspond to P_2. The first term in (49a) was calculated as the entropy of the alphabetic distribution of the Germanic component in Bunyan; the second term was calculated as the sum of the information values of the probabilities in the alphabetic distribution of the Romance component in Macaulay, each multiplied by $r_i = \dfrac{p_{1i}}{p_{2i}}$, the ratio of the probabilities of the initial letter i in the two etymological components, O-E. and

TABLE 26 (Yule, 1944)

Etymological analysis of the alphabetical distribution leaving out words not classed (57 from Bunyan and 106 from Macaulay).

1	2	3	4	5
Initial letter of noun	Bunyan		Macaulay	
	Number of nouns			
	I. O.E.-Teutonic	II. Latin-Romance	I. O.E.-Teutonic	II. Latin-Romance
A	19	92	13	232
B	105	34	89	67
C	52	156	51	326
D	49	102	42	193
E	19	49	20	142
F	62	47	53	92
G	40	28	39	61
H	76	28	63	44
I	6	65	12	157
J	2	19	—	23
K	18	—	19	—
L	56	27	56	61
M	50	73	52	153
N	22	16	18	32
O	12	28	18	52
P	33	150	34	295
Q	1	6	4	10
R	36	94	34	154
S	141	109	141	231
T	54	55	62	110
U	8	4	7	14
V	2	40	1	62
W	94	4	79	7
X	—	—	—	—
Y	5	—	8	—
Z	—	1	1	3
Total	962	1227	916	2521

L-R. Similarly, the first term in (49b) was calculated as the sum of the information values of the probabilities of the alphabetic distribution of the Germanic component in Bunyan each multiplied by $\frac{1}{r_i} = \frac{p_{2i}}{p_{1i}}$; the second term was calculated as the entropy of the alphabetic distribution of the Romance component in Macaulay.

The two terms according to (49a), resulted as

$$\text{L.L.R. for Germanic} \ldots 3.528 - 4.729 = -1.201$$

The terms, according to (49b), resulted as

$$\text{L.L.R. for Romance} \ldots 5.080 - 4.002 = 1.078$$

TABLE 27 (Yule, 1944)

*Bunyan and Macaulay, alphabetical distributions per 10,000 for the
two etymological groups.*

1	2	3	4	5
Initial letter of noun	I. O.E.-Teutonic		II. Latin-Romance	
	Bunyan	Macaulay	Bunyan	Macaulay
A	198	142	750	920
B	1091	972	277	266
C	541	557	1271	1293
D	509	459	831	766
E	198	218	399	563
F	644	579	383	365
G	416	426	228	242
H	790	688	228	175
I	62	131	530	623
J	21	—	155	91
K	187	207	—	—
L	582	611	220	242
M	520	568	595	607
N	229	197	130	127
O	125	197	228	206
P	343	371	1222	1170
Q	10	44	49	40
R	374	371	766	611
S	1466	1539	888	916
T	561	677	448	436
U	83	76	33	56
V	21	11	326	246
W	977	862	33	28
X	—	—	—	—
Y	52	87	—	—
Z	—	11	8	12
Total	10,000	10,001	9,998	10,001

2.   However, the distribution of the Romance and Germanic components only
could not be used for our purpose as stated at the beginning of this section, because
in English there are always both components present, and no actual piece of writing
could, therefore, be conceived as a random sample of either of these components.
For the practical work, therefore, the populations P_1 and P_2 must be actually occurring
alphabetic distributions from a writer with a strong preference for the Germanic,
and another with a strong preference for the Romance component, such as Bunyan
on the one hand and Macaulay on the other. The Romance vocabulary in the sample
from Bunyan is 54.6% of the total vocabulary and in Macaulay 71.2%, the former
being less than the percentage Romance vocabulary which we generally find in English
writers (between 55% and 60%) and the latter very much in excess of that figure.

Next we calculate the log-likelihood ratios for the alphabetic distribution of all nouns in Macaulay and Bunyan. The two terms according to (49a) were in this case the entropy of the alphabetic distribution of nouns in Bunyan and the sum of the information values of the relative frequencies of the alphabetic distribution of nouns from Macaulay each multiplied by the ratio $r_i = \dfrac{p_{1i}}{p_{2i}}$, the ratio of the probabilities of the initial letter i in the two writers, Bunyan and Macaulay. Analogously for (49b) the two terms were calculated as the sum of the information values of the relative frequencies in the alphabetic distribution of nouns from Bunyan each multiplied by $\dfrac{1}{r_i} = \dfrac{p_{2i}}{p_{1i}}$ and the entropy of the alphabetic distribution of nouns from Macaulay. The numerical values according to (49a) were:

$$\text{L.L.R. for Bunyan} \ldots 4.209 - 4.339 = -.130$$

and for (49b)

$$\text{L.L.R. for Macaulay} \ldots 4.294 - 4.180 = .114$$

The difference between the two log-likelihood ratios for all nouns in Macaulay and Bunyan is well within the difference between the log-likelihood ratios of the two etymological components. This is as it should be. Since each writer uses both components, though maybe one in excess of the other, the difference between the writers as regards the alphabetic distribution of nouns must be smaller than in the hypothetical case of writers using only the Romance or the Germanic component. In agreement with expectation, the log-likelihood ratio for Bunyan is negative like that for the English component only, and that for Macaulay is positive like that for the Romance component only.

Moreover, the log-likelihood ratio for the comparison of each etymological component in both writers was calculated and resulted, using again formulae (49a) and (49b), for the Germanic component as .003 and for the Romance component as .064. The values of the log-likelihood ratio are now not very different from zero. This is as it should be if the alphabetic distribution of a particular etymological component is, by and large, stable in the samples from the two writers.

3. As pointed out above, the method enables us to establish from a sample of the alphabetic distribution of an English writer whether he has a preference for either of the two etymological components of English vocabulary. More particularly, since we take Bunyan and Macaulay to provide standard or callibration values for a strong preference for one of these components, the answer to the question as to whether a writer has a preference for one of them would be that his style was in this respect more like Bunyan's or more like Macaulay's. The log-likelihood ratio for the sample is calculated according to the general formula as

$$\Sigma \, p_{Ni} \times \log \frac{p_{1i}}{p_{2i}}, \tag{55}$$

where p_{Ni} is the percentage of the initial i in a sample of N vocabulary items which we wish to examine, and p_{1i}, p_{2i} are the corresponding percentages in Bunyan and Macaulay respectively. The variance of the mean log-likelihood ratio is calculated as

$$1/(N-1) \left[\Sigma \left\{ p_{Ni} \log^2 \frac{p_{1i}}{p_{2i}} \right\} - \Sigma \left\{ p_{Ni} \log \frac{p_{1i}}{p_{2i}} \right\}^2 \right] \tag{56}$$

In a sample from Macaulay of approximately 4,000 occurrences, Yule found the following alphabetic distribution of the 1537 different vocabulary items:

TABLE 28

A	101	H	60	O	31	V	31
B	62	I	69	P	152	W	38
C	156	J	9	Q	6	X	—
D	105	K	10	R	86	Y	1
E	74	L	50	S	184	Z	3
F	76	M	84	T	71		
G	46	N	23	U	9	Total	1537

If it is a question of whether the "mean score" of this sample of the alphabetic distribution could be regarded as a random sample of the log-likelihood ratio for the population as represented by our large sample from Macaulay, we calculate the log-likelihood ratio of the sample according to formula (55), or using the information-theoretical method developed in this paper as

$$p_{Ni} \log p_{1i} - p_{Ni} \log p_{2i}$$

which can be written as

$$\frac{p_{Ni}}{p_{1i}} p_{1i} \log p_{1i} - \frac{p_{Ni}}{p_{2i}} p_{2i} \log p_{2i} \tag{57}$$

It results as

$$4.234 - 4.173 = 0.061.$$

In order to ascertain whether by the token of the log-likelihood ratio the sample from Macaulay could be regarded as a random sample in the technical sense of the term, of what we regard as the population of the alphabetic distribution in Macaulay, we compare the mean "score" of 0.061 with that of 0.114 for the population.

The variance of the mean log-likelihood ratio of the sample calculated by (11) results as

$$1/1536 (0.11896 - 0.00063) = .000076$$

and the standard deviation as .00872. Adding and subtracting three times the standard deviation from the mean log-likelihood ratio of the sample, we get the fiducial limits of .087 and —.035.

Although there is an appreciable difference of the upper limit from the population value .114, so that we cannot regard the quantity .061 as a random sample value of the basic log likelihood ratio from Macaulay, yet it is unmistakably nearer to it than to that for Bunyan.

If the sample is neither from writings by Macaulay or Bunyan, we can through a significance test of this sort, and thus, by the token of the sample log-likelihood ratio being nearer to that of Bunyan or Macaulay, establish whether the writer has, by and large, a preference for the Germanic or the Romance component.

Summary

1. The investigation has shown the information-theoretical structure of the log-likelihood ratio in its use for purposes of discrimination, which leads to its definition as a difference of two particular forms of the population parameter $c_{m,n}$.

2. Apart from its theoretical interest, the information-theoretical interpretation has certain advantages for computation. If a table of information values of probabilities is available, the computation of the log-likelihood ratio could be carried out by machine without the use of a table of logarithms.

3. The method was applied to the problem of establishing the preference of English writers for either the Germanic or the Romance component of English vocabulary.

XV

INFORMATION-THEORETICAL INTERPRETATION OF CHINESE WORD STRUCTURE

15.1 THE RELATION BETWEEN WESTERN PHONEMIC (ALPHABETIC) SYSTEMS AND THE SYSTEM OF CHINESE RADICALS

To the writer's knowledge, there are few, if any, serious attempts to apply information-theoretical ideas to Chinese language structure. In fact, there have been only very few such attempts for Western languages, the reason being evidently the antipathy on the part of the linguist to the numerical work needed for such investigations. But the virtual lack of any such investigation for Chinese has more intrinsic reasons.

There does not seem, at the first glance, anything comparable in Chinese to the phonemic (alphabetic) systems of our languages, to which information theory primarily applies. The correctness of this statement becomes obvious if we consider that what makes the Western languages amenable to information theory is primarily the independence of particular phonemes from meaning, or the independence of word from word meaning.

Now this axiom which, for our languages, it has taken the genius of de Saussure to put forward as a major characteristic of the linguistic code, is a matter of common-place for Chinese, if by "word" we understand the phonetic form only. The extraordinarily small number of Chinese words of the spoken language—420 in Mandarin each of which may be pronounced possibly in 4 different tones—compared with the equally extraordinarily high number of Chinese words in the written language, between 6000 and 8000 for ordinary requirements and more than 40,000 in the more complete dictionaries, leaves no doubt about the amount of independence of word sound from word meaning, let alone the independence of particular unit sounds (phonemes) from meaning.

But there is an important difference in this "axiom" when applied to our languages and to Chinese. What for our languages is regarded—and rightly so—as an asset of major importance for language as a symbolic system of communication, has become for Chinese a rather embarrassing feature of great disadvantage. This will be explained in a forthcoming publication.

Moreover, the role of sound and pronounciation of Chinese phonemes does not correspond to their role in Western languages. A fact that must strike everybody who studies Chinese is that in Chinese things are very often diametrically opposed to all that we are accustomed to in the West. In examining the oldest monuments of a Western language, i.e. inscriptions in stone and metal or written texts, the scholar would start by determining the sounds, the phonetic values of the written symbols; having done this, by trial and error, he would spell the words of the inscription, and this would enable him to identify these words with words of a later period of development of that language. It is only in this way, i.e. through tracking the old pronounciation in the new, that he arrives at the sense of the words.

In Chinese the procedure is exactly the reverse.[1] The ideograms were originally simply pictures of the objects they denoted. In the course of history their *form* has changed considerably, but the idea they represent is the same. Through the characters we arrive directly at the *sense* of the word. But as they do not constitute a phonetic script, they give no hint—apart from the ideograms of a later period containing the so-called "phonetic"—of the sounds of the words in ancient Chinese. The consequence is that one is able to read off the meaning of the ancient classics without knowing their old pronounciation. Thus, in the study of other languages the task consists in fixing the phonetic value of the old symbols; once this is done, the pronounciation, and with it the sense of the word, can be determined. In Chinese, on the contrary, we have to do with the characters as symbols for the whole words whose old pronounciation is unknown. Consequently the bridge between chronologically distant strata of the language is here not sound or pronounciation, but script. What corresponds in Chinese to the sound of Western languages is its script.

It would appear, therefore, that in equating our phonemic system with the sounds of Chinese, and our words with the monosyllables of Chinese, we are comparing like with unlike. It may lead to a more truly satisfying comparison if we abandoned the superficial similarity and made isomorphy the guiding principle for what is comparable in languages so far removed. As will be seen, this is actually the case. Concentrating, instead of upon the sound or phonetic property of phonemes, upon their *distinctive function as members of linguistic oppositions*, we shall find the corresponding feature in Chinese to be the *distinctive property of Radicals* (the significant part of an ideogram indicating, or at least suggesting, the sense of the word or giving the category to which it belongs, as different from the phonetic part indicating, or at least suggesting, the pronounciation of the word.)

A possible objection might be that it is not only the opposition between the Radicals but also that between the Chinese Phonetics which corresponds to the phonological opposition of our Western languages. But I think it will be agreed that however important the role of the phonetic for the distinction between the ideograms, yet as a first and basic opposition between them we must regard that between their radicals. The further development of our argument will be seen to lend support to this view, though it would not really invalidate our argument if this were not so. Assuming, provisionally, the correspondence between phonological (alphabetic) units in the

---

[1] B. Karlgren, *Sound and Symbol in Chinese* (London, 1933).

Western, or more generally the alphabetic languages, and the system of radicals in Chinese, we now proceed to test that assumption by binary coding of the latter system and comparing the results with the binary coding of English and Russian as representatives of the group of alphabetic languages, all with a view to deciding whether it is a case of isomorphy.

The isomorphy in which we are interested is that between phonemes, as the basic elements of our Western languages, and the radicals as the basic units of Chinese ideograms. It makes no difference to our argument, which is based upon the idea of binary coding as a means for establishing isomorphy, if instead of the distribution of phonemes we use that of alphabetic symbols. Not only can the distribution of letters be regarded as a true replica of their phonemic frequency distribution at a certain time of development of the language, namely the time when the sounds of the language were first coded into alphabetic symbols, but even though the two distributions are diverging in the language of today, the argument would be the same whether we established isomorphy between phonemes and radicals or between alphabetic symbols and radicals. Neither of the two distributions of phonemes and letters could exist without the other. In what follows, the binary coding of alphabetic symbols is therefore to be understood as embracing that of phonemes.

15.2   BINARY CODING OF CHINESE VOCABULARY ACCORDING TO RADICALS

As the empirical basis for our investigation, the vocabulary of a dictionary of medium size, C. W. Mathews' Chinese-English Dictionary, Peking, with 8926 characters, was used. This vocabulary is arranged in Tables 29a to h in the traditional manner of a Chinese dictionary, i.e. according to radicals, and under each radical the numbers of composite characters, consisting of radical plus phonetic according to the number of strokes in the latter.

Table 30 shows the result of binary coding of the character groups according to the radical under which they are listed. Columns 1 to 6 contain the number of the radical, the relative frequency of the symbols listed under a given radical, i.e. of the derivatives of that radical, (i.e. the column sums of Table 29 divided by the total number of derivatives, 8711), the cumulative relative frequencies, the binary coding symbol for each radical group, the average number of "bits", and the average stroke number of partial specified groups of ideograms.

TABLE 29. The 214 columns, one to each radical, contain the numbers of derivative ideograms entered in the rows according to the numbers of strokes of the phonetic. Thus, the top row has the 214 radicals in the conventional order, and the following rows, numbered from 1 to 26, give the numbers of the ideograms whose phonetic has 1, 2 ... 26 strokes.

	1	2	3	4	5	6	7	8	9	10	11	12	13	14	15	16	17	18	19	20	21	22	23	24	25	26	27	
	一	丨	丶	丿	乙	亅	二	亠	人	儿	入	八	冂	冖	冫	几	凵	刀	力	勹	匕	匚	匸	十	卜	卩	厂	
1	3	1		3	2	1	2	1	1	1	1					1		1		1				2				21
2	5	2	1	3	1		5	2	12	2	1	3		2		3	1	4	1	4	2	2	1	3	1	1	1	61
3	6	2	1	1	1	1			14	2	1		4		1		3	1	2	3	1	2		2	2	2		52
4	5	2	1	4	1		2	3	25	4	3	1	1		4			8	3	1		2	2	1		1		73
5	5			3	1		2	2	39	3		1			2			10	5	1					2	3	1	81
6	1	1			1	1	2	2	37	3	1	3		1	2	1	1	14	3	2		1	1	5		4	1	88
7	1			1	1	1		2	28	1	1			1				8	6	1		2		1	2	3	3	63
8								1	42	1		1	2	3	9			13	2			2					3	80
9		1		1					24				1		3	1		4	6	2	2		3	1			2	50
10	10			1	2				14	1			1		2	1		6	3			1		1		1	4	46
11								1	19					1				5	6			1					2	36
12					1				19	1						1		2	2			1					3	30
13									15							1		6	3			1					2	30
14									9						3			5	1									17
15									5					1	1				1									8
16									3						1													4
17									2					1					1									3
18																			1									1
19								1	4																			5
20									2									1										2
21									1																			2
22									1																			1
23																												—
24																												—
25																												—
26																												—
27																												—
Col. Sums	36	8	3	17	11	4	13	15	316	19	8	9	9	10	28	9	5	88	46	15	5	13	7	16	7	15	22	754

	28	29	30	31	32	33	34	35	36	37	38	39	40	41	42	43	44	45	46	47	48	49	50	51	52	53	54	
	厶	又	口	囗	土	士	夂	夊	夕	大	女	子	宀	寸	小	尢	尸	屮	山	川	工	己	巾	干	幺	广	廴	
1	1	1				1				5		1			1	1	2	1				1	1		1			17
2	1	7	22	2	1				2	2	2	1	4	1	1		2		1		3		2	1	1	1		57
3	1	1	14	5	7		1	1	2	2	8	3	4	1	2		1	1	3	3			1	2		2		64
4		1	34	7	16	2	1			1	12	5	4	1		3	5		5	2	1		1			5	2	109
5			35	3	16	2				3	20	4	9	2	1		6		11				9	2		6	3	133
6	1	5	34	1	10			1	1		22	1	6	1			3		3		1	1	4		2	4	2	101
7		4	31	3	12						13	2	9	3	1		4		8				5		1	4		102
8		1	35	4	20	1			1		20	1	9	3		2	2		20	1			7		1	6		132
9	1		40	1	17	3					12	1	7	2	1	1	3		10			1	7	2		4	1	113
10			28	2	16						16	2	5		1				6				1			8		88
11		1	24	3	16	1		1	3		12		10	1			2		5	1			4			6		88
12			28		14						7		4				2		5	1			5			8		75
13			19	1	9						6	1		1					3				4			3		47
14		1	8		6			1			4						1		6				3					31
15			2		2						1																	5
16		1	6		5						1	1											1					15
17			4		1						3								3				1					12
18			5									1					1		1									8
19			4	1							1	1					1		2									9
20			1					1											2									4
21					1																							2
22			3																								1	4
23																												—
24																												—
25																												—
26																												—
27																												—
Col. Sums	5	23	377	33	169	10	2	5	9	13	160	27	71	16	8	7	35	2	94	7	5	3	56	7	6	57	9	1216

	55	56	57	58	59	60	61	62	63	64	65	66	67	68	69	70	71	72	73	74	75	76	77	78	79	80	81	
	廾	弋	弓	彐	彡	彳	心	戈	戶	手	支	攴	文	斗	斤	方	无	日	曰	月	木	欠	止	歹	殳	毋	比	
1	1	1					1	2	1	1						1		2			5		1			1		17
2	1	1	2	1			1	5		4		2				1		5	2	1	8	1	1	1				37
3		1	1				10	2		7		3						3	1	1	19		1			1		50
4	1		2		2	3	16	3	4	32		2	1		1	1		15		2	30	2	3	2		1		123
5			5	1		5	27		2	38		7			1	3		18	1	1	40			4	1		2	156
6	2		2	1	1	7	35		5	25		1	1	1		6		8	1	3	33	2		2	2			138
7			2		1	3	26	2	1	26		8	1	2	1	6	1	10	2	3	39	4		1	1			140
8			5	1	4	7	34	2	2	53	1	8	2	2	2			10	4	3	42	6		5	3			196
9		1	3	1	1	4	32	7		40		2	2	1	1	2		14	1		30	3	1	2	2	1		151
10				1		4	24	2		42		1		1	2	1		4	1	1	28	2		1	1	1		117
11			1	1	1		28	1	3	52	6													2	2			97
12	1		1		1	3	25	1		32						2		10	1		24	4	1	3	1			110
13			1			2	17	1		24		2						2		1	13	1		2	1		1	68
14			1			1	8	2		16		2				1		4		1	10	1	1	1				49
15			1	1			3			12						2		2			1	1						27
16							5			3		1				1		3			7							23
17							1			4			1					1		1	6							15
18							5			3											1			1				11
19							2			4								1			2				1			9
20										3											1							4
21										1											2							3
22							1			2											1							4
23																												—
24							1														1							2
25																												—
26																												—
27																												—
Col. Sums	6	4	27	8	11	40	302	30	18	424	7	39	8	7	8	27	1	112	14	18	349	28	9	28	16	5	3	1549

	82	83	84	85	86	87	88	89	90	91	92	93	94	95	96	97	98	99	100	101	102	103	104	105	106	107	108	
	毛	氏	气	水	火	爪	父	爻	爿	片	牙	牛	犬	玄	玉	瓜	瓦	甘	生	用	田	疋	疒	癶	白	皮	皿	
1		2		2	1															1								6
2				5	2				1			2	1		1					2	3		2				2	21
3				14	6						1	5	2		2						6		3		2		5	42
4			3	30	6	2	1		1	1		3	6	1	5	2	1		1		8		6	1	1		6	85
5	2			48	12	1			1			3	4	2	11		1	1	1		6		19		3	2	5	123
6	2		3	32	14	1	1		1			5	4		9	1	1		3	1	4		7		2	1	3	93
7	3			31	5			1				4	11		9		1	1			5	1	12	2	1		3	95
8	2			48	13	1				2		3	11		15		3				4		18		2	2	2	123
9	3			53	25		1			2		2	14		14		2				1	2	11			2	1	134
10	1		1	34	14			1	1	1		3	6		9						2		14		4		3	94
11	1			44	9					2			3		9		4						12		1	1	1	90
12	4			35	22								3		4		2				1		9		2			83
13	2			21	10				1				6		8	1	2						4		1			55
14				21	5	1			1				5		3	1	1				2		2					42
15	1			9	3					1		1	3		1								3					23
16				11	2							2	3		1	1	2						3					24
17				5	1								1		2						1		3					14
18	1			3	1								1										2		1			9
19				3																			2					5
20													1															1
21				2																								2
22				2																								2
23				1																								1
24				1																								1
25					1																							1
26																												—
27																												—
Col. Sums	22	3	7	455	152	6	3	2	7	9	1	33	85	3	103	7	20	2	5	4	43	3	132	3	20	8	31	1169

	109	110	111	112	113	114	115	116	117	118	119	120	121	122	123	124	125	126	127	128	129	130	131	132	133	134	135	
	目	矛	矢	石	示	禸	禾	穴	立	竹	米	糸	缶	网	羊	羽	老	而	耒	耳	聿	肉	臣	自	至	臼	舌	
1					1							2					1											**4**
2			1		1		3	1		1					1							2	1			2	1	14
3	3		1	3	4		5	3		2	3	9	1	2	2			4	1	2		10			2	2	1	60
4	14	1	1	6	5	2	8	5	1	10	3	19	2	1	4	4	3		1	2		17		2		2	1	119
5	15		1	14	15		11	6	3	14	5	20		3	4	4	1		2	3		22				1	1	145
6	10			6	5		5	3	3	16	6	22		1	2	3	1			1		18		1		1	1	105
7	9	1	2	7	1	1	11	3	4	15	5	15		1	3	4			1	2	3	16				2		102
8	20		1	12	7	1	8	3	1	17	4	32	2	5	1	5			1	3	1	14	1				1	138
9	8			12	10		4	4	2	15	5	24	2	4	2	5			1	1		16				1		117
10	5			11	1		7	6		11	6	19	1	2	1	3			1	1		9		1	1			88
11	9			10	1		7	3		13	9	24	2	2	1	2			1	3		9	1					97
12	12		2	9	3		1	2		11	2	11	2	1	3	2				3		8				1		72
13	4			2	2		4	3		5		13	1	1					1			13				1	1	51
14	2			2	3		3	1		5	2	7	1						2			3						34
15	1			5				1	1	2	2	7	1		1				1			2						24
16	1			2	1		1	2		4	1	1		2								3						18
17				2	2		1	1		3	1	3	1						1			1						16
18				1						1	1	1		1								1						**6**
19	1									2		2		1								2						8
20	1																											1
21	1											1																2
22																												—
23																												—
24																												—
25																												—
26																												—
27										1																		1
Col. Sums.	**116**	2	9	104	62	4	79	47	15	148	55	232	16	27	25	32	6	4	14	25	4	166	3	4	3	13	7	**1222**

	136	137	138	139	140	141	142	143	144	145	146	147	148	149	150	151	152	153	154	155	156	157	158	159	160	161	162	
	舛	舟	艮	色	艸	虍	虫	血	行	衣	西	見	角	言	谷	豆	豕	豸	貝	赤	走	足	身	車	辛	辰	疋	
1			1				1							4			1		2					1			1	4
2					2	1	1			2		1	1	12		2	1	3	3		2	1		2		1	8	20
3		2			6	1	4	1	2	3	1			13	1	1	1		7	1	2	2	1	3			10	58
4		4			22	3	16	1		10		3	1	25			1	1	15	1		4	1	3		1	13	102
5		6		1	36	2	17	1	2	13	2	2	3	24			3	4	10		5	15		7	1		15	169
6	1	1			27	2	12	3	3	10	1	1	2	19	1	2	2	3	5	1	3	15	2	7	1		21	148
7					29	2	20		1	13		1	1	21		2	1		16		2	6	1	4	3		11	137
8	1	2			43		18			15		2	1	29			2		4	2	3	16	4	16	1		17	173
9		2			29	2	25		3	12		3	1	18	2	2	1	1	6		1	12		9	2		10	155
10		4			32		18		1	13		2	1	11		1	1	2	3			8		6			7	127
11		2	1		30	1	18			8		2	1	13			1		4		2	9	1	4			7	102
12		1			23	1	15			4	1	3	2	8					3		1	11	1	3			6	92
13		4			24		12			7	1	1	1	3					4		1	6	1	6			2	81
14		2		1	14		7			2				3					2			3		2	1		2	42
15		2			11		5	1		5		3		5								8		2				44
16					15		2			3				4				1	1			1		1				27
17					6		3			1	1			1								2						18
18					1		2		1	2		1	1	1							1	3						13
19					5		1			1				2													2	11
20																												2
21					1										1													2
22														1														1
23																												—
24																												—
25					1																							1
26																												—
27																												—
Col. Sums	2	32	2	2	357	15	197	7	13	124	7	25	16	217	5	10	15	15	85	5	25	122	12	76	9	2	132	1529

	163	164	165	166	167	168	169	170	171	172	173	174	175	176	177	178	179	180	181	182	183	184	185	186	187	188	189	
	邑	酉	采	里	金	長	門	阜	隶	隹	雨	青	非	面	革	韋	韭	音	頁	風	飛	食	首	香	馬	骨	高	
1			1				1								1				2									2
2		2		1	2		1			4					2	1			4			5						22
3	4	3			8		3	2		2	2				4		2	1	8	1		1	2		2	3		39
4	6	3		1	15		7	8		5	2				7	1		1	2	2		7			4	3		78
5	8	5	1	1	18		3	10		6	4	1			4				8	1		4		1	5	4		91
6	8	3			17		10	5		1	1				3				11			8			12	2		75
7	9	7			20		4	10	1		7	1	1	1	4	1		1	1	2		10			7	2		93
8	4	6			24		7	10	1	1	7	2			3	2			7	2		12	1		6	2		96
9	6	5			18		7	14	1	1	5				1	3		1	7	4		7		1	9	2		87
10	4	5			21		8	7		9	2	1	1		2	1			2	2		9			6	1		91
11	5	4		1	19		2	3		2	2				1				3	1		5			8	1		61
12	8	4			14		4	2			2			1	5			1	1			8			8	1		53
13	2	3	1		11		3	4			2								3			4		1	4	4	1	48
14	1	1			5			3			3			1	2	1			1			1			5			20
15	1				7			1							1				1			1			1			14
16					3			1			4				1							1				1		14
17	1	1			3						1				1							1		1	2	1		9
18	2	2			3														2						1			10
19	1				4																			1	1			7
20		1			1																				2			2
21															1										1			2
22																												—
23																												—
24	1																											1
25																												—
26																												—
27																												—
Col. Sums	71	55	3	4	213	—	60	80	3	31	44	5	2	3	42	10	2	5	63	15	—	84	3	5	84	27	1	915

	190	191	192	193	194	195	196	197	198	199	200	201	202	203	204	205	206	207	208	209	210	211	212	213	214	
	髟	鬥	鬯	鬲	鬼	魚	鳥	鹵	鹿	麥	麻	黃	黍	黑	黹	黽	鼎	鼓	鼠	鼻	齊	齒	龍	龜	龠	
1																										—
2	1					1	3		1								2					1				9
3	1					1	3				1		1	1			1			1	1	1	1			13
4	3				2	6	8		2	2	1		1	2		1			1	1		1	2			33
5	6	1			3	8	10		3				1	4	1	2			3	1		7			1	51
6	3	1				8	8		1	2				2				1		1		3			1	31
7	5			1	1	6	8		1						1			1			1		1		1	27
8	4	1		1	4	10	11		5	2				4				1	1			2			1	47
9	2					10	7	1	1					1					1	1		2				26
10	2	2			1	6	17	2	1	2										2		2			1	38
11	1					9	5		1					2		1										19
12	2			1		6	7		1	1						1										19
13	1				1	4	6	2		1	1			1		1										18
14	1	1			1	1	3							1		1										9
15	1													1												2
16						2	1			1																4
17		1					1																			2
18							2																			2
19			1				1																			2
20							1																			1
21																										—
22						1			1																	2
23																				1						1
24									1																	1
25																										—
26																										—
27																										—
Col. Sums	33	7	1	3	13	79	102	5	19	11	3	—	3	19	2	7	3	3	6	8	2	19	4	—	5	357

TABLE 30

Binary coding of Chinese vocabulary according to radicals

Number of radical	Rel. frequency of symbols listed under radical (%)	Cum. frequency (%)	Binary coding symbol, b_i	Average number of "bits"	Average number of strokes
1	2	3	4	5	6
85	5.23		0000		
64	4.87		00010		
30	4.33		00011		
140	4.10		0010		
75	4.01		00110		
9	3.63		00111		
		26.17		4.7	3.9
61	3.47		01000		
120	2.67		01001		
149	2.49		01010		
167	2.45		01011		
142	2.26		01100		
32	1.94		011010		
130	1.91		011011		
38	1.84		011100		
86	1.75		011101		
118	1.70		011110		
164	1.52		011111		
		50.17		5.6	5.3
162	1.52		100000		
145	1.43		100001		
157	1.40		100010		
109	1.33		100011		
72	1.29		100100		
112	1.20		1001010		
96	1.18		1001011		
196	1.17		1001100		
46	1.08		1001101		
18	1.01		1001110		
94	0.98		1001111		
154	0.98		1010000		
184	0.97		10100010		
187	0.97		10100011		
170	0.92		1010010		
115	0.91		10100110		
195	0.91		10100111		
159	0.87		1011000		
40	0.82		1011001		
163	0.82		1011010		
181	0.72		1011011		
113	0.71		1011100		
169	0.69		1011101		
53	0.66		1011110		
50	0.64		1011111		
		75.35		7.0	6.2

Number of radical	Rel. frequency of symbols listed under radical (%)	Cum. frequency (%)	Binary coding symbol, b_i	Average number of "bits"	Average number of strokes
1	2	3	4	5	6
119	0.63		1100000		
164	0.63		1100001		
116	0.54		11000100		
19	0.53		11000101		
173	0.51		11000110		
102	0.49		11000111		
177	0.48		1100100		
60	0.46		11001010		
66	0.45		11001011		
1	0.41		11001100		
44	0.40		11001101		
31	0.38		11001110		
93	0.38		11001111		
		81.64		7.8	4.8
190	0.38		11010000		
124	0.37		11010001		
137	0.37		11010010		
108	0.36		11010011		
172	0.36		11010100		
62	0.34		11010101		
15	0.32		11010110		
76	0.32		110101110		
78	0.32		110101111		
39	0.31		11011000		
57	0.31		11011001		
70	0.31		11011010		
122	0.31		11011011		
188	0.31		11011100		
123	0.29		110111010		
128	0.29		110111011		
147	0.29		11011110		
156	0.29		110111110		
29	0.26		110111111		
		87.70		8.3	5.2
27	0.25		11100000		
82	0.25		111000010		
98	0.23		111000011		
106	0.23		111000100		
10	0.22		111000101		
198	0.22		111000110		
203	0.22		111000111		
211	0.22		111001000		
63	0.21		111001001		
74	0.21		111001010		
4	0.20		111001011		
24	0.18		111001100		
41	0.18		111001101		
79	0.18		111001110		

Number of radical	Rel. frequency of symbols listed under radical (%)	Cum. frequency (%)	Binary coding symbol, b_i	Average number of "bits"	Average number of strokes
1	2	3	4	5	6
121	0.18		111001111		
148	0.18		111010000		
8	0.17		111010001		
20	0.17		111010010		
26	0.17		111010011		
117	0.17		111010100		
141	0.17		111010101		
152	0.17		111010110		
153	0.17		1110101110		
182	0.17		1110101111		
73	0.16		111011000		
127	0.16		111011001		
7	0.15		111011010		
22	0.15		1110110110		
37	0.15		1110110111		
134	0.15		111011100		
144	0.15		1110111010		
194	0.15		1110111011		
158	0.14		111011110		
5	0.13		1110111110		
59	0.13		1110111111		
		94.09		9.5	5.0
199	0.13		111100000		
14	0.11		1111000010		
33	0.11		1111000011		
151	0.11		1111000100		
178	0.11		1111000101		
12	0.10		1111000110		
13	0.10		1111000111		
16	0.10		111100100		
36	0.10		1111001010		
54	0.10		1111001011		
77	0.10		1111001100		
91	0.10		1111001101		
111	0.10		1111001110		
160	0.10		1111001111		
2	0.09		1111010000		
11	0.09		1111010001		
42	0.09		1111010010		
58	0.09		1111010011		
67	0.09		1111010100		
69	0.09		1111010101		
107	0.09		1111010110		
209	0.09		1111010111		
23	0.08		1111011000		
25	0.08		1111011001		
43	0.08		1111011010		
47	0.08		1111011011		

Number of radical	Rel. frequency of symbols listed under radical (%)	Cum. frequency (%)	Binary coding symbol, b_i	Average number of "bits"	Average number of strokes
1	2	3	4	5	6
51	0.08		1111011100		
65	0.08		1111011101		
68	0.08		1111011110		
84	0.08		11110111110		
90	0.08		11110111111		
97	0.08		1111100000		
135	0.08		1111100001		
143	0.08		1111100010		
146	0.08		1111100011		
191	0.08		1111100100		
205	0.08		1111100101		
52	0.07		11111001100		
55	0.07		11111001101		
87	0.07		11111001110		
125	0.07		11111001111		
208	0.07		1111101000		
17	0.06		1111101001		
21	0.06		1111101010		
28	0.06		11111010110		
35	0.06		11111010111		
48	0.06		1111101100		
80	0.06		1111101101		
100	0.06		1111101110		
150	0.06		11111011110		
155	0.06		11111011111		
174	0.06		1111110000		
180	0.06		1111110001		
186	0.06		11111100010		
197	0.06		11111100011		
214	0.06		1111110010		
6	0.05		11111100110		
56	0.05		11111100111		
101	0.05		1111110100		
114	0.05		11111101010		
126	0.05		11111101011		
129	0.05		11111101100		
132	0.05		11111101101		
166	0.05		11111101110		
212	0.05		11111101111		
3	0.03		11111110000		
49	0.03		111111100010		
81	0.03		111111100011		
83	0.03		11111110010		
88	0.03		111111100110		
95	0.03		111111100111		
103	0.03		11111110100		
105	0.03		111111101010		
131	0.03		111111101011		

Number of radical	Rel. frequency of symbols listed under radical (%)	Cum. frequency (%)	Binary coding symbol, b_i	Average number of "bits"	Average number of strokes
1	2	3	4	5	6
133	0.03		111111101100		
165	0.03		111111101101		
171	0.03		111111101110		
176	0.03		111111101111		
185	0.03		11111111000		
193	0.03		111111110010		
200	0.03		111111110011		
202	0.03		111111110100		
206	0.03		111111110101		
207	0.03		111111110110		
34	0.02		111111110111		
45	0.02		111111111000		
89	0.02		1111111110010		
99	0.02		1111111110011		
110	0.02		1111111110100		
136	0.02		1111111110101		
138	0.02		1111111110110		
139	0.02		1111111110111		
161	0.02		1111111111000		
175	0.02		1111111111001		
179	0.02		1111111111010		
204	0.02		1111111111011		
210	0.02		1111111111100		
71	0.01		1111111111101		
92	0.01		1111111111110		
189	0.01		11111111111110		
192	0.01		11111111111111		
		99.99		11.0	5.9
168	—				
183	—				
201	—				
213	—				

$$H_{cod} = 6.4360$$
$$H = 6.3360$$
$$h^* = H/H_{cod} = .985$$
$$R^* = 1 - h^* = .015$$
$$H' = 7.742$$
$$h = H/H' = .818$$
$$R = 1 - h = .182$$

15.3   ISOMORPHY BETWEEN THE BINARY CODING OF CHINESE CHARACTERS AND STROKE NUMBER

The results are most remarkable. For radicals with number of derivatives between 455 and 40, forming by far the greatest part of the vocabulary, the agreement between average stroke number and average number of binary units (columns 6 and 5) per symbol is excellent. To make the comparison easier, the results in columns 5 and 6 are condensed as follows:

Partial masses of vocabulary	b_i	Stroke no.
0 - 26.17%	4.7	3.9
- 50.17%	5.6	5.3
- 75.35%	7.0	6.2
- 81.64%	7.8	4.8
- 87.70%	8.3	5.2
- 94.09%	9.5	5.0
-100 %	11.0	5.9

For three-quarters of the vocabulary, the isomorphy of the series of b_i and stroke number is very good, both as regards the numerical agreement between b_i and stroke number for a specified part of the vocabulary and as regards the trend, viz. the increase of b_i and stroke number with decreasing size of the groups of derivatives per radical. This part comprises the radicals with the greatest number of phonetic compounds and the words of most frequent use.

This means that for the greater part of the Chinese dictionary the system of coding by stroke number is, to all intents and purposes, that of binary coding. For the moment we consider only the *number* of bits, and not the arrangement of 0's and 1's. It seems reasonable to assume that the arrangement has its counterpart in the order in which vertical and horizontal strokes must follow each other according to the rules of Chinese calligraphy.

For radicals with less than 40 derivatives the average number of bits per group is always in excess of the average number of strokes, but even so the trend is the same in each series: the averages of both b_i and stroke number increase as the groups of derivatives per radical become smaller. That the isomorphy between average binary coding symbol length and stroke number should apply fully only to one part of the dictionary need not invalidate our conclusion. We must not forget that the properties of artificial sign systems—such as that of binary coding—are never identical with those of the natural languages. Simplicity and regularity of the artificial system are often absent from the natural languages. However, some of the properties of these systems are found in natural languages, even if not in pure form.

The different relation between length of coding symbol and stroke number according to whether we deal with large or small groups of radical derivatives is not difficult to understand. First, we must keep clearly in mind that the conformity between stroke number and symbol length (number of bits) is by no means intentional, but the product of a very long, historical development. Only for the ideograms with radicals of frequent use in the formation of derivatives, which are, by and large, also the ideograms with greatest frequency, and which for that very reason, were also written with greater and greater speed as time went on, were the conditions given for an approach to settling the number of strokes per radical in accordance with the most efficient coding method—binary coding. For the rest of the dictionary it was more a matter of arbitrarily cutting down, or keeping low, the number of strokes per radical.

To use an analogy: the pebbles on the beach are steadily abrased by the action of waves according to their distance from the water. But only those near enough will be more or less continuously affected and will, by and by, assume the well-known polished appearance; those farther away, which will only occasionally come under the influence of the waves, will be little affected, and, consequently, will more or less retain their original shapes.

A word(ideogram) count of *Tung jen yü*, "The pupils of the eye that talked", from the "Liao Chai" by P'u Sung-ling in the version by Sir W. Hillier (1927) gave the number of occurrences as 1646 and that of different ideograms as 304, not counting the most frequent grammar forms (classifiers, particles etc.). Counting now the occurrences of ideograms belonging to radical groups with 40 or more derivatives, which thus constitute about 80% of the total vocabulary in the dictionary, that is of the first 53 radical groups in the order of Table 30, we find 908 occurrences of these radicals and their derivatives. Thus 53 groups or approximately 25% of 214, the total number of radical groups, provide 908 or 55% of 1646, the total text length. The average number of occurrences for the 53 radical groups is, therefore, $908/53 = 17$ approximately, whereas of the 161 remaining radical groups it is only $728/161 = 4.5$ approximately.

On the basis of all this, we consider the isomorphy between Western alphabetic (phonemic) systems and the lexicographic system of Chinese as established, if not as a 100% uniformity, so yet as a near-isomorphy.

The conclusion that the system of strokes in Chinese writing is nearly isomorph with binary coding of Chinese vocabulary finds support in the well-known fact that the radical, besides being an indicator of the meaning, has a further and most important function as a means of locating a Chinese character in the dictionary. Let us take the character *han*, to snore, for example, the radical of which is *pi*, a nose. If we look up the radical *pi* in the dictionary where it will be placed in the numerical order of radicals according to the number of strokes of which it consists (13, in our case), we shall find the character *han* among the derivatives of the radical in question in the sub-list of derivatives with 3-stroke phonetics ranged under that radical. This means that we are using the stroke number of each radical and phonetic exactly as a computing machine would use the binary coding symbol for identifying a linguistic form.

So far only the first part of the looking-up process was dealt with mathematically, i.e. looking-up of a character according to its radical. The isomorphy or near-isomorphy between stroke number of radicals and "bits" per radical group suggests extending the application of information-theoretical ideas to the sub-groups of ideo-grams listed under each radical according to the stroke number of the phonetic. This, as will be seen, shows the whole looking-up procedure in a Chinese dictionary to be essentially isomorph with machine-looking-up of linguistic forms, if the forms have been binarily coded.

Figure 6 is the graphical representation of the binary coding of a Chinese dictionary according to radicals.[2] Comparison with graphs 4 and 5 shows the number of dichotomies required for the binary coding of Chinese as exceeding by 6 that needed for the coding of English and by 5 that of the Cyrillic alphabet. The statistics H, H_{cod} are, of course, higher than the corresponding ones for the alphabet coding, due to the greater length of the series of radicals, h^* showing the redundancy for Chinese to be even less than for the alphabetic languages. It goes without saying that "redundancy" in this connection refers only to the suitability of the binary coding, and has nothing to do with the quality of the language in general as a means of communication. Attention was drawn in Section 12.4 to the fact that considering the deceptiveness of some terms of information theory, one must be very careful in their use and interpretation.

Although the scatter of points for the observed percentages around a mean value corresponding to $b_i = -ld\,p$ is wider than in graphs 4 and 5, yet it is not unreasonably so, i.e. not so as to make us doubt the linear correlation between p_i and b_i. In terms of mathematical statistics, although the dispersion of points along the straight line might well exceed the limits of chance fluctuations, using the .05 or the .01 limit— there being enough causes which would account for some of the deviations of the natural language (scatter of points) from the ideal sign system (continuous straight line)—yet, on the whole, we may regard the linear trend of the scatter as being fairly well represented by the straight line.

Important though this is for establishing isomorphy between the alphabetic (phonemic) systems of Western languages and the system of Chinese vocabulary items according to radicals, it would be rash to base a conclusion of such importance upon the mere conformity of graphical representation. After all, the coding graphs for widely and intrinsically different percentage series need not be strikingly different. Unless we can show that the graph of Figure 6 has a linguistic interpretation, just as we suggested the graphs of figures 4 and 5 to have, the inference of an essential isomorphism between the two types of systems, the alphabetic and that of the Chinese radicals, must remain tenuous.

For the linguistic interpretation of symbol length in the case of binary coding we

[2] Only the extent of scatter has been indicated by plotting the extreme points.

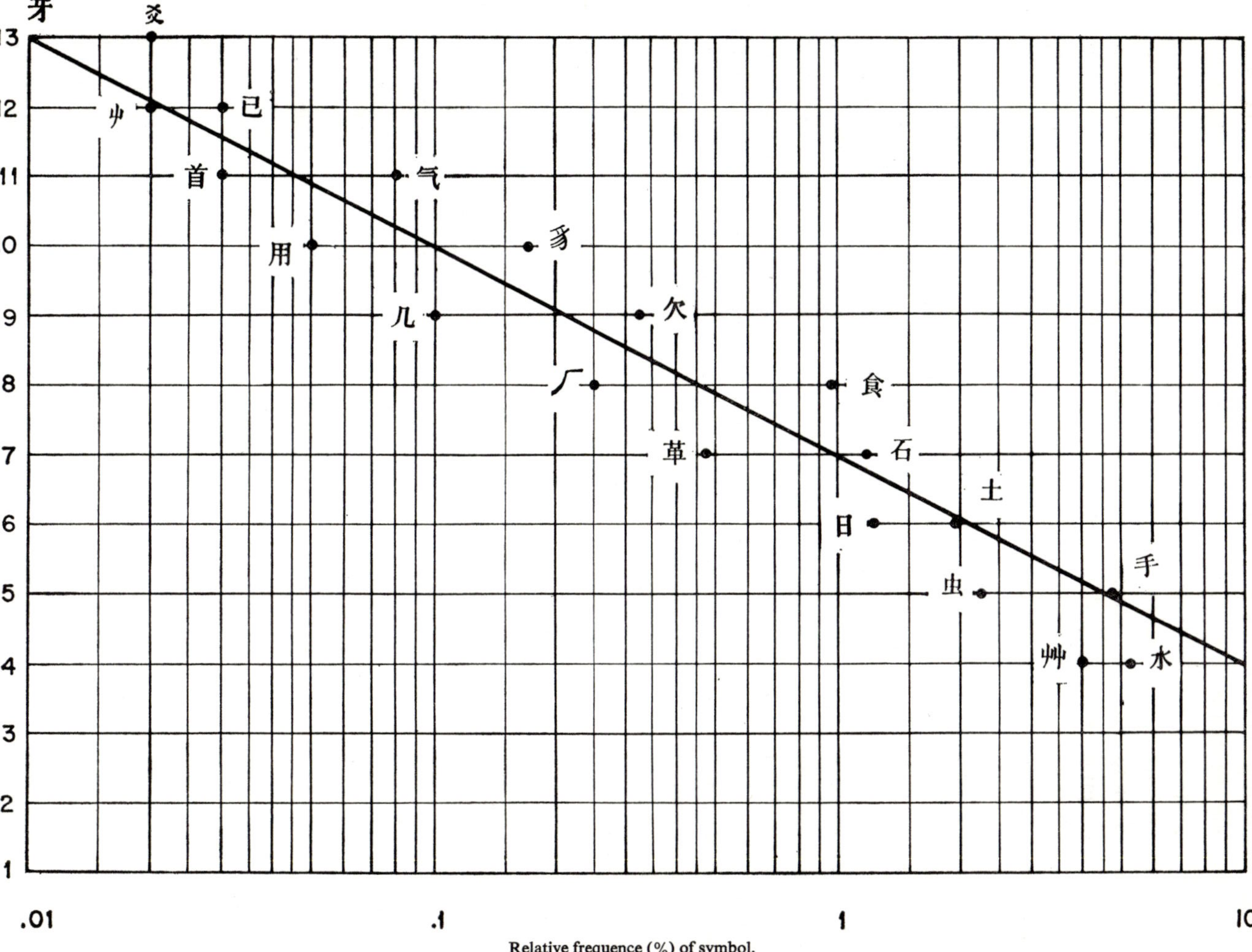

FIG. 6. Binary coding of Chinese vocabulary. (In the graph 13 dichotomies were used, thus leaving out the last two items of Table 29.)

have considered the number of strokes in the Chinese radicals, and as the counterpart of the frequency of use of the alphabetic symbol (phoneme) the number of derivatives—logical phonetic compounds—of the radical. This attempt turned out to be successful, which means that the so far only formal isomorphy between the graphs of figures 4 and 5, on the one hand, and of figure 6, on the other, i.e. between the binary coding of Western phonemic systems and of the Chinese vocabulary according to radicals, is supported and explained by a truly linguistic isomorphy, and thus exists not according to appearance only, but according to essence.

But let us dispose of a rather obvious possible objection, although it really means anticipating the argument to be developed in the forthcoming publication mentioned above, namely that the number of strokes in a Chinese character is so insignificant and so much a matter of chance that it could not very well be the counterpart of the number of distinctive elements in a phoneme. Now, whatever the historical development of the Chinese script—and we shall discuss it in some detail in that publication—so much is certain that as a result of the historical development of Chinese writing, both the *number* and *order* of the strokes in a Chinese character, and in particular in a radical, are an essential feature of the Chinese script and are stereotyped, not less than the number and order of the dots and dashes of the Morse code. It is the *exact number* of strokes required for a particular character, and in the *order* in which they are to be put, that the coding property of Chinese ideographic writing lies, even though historically some of the ideograms may have started as pictorial representations of objects of the manifold.

PART V

QUANTUM THEORY OF LANGUAGE

XVI

CHANCE, THE EVER-PRESENT ALTERNATIVE

16.1 INTRODUCTION

A fact which has received hardly any attention is that information theory is of very little use when applied to anything but the smallest linguistic units: phonemes and letters. I know of only one application to the word frequency distribution (Shannon, 1951), and that only with a view to obtaining an improved estimate of the entropy, H, for the letter distribution in English. Shannon calculates the entropy first from the frequency distribution of words according to rank, and uses this for obtaining an estimate of the entropy per letter. There is no attempt to improve the first estimate by taking the transition probabilities between words into account. Nor is there any method available by which this could be done.

This appears to be the real reason why information theory is so little, or hardly at all, applied to the word distribution: we do not know how to improve a first approximation of H calculated from only the global frequencies by bringing in the transition probabilities of words. What is quite feasible for the 26 letters of the alphabet, or the 43 phonemes of English, is not only impracticable for the 50,000 or so vocabulary items of our language, but simply impossible.

One might perhaps point to Sect. 13.3 where I have calculated H for the distribution of species according to the number of individuals. But the names of species are not items in a continuous text, and therefore have no transition probabilities. Neither are there any transition probabilities to be taken into account in Sect. 15.2 where H is calculated for the Chinese vocabulary according to the number of strokes in the Phonetic.

In this part we shall develop a statistical method by which the transition probabilities between words are indirectly taken into consideration, and, in consequence of this, obtain a satisfactory estimate of the amount of information per word, which will be in agreement with the facts. What is surprising in this development is that it requires a new type of statistics. The step is similar to that from number statistics, as used in the field of language before 1948, to statistical physics in the form of Maxwellian statistics introduced in 1948 by Shannon's information theory. When extending the concept of "information" to the words of a language, we find it necessary to introduce another type of statistical physics, viz. Bose-Einstein (B-E) statistics as the appropriate method for assessing the information value of words.

16.2   THE DETERMINISTIC VIEW OF THE USE OF WORDS
AND SOME FACTS AGAINST IT

The determinist linguist believes that every word a speaker or writer uses has its particular motivation; as a rule, he is disinclined to generalise about the use of different vocabulary items. He even objects against occurrences of the same vocabulary item in different contexts being regarded as sensibly the same thing, and still less does he believe in grouping different vocabulary items according to a formal characteristic, such as occurrence frequency. The deeper his analysis, the more does he tend to regard every word as a law of its own.

This, in a way, is the negation of general rules such as one would strive after in any other branch of knowledge. The question is: is the determinist linguist right in his assumption of the absence of any regularity in the use of words, i.e. the absence of any law which would apply to certain numbers of words in the same way, irrespective of their particular meaning and context? We shall try to answer this question starting from empirical observations.

From Macaulay's essay on Bacon four samples of increments of pages spread over the whole text were taken, and the nouns in each recorded together with their occurrence frequencies (Yule, 1944). They were then sorted according to whether they occurred in one sample only, in two samples, three samples and all four samples together. We shall use the following notation. The capital A (positive symbol) denotes "noun occurring in sample A", the corresponding Greek letter α (negative symbol) "not occurring in sample A", and so on. There are four letters in each class symbol for the figures of Table 31, and each letter may be either a capital or a Greek letter, so there must be in all 2^4, or 16 classes.

A class frequency is denoted by putting the class symbol in brackets. According to the number of letters within the brackets, we speak of first-order, second-order, third-order and fourth-order frequencies. The numbers for each of these categories are shown in Table 31.

TABLE 31

	Samples			
	A	B	C	D
Words peculiar to a sample, e.g. $(A\beta\gamma\delta)$	268	280	275	312
Words common to two samples, e.g. $(AB\gamma\delta)$	68	68		
	64		64	
	59			59
		67	67	
		66		66
			81	81

Words common to three samples, e.g. ($ABC\delta$)	62	62	62	
	58	58		58
	53		53	53
		64	64	64
Words common to all four samples ($ABCD$)	271	271	271	271

We note that there is a high degree of conformity in respect of the four categories of words, which points to similarity in linguistic behaviour regardless of the meaning of particular words, and of the content. This suspicion of a certain regularity in the use of words is considerably strengthened when we compare the ratio $\dfrac{(A\beta\gamma\delta)+(ABCD)}{(A)}$ in the four samples (Table 32).

TABLE 32

Sample	$100\,\dfrac{(A\beta\gamma\delta)+(ABCD)}{A}$
A	59.7
B	58.9
C	58.3
D	60.5

That ratio which can be regarded as the *alternative probability of a word being peculiar to a sample or common to all four*,[1] is remarkably close for our four samples. To overcome the objection that this may just be a "fluke of chance"—though it should be understood that a statistician does not share the common contempt if a result should turn out to be a fluke of chance; on the contrary he considers this as a most interesting result—, I give in Table 34 the values of that ratio for two other groups of literary texts.

There seems to be sufficient reason for suspecting a mechanism to be responsible for the regularity observed, or, in other words, for assuming a general law of the language code which would provide that effect.

16.3   CHANCE, THE EVER-PRESENT ALTERNATIVE

When trying to devise a mathematical model for these regularities in linguistic behaviour, a perfectly analogous case in statistical physics comes to our mind, which suggests using chance as the ever-present alternative for explaining certain events.[2]

Physical systems with a small number of degrees of freedom, such as the planets in the gravitational field of the sun, can be studied by the methods of classical mechanics. By constructing the equations of motion of the system (as many as there are degrees of freedom), and integrating them, complete information about the motion of the system can be deduced. When, however, we are dealing with systems which

---

[1]   *TTM*, p. 251.
[2]   L. Landau and E. Lifshitz, *Statistical Physics* (Oxford, 1938).

have a very large number of degrees of freedom (for instance, macroscopic bodies consisting of, say 10^{25} particles), the number of equations of motion, one for each particle, becomes too large to solve in practice.

These considerations might, at first sight, suggest that as the number of degrees of freedom increases, the properties of a mechanical system should become more and more complicated, and that it should become increasingly difficult to find any regularity of behaviour. Fortunately, this is not true. Just when there is a very large number of degrees of freedom, the system obeys laws of a very special kind. The investigation of these laws forms a special branch of physics, called statistical physics. In other words: chance, the ever-present alternative, comes to our rescue. The analogy between the dilemma when investigating physical systems and when investigating language systems, both with very high numbers of degrees of freedom, is so close that it suggests trying also for our problem chance as the ever-present alternative.

The random partitioning of vocabulary may be visualised by the following thought experiment. Let us suppose we write out all the nouns of the total frequency distribution of words from Macaulay's essay on Bacon on counters, giving a noun that occurs x times x counters, and then deal them at random into four trays labelled A, B, C and D. To ensure approximate randomness we might toss the counters into a spinning circular tray with four equal quadrants A, B, C and D. Sorting the counters in each quadrant by nouns, and listing and counting the nouns in each—not the number of counters—, we shall then have the 4th-order word classes.

Our samples represent a linear sequence of ca. 8,000 occurrences which is divided into four samples of 2,000 occurrences each. The probability of a counter appearing in one quadrant is $2,000/8,000 = .25$ and, consequently, that of its not appearing $.75$.

In general, for r samples the probability of a counter appearing in one of k quadrants is k/r and that of its not appearing in k quadrants

$$\frac{r-k}{r} \tag{1}$$

The most convenient set of quantities for our purpose is that of the probabilities of non-appearance, from which the probabilities, and expected numbers of words in the various classes, can easily be obtained.

If the word is written on two counters, the above probabilities for appearance and non-appearance in a quadrant apply to each occurrence of the word, and are, by the multiplication theorem of probability, $(.25)^2 = .0625$ and $(.75)^2 = .5625$, respectively; if the word is written on three counters the probability of its appearance and non-appearance in a quadrant are $(.25)^3 = .01562$ and $(.75)^3 = .4219$.

Generally, for x occurrences and r quadrants, the probability of non-appearance in k quadrants is

$$\left(\frac{r-k}{r}\right)^x \tag{2}$$

If there are f_x such words (the sum of all f_x being the number of words in the total, 2048 in our illustration), the expected number of them not appearing in any of the k quadrants is therefore

$$f_x\left(\frac{r-k}{r}\right)^x \tag{3}$$

and the entire number of words not falling into any one of the k quadrants is the sum of such expressions for all values of x

$$S\left\{f_x\left(\frac{r-k}{r}\right)^x\right\} \tag{4}$$

The arithmetic is most briefly and simply carried out directly as indicated by this expression. With $r = 4$, as in our experimental material, we evaluate the three frequencies

$$(\alpha) = S\{f_x(\tfrac{3}{4})^x\}, \quad (\alpha\beta) = S\{f_x(\tfrac{1}{2})^x\}, \quad (\alpha\beta\gamma) = S\{f_x(\tfrac{1}{4})^x\} \tag{5}$$

which actually give us fourteen frequencies since $(\alpha) = (\beta) = (\gamma) = (\delta)$, and so forth. We know the value of N (the total number of nouns in the frequency distribution) and are also given $(\alpha\beta\gamma\delta) = 0$, and can then calculate the complete set of fourth-order frequencies, or the frequencies of the positive classes or any other set we like. For the sake of more clearly exhibiting how $(ABCD)$, $(ABC\delta)$, $(AB\gamma\delta)$ and $(A\beta\gamma\delta)$ are built up—and we need only concern ourselves with these four since obviously $(ABC\delta) = (AB\gamma D) = (A\beta CD) = (\alpha BCD)$ and so on—, the reader is referred to Table 16, Chpt. 11, for a 5th-order vocabulary partition. The equations, derived from equation (5), are

$$\begin{aligned}
(ABCD) &= S\{f_x[1 - 4(\tfrac{3}{4})^x + 6(\tfrac{1}{2})^x - 4(\tfrac{1}{4})^x]\}\\
(ABC\delta) &= S\{f_x[(\tfrac{3}{4})^x - 3(\tfrac{1}{2})^x + 3(\tfrac{1}{4})^x]\}\\
(AB\gamma\delta) &= S\{f_x[(\tfrac{1}{2})^x - 2(\tfrac{1}{4})^x]\}\\
(A\beta\gamma\delta) &= S\{f_x(\tfrac{1}{4})^x\}
\end{aligned} \tag{6}$$

Their derivation follows these lines.

Starting from the last equation, it is obvious that the probability of a word of frequency x_i belonging to one sample only is equal to its not appearing in the other three, $(\tfrac{1}{4})^x$. The probability of occurring in a particular pair of samples, say AB, implies its non-occurrence in the other two $\gamma\delta$ and equals, therefore, the probability of not occurring in any pair of samples, $(\tfrac{1}{2})^x$, minus the combination of $\gamma\delta$ with α or β, which is $2(\tfrac{1}{4})^x$. In this way, the frequencies of the random partitioning of vocabulary are built up by a process of stepwise substitution according to the theory of attributes (Yule and Kendall, 1937, Chapter I), the coefficients being those of the binomial expansion $(1+1)^n$.

For once-words, in particular, the last line of formula (6) gives the expected frequency of such words in each sample as $\tfrac{1}{4}$ of the hapax legomena in the total.

The general form of the random partitioning function is as follows:

$$S\left\{f_x\left(\tfrac{1}{r}\right)^x\right\}$$
$$S\left\{f_x\left[\left(\tfrac{2}{r}\right)^x - 2\left(\tfrac{1}{r}\right)^x\right]\right\}$$
$$S\left\{f_x\left[\left(\tfrac{3}{r}\right)^x - 3\left(\tfrac{2}{r}\right)^x + 3\left(\tfrac{1}{r}\right)^x\right]\right\}$$
$$S\left\{f_x\left[\left(\tfrac{4}{r}\right)^x - 4\left(\tfrac{3}{r}\right)^x + 6\left(\tfrac{2}{r}\right)^x - 4\left(\tfrac{1}{r}\right)^x\right]\right\}$$

$$\cdot\ \cdot\ \cdot\ \cdot\ \cdot\ \cdot\ \cdot\ \cdot\ \cdot\ \cdot\ \cdot\ \cdot\ \cdot\ \cdot\ \cdot$$

where r = number of text samples in a series

          x = frequency of occurrence of a word in the total frequency distribution

          f_x = number of different words with frequency x

          S = sign of summation.

For instance, for a series of 7 partial texts ($r = 7$), the series of formulae is as follows:

$$S\left\{f_x\left(\tfrac{1}{7}\right)^x\right\}$$
$$S\left\{f_x\left[\left(\tfrac{2}{7}\right)^x - 2\left(\tfrac{1}{7}\right)^x\right]\right\}$$
$$S\left\{f_x\left[\left(\tfrac{3}{7}\right)^x - 3\left(\tfrac{2}{7}\right)^x + 3\left(\tfrac{1}{7}\right)^x\right]\right\}$$
$$S\left\{f_x\left[\left(\tfrac{4}{7}\right)^x - 4\left(\tfrac{3}{7}\right)^x + 6\left(\tfrac{2}{7}\right)^x - 4\left(\tfrac{1}{7}\right)^x\right]\right\}$$
$$S\left\{f_x\left[\left(\tfrac{5}{7}\right)^x - 5\left(\tfrac{4}{7}\right)^x + 10\left(\tfrac{3}{7}\right)^x - 10\left(\tfrac{2}{7}\right)^x + 5\left(\tfrac{1}{7}\right)^x\right]\right\}$$
$$S\left\{f_x\left[\left(\tfrac{6}{7}\right)^x - 6\left(\tfrac{5}{7}\right)^x + 15\left(\tfrac{4}{7}\right)^x - 20\left(\tfrac{3}{7}\right)^x + 15\left(\tfrac{2}{7}\right)^x - 6\left(\tfrac{1}{7}\right)^x\right]\right\}$$
$$S\left\{f_x\left[1 - 7\left(\tfrac{6}{7}\right)^x + 21\left(\tfrac{5}{7}\right)^x - 35\left(\tfrac{4}{7}\right)^x + 35\left(\tfrac{3}{7}\right)^x - 21\left(\tfrac{2}{7}\right)^x + 7\left(\tfrac{1}{7}\right)^x\right]\right\}$$

To simplify the calculation, which becomes rather cumbersome for high values of x' numerical tables have been prepared from which to read directly the probability of a word belonging to a specified number of samples or text parts. These tables are given in Appendix G (pp. 341-412) of the author's *Type-Token Mathematics* (The Hague, 1960), and cover a range of r from 1 to 30 and x from 1 to 100.

16.4   FITTING THE RANDOM PARTITIONING FUNCTION TO THE RESULTS OF EMPIRICAL VOCABULARY PARTITIONING

In order to ascertain whether the empirical results of random partitioning are satisfactorily fitted by the random partitioning function, we compare observation and theory in the following tables. The numbers in brackets in Table 34 are the theoretical figures obtained by the random partitioning function.

TABLE 33

Lines (of Table 31)	Mean Frequency	Theoretical
1	283.75	273.66
2-7	67.50	71.58
8-11	59.25	61.60
12	271.00	277.51

TABLE 34

Probability of a word being peculiar to one sample or common to all four samples (in %)

Sample	Four samples from essay on Bacon	Four essays of Macaulay	Four works of Bunyan
A	59.7 (58.1)	55.2 (57.8)	51.8 (60.9)
B	58.9 (58.1)	51.4 (57.8)	54.5 (60.9)
C	58.3 (58.1)	55.6 (57.8)	59.3 (60.9)
D	60.5 (58.1)	54.3 (56.5)	60.0 (60.9)
Average	59.4	54.1	54.4

Inspection of the above tables does not leave any reasonable doubt about the random partitioning function providing a satisfactory fit for the observed regularities in the use of vocabulary (but see Sect. 18.4 for a more detailed discussion of the problem of fitting by the random partitioning function).

16.5   CONCLUSIONS

We have thus proved that chance is in fact the ever-present alternative to the deliberate word-picking assumed by the determinist linguist. Does this mean that we have disposed of any intention and motivation for the use of particular words? By no means. We have done that just as little as the Maxwellian law disposes, or negates, a cause-and-effect relation in the movement of the individual particles. But we have, by disregarding individual behaviour, succeeded in establishing laws for the behaviour of words in general, which the consideration of the individual words would never have enabled us to do.

This is a formulation of our results with which everybody, including the determinist linguist, will agree. But it need not be the end of the conclusions to be drawn from this. If what is considered at first sight to be the result of the strictest motivation in the use of words, turns out to be also obtainable by a chance mechanism, does this not point to some unwarranted assumption about what we call "strict motivation" in the use of words? And may there not be more chance in this than the determinist takes for granted?

The same type of problem has arisen in modern physics and has led to virtually abandoning the assumption that the path of a mass point (particle) could ever be described strictly in terms of cause and effect. This, in fact, was the starting point for the *Principle of Indeterminacy* in physics. Since the distribution of vocabulary over the whole text (*TTM*, Table 14, col. 6) is the result of the dynamic forces of composition and writing, the random partitioning function leading to sensibly the same result can be taken as providing the explanation of the dynamic process, i.e. the process by which the global distribution accumulates with time.

An important item in support of this conclusion is that the statistics of the random partitioning function are in structure similar to a type of statistics needed for the description of a most fundamental dynamic process in nature. This will be shown in the next chapter.

XVII

VOCABULARY PARTITION AND QUANTUM STATISTICS

17.1 COMMON CHARACTERISTICS OF BOSE-EINSTEIN STATISTICS AND THE RANDOM PARTITIONING FUNCTION

The statistics of the random partitioning function seem deceptively close to what is known as classical statistics, used in economics, demographic studies and also in physics as Maxwell-Boltzmann statistics, but they are, in fact, of a fundamentally different type. They have the nature of the "New Statistics" or Bose-Einstein (B-E) statistics, used in Quantum theory (*TTM*, Sect. 20.7).

The conceptual model for the statistics required is that of the distribution of r balls in n cells. Table 35 describes all possible outcomes of the experiment of placing 3 balls into 3 cells according to the classical conception of probability. Each of these arrangements represents a simple event, or, as we say, a point in sample space which corresponds to the phase space of statistical physics. The total number of arrangements is n^r and, thus, for our example $3^3 = 27$. The probability of a particular arrangement is n^{-r}.

TABLE 35

1	abc	—	—	10	a	bc	—	19	—	a	bc
2	—	abc	—	11	b	a c	—	20	—	b	a c
3	—	—	abc	12	c	ab	—	21	—	c	ab
4	ab	c	—	13	a	—	bc	22	a	b	c
5	a c	b	—	14	b	—	a c	23	a	c	b
6	bc	a	—	15	c	—	ab	24	b	a	c
7	ab	—	c	16	—	ab	c	25	b	c	a
8	a c	—	b	17	—	a c	b	26	c	a	b
9	bc	—	a	18	—	bc	a	27	c	b	a

So far, we have assumed that the balls are distinguishable as *a*, *b* and *c*. If we suppose that the balls are indistinguishable, it means that we no longer distinguish between three arrangements such as 4, 5, 6, and Table 35 reduces to Table 36.

In the scheme above, we have considered indistinguishable balls, but Table 36 still refers to a first, second, third cell. That is, it still refers to an ordered arrangement of the balls. We can go a step further and assume that even cells are indistinguishable.

TABLE 36

1	***	—	—	6	*	**	—
2	—	***	—	7	*	—	**
3	—	—	***	8	—	**	*
4	**	*	—	9	—	*	**
5	**	—	*	10	*	*	*

With both balls and cells indistinguishable, only three different arrangements are possible, namely:

$$*** \quad — \quad —, \qquad ** \quad * \quad —, \qquad * \quad * \quad *$$

with probabilities $^3/_{10}$, $^6/_{10}$, $^1/_{10}$ respectively, each possible arrangement being equally probable, and this is, in effect, the step which leads from classical statistics to quantum statistics.

The mathematical model for the B-E statistics assumes both balls and cells to be indistinguishable. This has the consequence that whereas the 10 points of Table 36 have, according to classical statistics, the following probability distribution

Sample number:	1	2	3	4	5	6	7	8	9	10
Probability:	$\frac{1}{27}$	$\frac{1}{27}$	$\frac{1}{27}$	$\frac{1}{9}$	$\frac{1}{9}$	$\frac{1}{9}$	$\frac{1}{9}$	$\frac{1}{9}$	$\frac{1}{9}$	$\frac{2}{9}$,

the B-E model attributes a probability of $^1/_{10}$ to each of the 10 sample points.

Generally, the number of distinguishable arrangements if both balls and cells are indistinguishable is no longer n^r, but

$$\binom{n+r-1}{r} = \binom{n+r-1}{n-1} \tag{7}$$

all arrangements being equally probable. For our example the number of distinguishable arrangements is

$$\frac{(3+3-1)!}{3!\,2!} = 10 \tag{8}$$

each arrangement having the probability $^1/_{10}$.

The operative word in B-E statistics is the indistinguishability of both balls and cells, and we shall find this feature to be characteristic for the random partitioning function, and with it for the distribution of vocabulary.

Let us recall the statistical model of the random partitioning function (Sect. 16.3). When distributing randomly the word occurrences over a specified number of cells, the linear order of these occurrences in the literary text is, of course, abandoned. The arrangement of the words within a cell, and that of the cell totals, simulate statistically the original text, and must, therefore, be imagined as a linear sequence of words. According to the model of the random partitioning function, the order of words within a cell is indistinguishable from any other arrangement of these words, and so is that of the cell totals. Moreover, it is immaterial *which word* will partake in any of the combinations of a stated complexity. This means indistinguishability of words to be a characteristic of the random partitioning function. Thus, if we consider a two-part combination, any vocabulary item with a particular frequency

X_i will have the same probability of belonging to such a combination, which means that all that matters for the allocation of a word to a specified (as to type) combination is the probability of words with a given X_i to fall into that combinatory class, not their individual meaning, which corresponds to indistinguishability of "balls". And lastly, since all that these probabilities tell us is the chance a word with a given X_i has of falling into one of the *nth*-order classes, but not into which particular combination of that class, there is indistinguishability as to "cells". It follows that the random partitioning function is characterised by those features which distinguish B-E from classical statistics, indistinguishability of words and combination, or *nth*-order classes, standing for "balls" and "cells" respectively.

17.2   THE RANDOM PARTITIONING FUNCTION AND TRANSITION PROBABILITIES BETWEEN WORDS

In order to fully appreciate what we are doing when replacing the classical method by that of the "new statistics" in dealing with the distribution of words (morphemes), it is not enough to be clear about the formal difference only in the basic concepts of the two methods. We shall appreciate the importance of the change in method better when we understand the influence which such a change has on the independence of word occurrences from one another, which is characteristic for random *sampling*. Our contention is that empirical vocabulary partitioning, and the random *partitioning* function, take the association values of words, their "valeur", implicitly into consideration. It is in this way that the transition probabilities between words are fully taken account of, though in a statistical way only, that is in a summary manner which, however, is the only way in which they can be completely taken into account.

The somewhat lengthy argument of the following section should not make the reader miss the object, which is to establish that the random partitioning function takes the transition probabilities between words implicitly into account.

17.2.1   *Vocabulary Association*

For the investigation of the degree of association between writers or texts as regards vocabulary, it is customary to use the statistical methods of association. If the vocabulary of a group of texts, two of which are A and B, contains N different vocabulary items, and we denote the number of words occurring in text A by (A), those not occurring in A by (α); those occurring in B by (B); those not occurring in B by (β), we get the following table which is called an Association Table.

Attribute	Attribute		Total
	B	β	
A	(AB)	$(A\beta)$	(A)
α	(αB)	$(\alpha\beta)$	(α)
Total	(B)	(β)	N

We may now ask whether the distribution of vocabulary is such as to signify an association between the two texts as regards vocabulary and, if so, to what extent. It is sometimes convenient to summarise the whole matter into a single numerical measure or "coefficient" which will take the value zero if the attributes are independent, positive values if the association is positive and negative values if it is negative. The simplest of such coefficients is the association coefficient[1]:

$$Q = \frac{(AB)(\alpha\beta) - (A\beta)(\alpha B)}{(AB)(\alpha\beta) + (A\beta)(\alpha B)} \tag{9}$$

According to this equation, Q takes the value zero as required, when the attributes are independent. It takes positive values if the association is positive, the values in this case ranging from $+1$ if $(A\beta) = 0$ (all A's are B) or $(\alpha B) = 0$ (all B's are A), or both. It takes a negative value if $(AB) = 0$ (the two texts having no word in common) or $(\alpha\beta) = 0$ (if all the words of the total N which are missing in one text, A or B, are also missing in the other).

In spite of the appropriateness of Q for judging vocabulary association, there is an element of arbitrariness as regards the exact value of Q. It is evident from the formula that since its value depends on the quantity $(\alpha\beta)$, that is on the words missing in both texts, its value will ultimately depend on the background against which the connection of A and B is judged. In other words, the *field or universe* with which we are dealing must always be borne in mind.

17.2.2 *Vocabulary Association from Experimental Data*

Our material consists of four spatially different samples from the same work, Macaulay's Essay on Bacon (A-D); samples from four different essays by Macaulay: on Milton (A), John Hampton (B), Frederick the Great (C) and the total count from the Essay on Bacon (D), and samples from four works by Bunyan: The Pilgrim's Progress, Parts I & II (A, B), The Life and Death of Mr. Badman (C), The Holy War (D).

The association coefficient Q from the three sets of data are given below.

For the sampling experiment (four samples from Macaulay's Essay on Bacon), the values of Q for particular pairs of samples are not very different from one another, and therefore also not sensibly different from their average. This is no longer true for the four works by Bunyan, but we can easily account for the differences. The most substantial association $Q = 0.310$ is naturally that between Parts I and II of The Pilgrim's Progress (AB), the intensity of association being much less between one part of The Pilgrim's Progress and either of the two remaining works (C, D) or between the remaining works, because of heterogeneity in the vocabulary in the

---

[1] G. Udny Yule and M. G. Kendall, *An Introduction to the Theory of Statistics*, 11th edition (London, 1937).

TABLE 37

Pair of attributes	Association Coefficient Q		
	Sampling Experiment	Macaulay	Bunyan
AB	+0.183	+0.216	+0.310
AC	+0.146	+0.072	+0.105
AD	+0.063	−0.076	+0.078
BC	+0.141	+0.215	−0.046
BD	+0.073	+0.176	+0.053
CD	+0.110	−0.080	−0.025
Mean	+0.119	+0.087*	+0.079

* Mean of three associations not involving D + 0.168, of three involving D + 0.007.

different works, which necessarily means an inhomogenous field of discourse. It is similar with the four essays by Macaulay, though the differences are not so easily accounted for, but there is little doubt that a comparison of the essays as regards universe of discourse would explain the differences in the value for Q.

17.2.3 *Vocabulary Association due to Random Sampling*

What is more difficult to explain is that the value of Q appears so unexpectedly small. The mean value of Q for the sampling experiment is +0.119, for Macaulay only +0.087, for Bunyan still less, +0.079. Two of the coefficients both for Macaulay and Bunyan are actually slightly negative. One would expect much more substantial associations between parts of one text or between texts by the same author, say of the order 0.5 or so. The first question would seem to be: how are we to account for these small associations? The values of Q are so small that one could hardly avoid the surmise that they may be accounted for by chance, in which case one could not even speak of a significant association.

We shall first test this assumption. If we wanted to draw from a given distribution of vocabulary according to frequency of occurrence four equal samples by simple random sampling, we might write out all the words of the total frequency distribution on counters, giving each noun that occurs x times x counters, and mix them up in a bag. Then we should draw a counter, note the word, *return the counter to the bag* and stir it up; draw another counter, note the word and again return the counter, and so on, until we had accumulated a sample of the required size. Then we should proceed to form another sample in precisely the same way, and so on. For words with a given number of occurrences x, the total number of occurrences being S_1, the chance of a word with x occurrences being drawn at any one drawing is x/S_1, and the chance of its not being drawn in, say, s_1 drawings is

$$q_x = \left(1 - \frac{x}{S_1}\right)^{s_1} = e^{\,x(s_1/S_1)} \tag{10}$$

using the exponential approximation; for the special case of a sample one-fourth the size of the original

$$q_x = e^{-x/4} \tag{11}$$

If $p_x = 1 - q_x$, we then have

$$
\begin{aligned}
(AB) &= S(f_x p_x^2) \\
(A\beta) = (\alpha B) &= S(f_x p_x q_x) \\
(\alpha\beta) &= S(f_x q_x^2)
\end{aligned}
\tag{12}
$$

The probabilities of a word occurring in any of the four cells of the association table, if the total text is divided into four parts, are listed in Table 38.

TABLE 38

x	p_x^2	$p_x q_x$	q_x^2
1	.049	.172	.607
2	.154	.239	.368
3	.278	.249	.223
4	.400	.233	.135
5	.509	.204	.082
6	.603	.173	.050
7	.683	.144	.030
8	.748	.117	.018
9	.800	.094	.011
10	.842	.075	.007
11	.876	.060	.004
12	.903	.047	.003
13	.924	.037	.002
14	.940	.029	.001
15	.954	.023	.001
16	.963	.017	—
17	.972	.014	—
18	.979	.011	—
19	.983	.008	—
20	.986	.006	—
21	.990	.007	—
22	.993	.005	—
23	.994	.003	—
24	.995	—	—
25	1.000	—	—
26	1.000	—	—
27	1.000	—	—
28	1.000	—	—
29	1.000	—	—
30 up	1.000	—	—

The vertical scale of Table 38 is that of word frequency, the horizontal scale that of the probabilities of a word occurring in one of the 4 compartments of Table 39, viz. $p_x{}^2$, p_xq_x, $q_x{}^2$. In the body of the table are listed the probabilities of a word with a particular frequency of occurrence to occur in one of the 4 compartments of the Association Table. Multiplying these probabilities by the appropriate frequencies of a given distribution (sampling experiment on Bacon, four essays by Macaulay, four works by Bunyan) and summing over the whole range of x gives the totals for the four compartments of the association table.

Since for words with a given number of frequency x, the drawing of words for one sample has nothing whatever to do with the drawing of words for any other, they must tend to be quite independent, and for each elementary or component association according to Table 38, Q is zero. It is only in the pool of these elementary or component tables as given in Tables 39a-c that the association differs from zero—a well-known fact of pooling.[2] We obtain in this way for the sampling experiment on Bacon:

TABLE 39a

	B	β	Total
A	512.29	367.89	880.18
α	367.89	799.96	1167.85
Total	880.18	1167.85	2048.93

$$Q = 0.503$$

For Macaulay's four essays

TABLE 39b

	B	β	Total
A	1084.29	613.23	1697.52
α	613.23	1231.91	1845.14
Total	1697.52	1845.14	3542.66

$$Q = .561$$

For Bunyan

TABLE 39c

	B	β	Total
A	707.80	380.83	1088.63
α	380.83	776.38	1157.21
Total	1088.63	1157.21	2245.84

$$Q = .582$$

From Table 39a we obtain $Q = +0.503$, from Table 39b we have $Q = .561$, and from Table 39c, $Q = .582$, which is just the sort of association one might expect intuitively for the presence of a word in two samples from the same author. But

[2] G. U. Yule (1937), p. 57, 58.

these values of Q are very different from the observed values (Table 37). It follows that there must be something wrong with the theoretical model of random sampling for the event in question. Since it agrees only with our intuitive idea about what the association should be like, it would seem that our intuition in that case is based upon the idea of random sampling. But since it does not agree with the actual intensity of association as observed for two samples, it follows that our intuition is not correct in this case, and random sampling does not provide the appropriate model for the event in question.

Instead, therefore, of trying to construct the model using the random *sampling* methods of classical statistics, let us now construct a model of random *partitioning* using a particular kind of occupancy statistics, and see whether the results agree better with our observations. In theoretical terms, we shall use a model, not of random sampling, but of occupancy statistics with the special provision of indistinguishability of either, the word belonging to a frequency group and the parts (samples).

17.2.4 Application of Random Partitioning to our Data

For two classes A, B we have, by the random partitioning function, the expected frequencies:

$$(\alpha) = S\{f_x(\tfrac{3}{4})^x\}, \; (\alpha\beta) = S\{f_x(\tfrac{1}{2})^x\} \tag{20}$$

Hence also

$$(AB) = S\{f_x[1 - 2(\tfrac{3}{4})^x + (\tfrac{1}{2})^x]\} \tag{21}$$

$$(A\beta) = (\alpha B) = S\{f_x[(\tfrac{3}{4})^x - (\tfrac{1}{2})^x]\} \tag{22}$$

The probabilities for a word to appear in one of these groups are listed in Table 40.

The vertical scale of Table 40 is that of word frequency, the horizontal scale that of the probabilities of a word to appear in both texts (AB), in one text only $(A\beta)$ or (αB) or in neither $(\alpha\beta)$. In the body of the table are listed the probabilities of a word with a particular frequency of occurrence to occur in one of the 4 compartments of the association table. The probabilities for any number of samples or text parts up to 30 and frequency x up to 100 could be read off directly from the numerical table of the random partitioning function given in Table 38. Multiplying the probabilities by the appropriate frequencies f_x of a given vocabulary distribution, and summing over the whole range of x gives the totals for the 4 compartments of the association table.

TABLE 40

x	$1 - 2(\tfrac{3}{4})^x + (\tfrac{1}{2})^x$	$(\tfrac{3}{4})^x - (\tfrac{1}{2})^x$	$(\tfrac{1}{2})^x$
1	—	.250	.500
2	.124	.312	.250
3	.281	.296	.124
4	.429	.253	.063
5	.566	.206	.031
6	.659	.162	.015
7	.741	.125	.007
8	.804	.096	.004
9	.851	.073	.002
10	.888	.055	.001
11	.915	.042	—
12	.936	.032	—
13	.953	.024	—
14	.964	.018	—
15	.973	.014	—
16	.980	.010	—
17	.985	.008	—
18	.988	.006	—
19	.992	.005	—
20	.994	.004	—
21	.999	.003	—
22	.998	.003	—
23	.997	.001	—
24	1.000	—	—
25	1.000	—	—
26	1.000	—	—
27	1.000	—	—
28	1.000	—	—
29	1.000	—	—
30 up	1.000	—	—

Curiously enough, each elementary or component association for a particular x according to Table 40 is now negative, but on consideration it is evident that random partitioning must lead to such a result. Let us suppose a word occurs 4 times and is consequently written on 4 counters. If in our mechanical illustration of random partitioning the first counter falls into quadrant A, there are only 3 left which have a chance of falling into B. Thus, the chance of a counter appearing in B is reduced, if a counter has already appeared in A. If it has not fallen into A, it may itself have fallen into B, and anyway there are still 3 others left that have a chance of doing so. Hence, the proportion of A's that are B will tend to be less than the proportion of non-A's that are B. It is only in the pool of the elementary or component tables, given by the totals in Table 41 that the association becomes positive as an effect of pooling. Evidently if the association had been zero for each row instead of negative, the association for the row of totals would have been considerably higher (see the preceding Section whose results are in full agreement with this conclusion). For the sampling experiment on Macaulay's Essay on Bacon we get:

TABLE 41a

	B	β	Total
A	472.27	478.43	950.70
α	478.43	618.89	1097.32
Total	950.70	1097.32	2048.02

$$Q = 0.122$$

For the four works by Bunyan, we obtain from random partitioning the following association table:

TABLE 41b

	B	β	Total
A	676.79	487.21	1163.00
α	487.21	594.83	1082.04
Total	1163.00	1082.04	2245.04

$$Q = 0.261$$

Proceeding in the same way with Macaulay's pairs AB, AC and BC we obtain $Q = 0.334$ and for the pairs AD, BD, CD, we get $Q = 0.114$.

The expected values of Q for the sampling experiment (0.122) is in close agreement with the mean of the observed values from that experiment (0.119). The same cannot be said for Macaulay and Bunyan, the expected values of Q on random partitioning being greater than the means of the observed values. There is, however, good agreement between the theoretical and some of the observed values, e.g. for Macaulay's essays: 0.216 (AB), 0.215 (BC), 0.176 (BD) against theoretical values of 0.334 and 0.114; for Bunyan's works: 0.310 (AB) against a theoretical value of 0.261. There is little doubt that the heterogeneity of the essays on the one hand, and of Bunyan's works, on the other, must have the effect of reducing the association below expectation.

On the whole, *the values of Q on random partitioning are much nearer to the observed values than are the theoretical values obtained on random sampling*, which shows that the appropriate statistics for vocabulary distribution is not that of random sampling, or classical statistics, but that of occupancy in the form of the random partitioning function. Such differences as we notice between expectation on random partitioning and observation may be traced to differences between the text contents, and thus to inhomogeneity of the universe of discourse.

17.2.5 *Vocabulary Association and Random Partitioning*

The importance of these results for the system of mathematical linguistics, can be summed up in one sentence. With regard to phonemes, word length, grammar forms, the parts of the universe of discourse behave, by and large, like random samples (which is the essence of ergodicity of word masses from running texts, Sect. 1.5); with regard to vocabulary items, on the other hand, running texts and their parts behave, not like random samples, but according to the random partitioning function. Hence, the dilemma of Sect. 17.2.1 because, although they can be regarded as a statistical mass, they do not in all respects behave like one.

The explanation of this phenomenon can be given in very simple form, which is, at the same time, the answer to the problem set at the beginning of Sect. 17.2. *The appearance of a word in one, two, three ... all parts of a text will depend upon the frequency of its association with other words in the text.* It is this frequency of association which, in the last resort, also determines its global frequency of occurrence in the text. It follows that, whereas the correlation coefficient, Q, between random samples assumes a random occurrence of words in the text, that calculated from random partitioning *takes the transition probabilities between words into account.* This explains why *different texts* could behave in this respect in the same way as do the different parts or samples from *one text.* The transition probabilities of words are, to a great extent, determined by their "valeur" in the language, which, of course, may undergo fluctuations according to subject and style.

The difference in the amount of Q as a measure of the relationship between groups of words according to whether it is calculated under the assumption of a pure random association of words or by taking their transition probabilities into account is quite analogous to the difference between the entropy of the phonemes in a language according to whether it is calculated from their global probabilities or by taking the transition probabilities between them duly into account.

The parameter which, in this domain, corresponds to the repeat rate $\Sigma\, p_i^2$ and to $H = \Sigma\, p_i \log p_i$, is one which is like the repeat rate and H independent of sample size, but is dependent upon the number of parts. This is the alternative probability V of the number of words peculiar to a part and the number of words common to all parts (Sect. 16.2 and *TTM*, Sects. 3.2, 18.4).

If the conclusion reached in this section is correct, we should expect the entropy of the word distribution calculated with due consideration of the facts of vocabulary partitioning to be considerably reduced against that calculated from the global frequency distribution of vocabulary. As will be shown in the next chapter, this is actually the case.

17.3 'NEW STATISTICS' VS. CLASSICAL STATISTICS

The conclusion reached in the previous section receives full support from the structure of the B-E statistics whose difference from classical statistics was explained by the English mathematician, E. Whittaker,[3] as follows:

"Altogether there are three kinds of statistics that are commonly found in as-

---

[3] E. Whittaker, *From Euclid to Eddington* (Cambridge, 1949).

semblages of particles: the *Maxwellian* statistics, the *Fermi-Dirac* statistics, and a third kind called *Bose-Einstein* statistics. The differences between them may be explained roughly in this way. Suppose an empty railway train is standing at a platform and passengers are getting into it. If we make the assumption that every passenger chooses his compartment blindfold, so to speak, without noticing whether other passengers are getting into it or not, then it would be possible to calculate the probability of any particular allocation of the passengers among the compartments. This set of probabilities would constitute a statistics, and we may compare it to the Maxwellian statistics. If, however, we make the assumption that passengers like to have compartments to themselves, or at any rate like to have corner seats, then the probabilities of the different distributions of passengers among compartments would be altered. The probability would be raised for those distributions in which every compartment has at least one occupant and no compartment is crowded. This set of probabilities may be compared to the Fermi statistics. If, lastly, we make the contrary assumption that the passengers are very friendly and gregarious people, who don't like to be alone and who choose by preference compartments into which a lot of other people are going, then the probabilities of the different distributions would again be modified, this time in favour of those distributions in which some compartments are crowded and others quite empty. This set of probabilities may be regarded as analogous to the Bose statistics. The Maxwellian statistics is a kind of limiting case, between the Fermi statistics and the Bose statistics, just as the parabola is the limiting case between the ellipse and the hyperbola. Fermi statistics and Bose statistics deviate from Maxwellian statistics in opposite directions, and tend to Maxwellian statistics in the limit when the temperature increases indefinitely."

Thus, both Bose-Einstein and Fermi-Dirac statistics are based upon the selectivity of passengers as regards compartments and companionship, just as we have explained vocabulary partitioning to come about. That we have only considered B-E statistics in this respect, does not mean that F-D statistics have no place in vocabulary partition.

XVIII

THE ENTROPY ACCORDING TO BOSE-EINSTEIN STATISTICS
AND THE INFORMATION VALUE OF WORDS

Calculation of the entropy per linguistic unit—be they letters, phonemes or morphemes (words)—requires the knowledge of the number of all possible combinations of the units contained in the sample of the units under consideration. This yields what in information theory is called the information per unit, and if logarithms to the base 2 are used, the number of binary units or "bits" of information per linguistic unit.

In information theory, the statistics used for arriving at the entropy are those of Maxwell. In order to develop a corresponding measure of information when using B-E statistics, let us first consider in detail the transition from the global frequencies X_i to the numbers of words in the different classes of combinations of samples or text parts. We shall in the following, speak of the different classes of combinations as *nth*-order classes, n being the number of parts or samples into which the text has been divided. Table 20 (Chpt. XI) shows the contributions of each word group with a given frequency X_i to the different classes of combinations; any such contribution is the product of the global frequency X_i, i.e. that of the total frequency distribution (Table 19) by the probability of a word of that frequency group appearing in a specified 5th-order class (which probability can be read off directly from the numerical table in TTM, pp. 341-412). To check each step of the work the "check total" (Col. 7) was calculated as the sum

(Fig. in col. 2) $+$ 5 (col. 3) $+$ 10 (col. 4) $+$ 10 (col. 5) $+$ 5 (col. 6).

Now note how the contributions to each class are made up. In col. 2, since words with only 1, 2, 3, 4 occurrences obviously cannot occur in all five samples, they contribute nothing to the total. For $X = 5$, the probability of a word appearing in the class $ABCDE$ is only .038400, but as X_5 is large (159), we get the substantial contribution of 6.11. The probability for a word appearing in that class of combination rises rapidly to a value of .522547 at $X = 10$, and to values of .828769 at $X = 11$, .987921 at $X = 27$. The rise in probability is so rapid at first that it more than overtakes the fall in the frequencies, and contributions to $(ABCDE)$ actually increase. As the frequencies continue to fall away, the contributions must finally do so, too— after $X = 10$—, but words occurring 27 times or more must, with random partitioning, practically all fall into $(ABCDE)$.

Column 3 for the class $ABCD\varepsilon$ is quite a contrast. Words occurring only once, twice or three times cannot be found in four samples, and the probability of a word falling in this class starts, therefore, with .038400 at $X = 4$, but reaches a maximum of .095478 at $X = 9$, and then diminishes again.

For the class $ABC\delta\varepsilon$ (col. 4), the initial probability for a word to appear is .048000 at $X = 3$, reaching a maximum of .107520 at $X = 7$, falling rapidly from then on. The bulk of the contributions to this class comes from words occurring 2, 3 and 4 times. For the class $AB\gamma\delta\varepsilon$ the initial probability for a word to appear, which is also the maximum, is .080000 at $X = 2$; from then it falls rapidly, the probability for $X = 3$ being already .0480000, and that at $X = 10$ being .000105.

Finally, for the class $A\beta\gamma\delta\varepsilon$, the probabilities are the rapidly converging series $\frac{1}{5}$, $\frac{1}{25}$, $\frac{1}{125}$ etc., and over 91 % are contributed by the once-words (hapax legomena) alone. Table 16 brings out very clearly how the partition of vocabulary over the five classes of combinations is dependent on the form of the global frequency distribution. The number of words in class $ABCDE$ is high because it includes a considerable proportion of words with even a moderate number of occurrences and nearly all the words with, say, 25 occurrences or more, and these come to a large total in the long tail of the frequency distribution; on the other hand, class $A\beta\gamma\delta$ is high because it is mainly dependent upon the number of once-words, the highest frequency in the whole distribution.

This U-shaped curve—decreasing in steepness with increasing number of segments —of the distribution (Fig. 2, Chpt. 11) is in accordance with the nature of the B-E distribution as explained by Whittaker, and we have already drawn attention to the fact that Whittaker's interpretation of the B-E distribution, as produced by the social tendencies of the units, their "gregariousness", is in complete agreement with our interpretation of the random partitioning function as taking the transition probabilities between words implicitly into account.

18.2   THE DYNAMICS OF VOCABULARY DISTRIBUTION

The probabilities for a word occurring X_i times to appear in one of the 5th-order classes—each such probability multiplied by the number of combinations of the same class—, must, of course, add up to unity. E.g.

$$
\begin{array}{lll}
\text{For } X = 2 & (A\beta\gamma\delta\varepsilon) & = \quad .040000 \times 5 \\
& (AB\gamma\delta\varepsilon) & = \quad .080000 \times 10 \\
\hline
& \text{Sum} & \quad\quad 1.000000
\end{array}
$$

$$
\text{For } X = 5 \qquad
\begin{aligned}
(A\beta\gamma\delta\varepsilon) &= .000320 \times 5 \\
(AB\gamma\delta\varepsilon) &= .009600 \times 10 \\
(ABC\delta\varepsilon) &= .048000 \times 10 \\
(ABCD\varepsilon) &= .076800 \times 5 \\
(ABCDE) &= .038400 \times 1 \\
\hline
\text{Sum} &\qquad 1.000000
\end{aligned}
$$

From this it is evident that although there are different probabilities attached to a word with mean frequency X_i for appearing in the different 5th-order classes, the word has the same probability for appearing in any of the combinations belonging to the same class. There is thus no gainsaying as to where a particular word will appear.

This is, of course, how the statistician would put it having worked out the number of words in different combinations of the parts of a text from the global frequency distribution as the starting point. What the linguist has in mind is the use of words during the composition of the text. But, as observed above, Sect. 17.5, the fact of the random partitioning of vocabulary resulting in, by and large, the same numbers of words in the different classes of combinations as observed empirically, must make us reconsider our pre-conceived views about the deterministic use of words. It justifies, at least, the view of chance as playing a prominent part in the use of vocabulary.

The conception of different probabilities being attached to words of a certain occurrence number X_i, for appearing in the different classes of combinations of parts of a text, and of the *same* probability for appearing in any of the combinations belonging to the *same* class, shows the statistics applied here to be of the B-E type, since it implies both indistinguishability of combinations (at least, those belonging to the same class) and of words, every word belonging to a frequency group X_i having the same probability for appearing in a specified class of combination.

Observe how the usually long series of frequencies X_i—and corresponding probabilities—has been transformed into that of the frequency—probability—of nth-order combinations, and that the probability of a word belonging to one type of combination is the same for all variants of that type. This corresponds exactly to the transformation of the series of probabilities of combinations according to classical statistics into that of B-E statistics (Sect. 17.1). In our example, the number of terms in the series of probabilities of different arrangements of three balls in three cells, which according to classical statistics was 10, is reduced to 3, with equal probability for any of the former arrangements now comprised in any of the new terms.

18.3   THE ENTROPY ACCORDING TO BOSE-EINSTEIN STATISTICS

As a consequence of the indistinguishability of both words and classes of combinations, the number of the possible different arrangements of words over the various classes of combinations is very great, and it is this number, denoted usually in physics by Z or W (for the number of possible arrangements of N units, of which n_1 units belong to class 1, n_2 units to class 2, ... n_r units to class r, the subsidiary condition being $n_1 + n_2 + \ldots + n_r = N$) which is the basis for the calculation of the entropy according to information theory using classical statistics. If we wish to calculate a corresponding parameter for the word distribution, we must first have the equivalent of W for B-E statistics.

The model from which the formula for W according to B-E statistics was derived is as follows:[1] the individual cells on a given level or sheet with index s of a physical system are denoted by z_1, z_2, $z_3 \ldots z_{g_s}$; their number is, by definition, given by the weight factor g_s of the sheet. On the other hand, let there be n_s particles in the sheet, which we denote by a_1, a_2, $a_3 \ldots a_{n_s}$. We have to distribute these particles among the g_s cells of the sheet and determine the number of distinguishable arrangements, when both particles and cells are indistinguishable. To this end we describe a definite arrangement in the following way: we write down purely formally the elements z (cells) and a (particles) in an arbitrary order

$$z_1 a_1 a_2 z_2 a_3 z_3 a_4 a_5 a_6 z_4 z_5 a_7 \ldots$$

with the understanding that the particles standing between two z's are in each case supposed to be in the cell which stands to their left in the sequence. The above sequence means, therefore, that the particles a_1 and a_2 are in the cell z_1; the particle a_3 in the cell z_2; the particles a_4, a_5, a_6 in the cell z_3, no particle in z_4, and so on; that being so, the first letter in the symbolic arrangement must obviously be a z. We then obtain all possible arrangements, by first setting down a z at the head of the sequence —which can be done in g_s different ways—and then writing down the remaining $g_s - 1 + n_s$ letters in arbitrary order one after the other. The total number of these arrangements is therefore

$$g_s (g_s + n_s - 1)!$$

Distributions which can be derived from one another by mere permutation of the cells among themselves or of the particles among themselves do not, however, represent different states, but one and the same state; the number of these permutations is $g_s! \, n_s!$. We thus obtain for the number of distinguishable arrangements in the level, or sheet, which is characterised by the index s, in the case of the B-E statistics

$$\frac{g_s(g_s + n_s - 1)!}{g_s! \, n_s!} = \frac{(g_s + n_s - 1)!}{(g_s - 1)! \, n_s!} = \binom{g_s + n_s - 1}{n_s} \tag{9}$$

Altogether, the number of distinguishable arrangements for the case when there are n_1 particles in the first sheet, n_2 particles in the second and so on, is given by the product of the expressions of the above type for the sheets

[1] M. Born, *Atomic Physics*, 3rd ed. (London-Glasgow, 1944).

$$W = \prod_s \frac{(g_s + ns - 1)!}{(g_s - 1)! \, n_s!} \qquad (10)$$

Taking logarithms, formula (10) becomes

$$\log W = \sum_s \{(g_s + n_s) \log (g_s + n_s) - g_s \log g_s - n_s \log n_s\} \qquad (11)$$

We call W the "probability" of that distribution of the particles among the various sheets which is defined by the numbers $n_1, n_2 \ldots$ It takes the place here of the probability found in the Boltzmann statistics, viz.

$$W = \frac{n!}{n_1! \, n_2! \, \ldots} \, g_1{}^{n_1} \, g_2{}^{n_2} \ldots \qquad (12)$$

Without going into further detail, it shall only be mentioned that what is known as the Fermi-Dirac statistics for the distribution of electrons, neutrons and protons can be derived by a further alteration of the assumptions which have led to the model of the B-E statistics.

Formula (10) was derived with a view to accounting for the distribution of the statistical units (protons and electrons) in three-dimensional systems. For this reason, and also because of the field of investigation being the distribution of photons and electrons, it cannot be expected as it stands to fit the distribution of words, whose arrangement is along the line of discourse, and thus in one dimension only, and whose "appearance" could only by analogy be compared with the physical appearance of electrons. However, if we are right in concluding that both distributions, that of electrons and that of words, obey B-E statistics, there should be a close similarity in form between the formula of W for the number of possible arrangements of electrons, and for that of possible arrangements of words. And this is actually the case.

Formula (11) for the distribution of n particles in g cells, which can be written as

$$\log W = \sum_s (g_s + n_s) \log (g_s + n_s) - \sum g_s \log g_s - \sum n_s \log n_s$$

is in form, if not identical—because of the difference as regards both, type of unit and number of dimensions of the system—, so yet very similar to that for the redundancy in a bi-variate system of linguistic units

$$R = H(x) + H(y) - H(x,y) \qquad (13)$$

or explicitly, since H is the negative average logarithm of the probabilities p_i,

$$R = \Sigma p(x,y) \log p(x,y) - \Sigma p(x) \log p(x) - \Sigma p(y) \log p(y) \qquad (14)$$

for whose derivation the reader is referred to *LCC*, Sect. 11.1, and also to Sect. 13.3 of this book.

In our case, we let x stand for the number of vocabulary items according to occurrence frequency, and y for the number of vocabulary items according to the nth-order classes of combination.

TABLE 42

Table 16, Chpt. 11, transformed into one of relative frequencies through dividing every item by the grand total 3540. At the end of each column, the entropy for the 5th-order class is entered.

X_i	$(ABCDE)$	$(ABCD\varepsilon)$	$(ABC\delta\varepsilon)$	$(AB\gamma\delta\varepsilon)$	$(A\beta\gamma\delta\varepsilon)$	Check Total
1	—	—	—	—	.412	.412
2	—	—	—	.137	0.34	.170
3	—	—	.043	.043	.004	.088
4	—	.011	.035	.013	.001	.060
5	.002	.017	.022	.004		.045
6	.004	.017	.012	.001		.034
7	.005	.013	.006		$H(x,y)=.775$	.024
8	.006	.010	.003			.019
9	.007	.008	.002	$H(x,y)=.711$		.016
10	.007	.005	.001			.013
11	.007	.004				.011
12	.005	.002				.007
13	.006	.002	$H(x,y)=.659$			.008
14	.005	.001				.007
15	.005	.001				.006
16	.005	.001				.005
17	.006	.001				.007
18	.006	.001				.007
19	.003					.003
20	.002					.003
21	.003	$H(x,y)=.631$				.003
22	.003					.003
23	.001					.001
24	.002					.002
25	.001					.001
26	.001					.001
27	.002					.002
28						
	$H(x,y)=1.064$					$H(x,y)=3.220$
459						
Totals	.133	.096	.122	.199	.451	1.001

I need hardly stress that, purely algebraically, there is no transition from formula (11) to formula (14), since the latter has no exact equivalent of the sum $(g_s + n_s)$. Ideologically, however, and substituting for the assumptions needed for deriving (11) other assumptions suitable for the field of language, formula (14) can be obtained.

Failing, so far, however, a strict derivation of (14) from (11), I cannot ask the reader to take this as proved and must, therefore, let the numerical facts speak for themselves. As will be seen, they are in favour of my conclusion.

We have above (Sect. 17.2.4) established that in the vocabulary partitioning function the transition probabilities between words are implicitly taken into account. If now the calculation of the bi-variate entropy for the word distribution according to vocabulary partitioning (Table 42), representing an application of the random partitioning function which we have recognised as being of the nature of B-E statistics, results in a *significantly reduced value of the entropy* compared with what it is when calculated from the global frequencies and those of the nth-order classes independently, *which means that the transition probabilities between words have been taken into account*, then the conclusion is justified that the formula for R is, in the field of language, equivalent to that for W of Quantum statistics.

The sum of the partial entropies for the different 5th-order classes is

$$1.064 + 0.631 + 0.659 + 0.711 + 0.735 = 3.800 \tag{15}$$

and by formula (13) we have for the redundancy

$$R = 3.220 + 2.036 - 3.800 = 1.483. \tag{16}$$

The gain in information—1.483 "bits"—through the use of the random partitioning function represents the difference in "bits" between guessing without taking the connection of frequency and vocabulary partitioning into account ($3.228 + 2.063 = = 5.283$), and when taking it into account (3.800).

This means that if—as it actually happens in the act of composition—the transition probabilities between words are implicitly taken into account through the use of the random partitioning function, the uncertainty per word is reduced by 1.483 "bits". This can also be regarded as the numerical confirmation of our contention, Sect. 17.2.4 that the effect of random partitioning is the same as if transition probabilities had been duly taken into account.

According to how the argument was put above, the substantial reduction of the entropy, implying the due consideration of transition probabilities between words through the use of statistics based upon indistinguishability of words and cells, justifies our conclusion about the *equivalence of formulae (11) and (14)*.

However sceptical the determinist linguist might be about our general contention at the end of Chapter 16, and about the result reached in this section, he cannot deny its purely practical value, viz. that chance as the ever-present alternative has come to our rescue in the seemingly hopeless matter of taking transition probabilities into account when calculating the entropy of words.

18.4   WORD COUNTS IN THEIR RELATION TO VOCABULARY, WORD ASSOCIATION AND GRAMMAR

Quite independent from the Quantum theory of language, Table 42, in conjunction with the basic table 20 in Chpt. 11, can be regarded as a succinct presentation of language statistics in all its aspects.

(1) Column 7 gives the distribution of vocabulary according to relative frequency of occurrence (col. 1). Its appropriate parameter is the Repeat Rate of a vocabulary item, that is the probability that, having picked a word at random, the next occurrence again chosen at random, should be the same vocabulary item; an estimate of the Repeat Rate obtainable from samples of any size is the Characteristic K or v_m, the coefficient of variation of the mean occurrence frequency.

(2) The last row gives the partition of vocabulary due to the different tendencies of words for associating with one another. The parameter epitomising this feature in the whole distribution is the alternative probability for a word to be peculiar to one or common to all samples

$$V = \frac{(A\beta\gamma\delta)}{(A)} + \frac{(ABCDE)}{(A)} \tag{17}$$

It should be noted that this quantity is dependent upon (a) the number of segments in which the text has been divided—decreasing systematically with the increase in segment number—, and (b) the homogeneity of the segments—increasing as the homogeneity decreases. The difficulty is here to define "homogeneity" in this respect. But again, as before, chance comes to our rescue by providing a method for simulating homogeneity—and inhomogeneity—statistically.

Having decided upon the number of segments into which the text is to be divided, the next thing is to decide about the size of sampling increment. In order to avoid "patchiness" of the samples, we may decide to spread each sample over all the pages of the text, taking from every page a certain increment in terms of, say, number of lines and, thus, number of word occurrences. The limiting values of these sampling increments are obviously the single word occurrence or the sampling unit, as the lower limit, and the whole sample or segment, as the upper limit. In the first case, our sample is collected precisely as if by random partitioning, where every counter represents one word occurrence; the more word occurrences are comprised in the sampling increment, the more will the method deviate from the theoretical or random partitioning, and the epitomising parameters calculated from the observed or empirical data will differ—though very slightly at first—from the theoretical values.

When the other extreme is reached, and the sampling increment has become the sample itself, which means that we have just divided the whole into blocks, one for each sample, the difference in content between the blocks will make itself felt, and find its numerical expression in a more appreciable difference between observed and theoretical value of the epitomising parameter. The amount of that difference is, therefore, to be regarded as an *index of inhomogeneity* between the samples. This makes it at once clear that, as regards inhomogeneity, there is no absolute difference, but only one of degree, between samples from one and the same text and samples from different texts, or between vocabulary connectivity in samples from one text and vocabulary connectivity in different texts.

(3) Finally, from the data in the body of Table 42, we get an index of the dynamic

behaviour of words during the composition of the text, in terms of the numerical expression of the transition indeterminacy per word occurrence.

Considering now that what is meant by transition between words is their connection through either grammar words, bound grammar forms or word order as a means of indicating grammatical function, the value of the entropy per word when taking transition probabilities into account reveals itself as a measure of indeterminacy, or hesitation, in establishing the grammatical connection between vocabulary items, since the very idea of vocabulary items combining or joining in form of sentences implies finding the appropriate grammatical unit for their connection. R then appears to be as the reduction in the indeterminacy per word occurrence in a given text when the word is about to enter a sentence with the grammatical structure appropriate to its association with another word.

Considering the different function of the three parameters, the Repeat Rate, the ratio V and R, it may be said that the statistical analysis of word frequency when carried out on the lines indicated in this Part, takes the linguistically relevant features of language: vocabulary, word association and grammar, duly into account.

XIX

THE QUANTUM THEORY OF LANGUAGE

19.1   CHARACTERISTICS OF THE WORD FREQUENCY DISTRIBUTION AND QUANTUM NUMBERS

The introduction of quantum-theoretical concepts into linguistics is not so strange as it may seem at the first glance. We have learnt to live with information-theoretical ideas applied to language, which meant the introduction of statistical physics of the classical type. Having found that the arrangement of the letters of the alphabet, and of the phonemes of a language, when considered in great masses, can be described in terms of classical (Maxwell-Boltzmann) statistics, because the smallest linguistic units behave in some respects like the molecules of physical systems, it stands to reason that the extension of the method so as to comprise the "New Statistics" of quantum theory may prove equally useful. Having found that the word distribution can be satisfactorily described by a method whose characteristic features are those of B-E statistics, we can hardly avoid the conclusion that the units of both these distributions, words and electrons, should have something in common. It is, of course, feasible that one and the same statistical method should apply in fields which have nothing in common except a particular formal structure. But in any such case it is well worth enquiring whether behind the formal similarity in structure there is a deeper meaning.

Let us first consider briefly the properties of the unit of energy, the Quantum. It was experiment which showed that there could be no doubt as to the existence of an elementary quantum of energy. "The negative electric fluid is constructed of grains, just as a beach is composed of grains of sand, or a house built of bricks... The elementary quanta of negative electricity are called *electrons*. Thus every negative electric charge is composed of a multitude of elementary charges represented by electrons. The negative charge can, like mass, vary only discontinuously... Thus, the atomic and electron theories introduce into science discontinuous physical quantities which can vary only by jumps."[1]

"According to quantum theory, three quantum numbers are required for the description of a chemical element. An atom of a chemical element may exist in its

---

[1]   A. Einstein and L. Infeld, *The Evolution of Physics* (Cambridge, 1938).

ground or normal or fundamental state and also in various excited states or levels, and these levels are indicated by numbers. Now, when objects are described by numbers, it sometimes happens that more than one number is used to describe each object: thus a particular telephone may be described as No. 56132, Extension 36; or the home of a friend in an American city might be described as No. 231, 59th Street. The numbers 56132 and 36 in the case of the telephone, or the numbers 231 and 59, in the case of the address, are what in atomic physics would be called quantum numbers. The state or level of an atom at any instant, then, is described by a set of quantum numbers. At first only two numbers were used: for definiteness we can picture the atom as consisting of an electron circulating in an orbit round a nucleus, and we can think of one of the numbers as corresponding to the energy of the system, and the other as corresponding to the angular momentum of the orbital motion.

In 1925 it was discovered that a third quantum number was needed in order to describe a level. It was as if the houses in a street, which had hitherto been supposed to accommodate one family apiece, had been found to be divided into flats, so that in order to have an address precisely, it would be necessary to know not only the number of the street and the number of the house in the street, but also the number of the flat within the house. The question was at once asked, to what physical character in the atom does this new third quantum number correspond? Spectroscopic evidence showed that it must be of the same nature as the second quantum number: and reasons were found for believing that while the second number represented the angular momentum or spin of the orbital motion of the electron, the third number corresponded to the total spin of the whole atom. The further question had then to be settled, what was the character of the additional spin, which when compounded with the orbital spin, yielded the total spin? There were two possibilities: it might be a spin of the nucleus, or it might be a spin of the circulating electron. The former alternative was soon shown to be impossible: and so the final conclusion was that the electron has a spin—that is, an intrinsic mechanical angular momentum.

The amount of the electron-spin is connected with the only physical constant then known which had the dimensions of a spin, namely the "constant of action", which had been introduced by Planck in 1900 in his theory of radiation, and which was later termed "quantum".[2]

The transition now from quantum numbers of physics to certain characteristics of the word frequency distribution is similar to that we had to make in Chpt. 11 when passing from the concept of frequency of vibration, or oscillation, of physical particles to that of frequency of occurrence of words. A word, like an atom, is characterised by three numbers which determine its appearance when "in action". It has a global frequency X_i which will fluctuate in "la parole" around a basic frequency λ_i in "la langue"; the partition of vocabulary provides the other two numbers. In order to see the close similarity between quantum number and word characteristic, we intro-

---

[2] E. Whittaker, *From Euclid to Eddington* (Cambridge, 1949).

duce the following very slight alteration in our model for obtaining the vocabulary partition by experiment. Originally, we assumed that the counters representing word occurrences were dropped on to a *spinning tray*; however, the effect would remain physically and mathematically exactly the same if the tray bearing the compartments or cells remained quiet and we let the *counters representing word occurrences spin* before dropping them.

For example, let us assume a word occurring $X = 5$ times is about to be dropped on to a tray with 5 cells of equal size. Spinning the counters belonging to a vocabulary item before dropping them will attach to each such item a probability of 0.0384 of falling into any of the 5 cells, a probability of 0.0768 of falling into any of 4 cells, a probability of 0.048 of falling into any group of 3 cells, a probability of 0.0096 of falling into any group of 2 cells and a probability of 0.00032 of falling into any one cell only. These probabilities due to the spinning of the counters are comparable to the second quantum number, which describes the spin of the orbital motion of the electron. Corresponding to the angular momentum denoted by the second quantum number, if the spin is such as to distribute the counters over all 5 cells, the angle of distribution is 360°, if over 4 cells 288°, if over 3 cells 216°, if over 2 cells 144°, and if all go in one cell, about 72°.

But the precise place where the counters are to land on the tray has not yet been determined. Apart from the counters for a given vocabulary item falling into all 5 cells, there is a choice of any of the 5th-order combinations of a given type: there are five 4-cell combinations, ten 3-cell, ten 2-cell, and five 1-cell combinations.

Having "decided" about the type of nth-order class to which a word is to belong, or, in other words, the angular momentum of the word being fixed, its probability to fall into one particular class is 1.00 for class $ABCDE$, 0.204 for $ABCD\varepsilon$, 0.10 for $ABC\delta\varepsilon$, 0.10 for $AB\gamma\delta\varepsilon$, 0.20 for $A\beta\gamma\delta\varepsilon$, and these quantities are what corresponds to the electronic spin, or the third quantum number.

19.2 WORD FREQUENCY AND SECOND QUANTUM NUMBER

One of the most interesting consequences of the quantum theoretical conception of the behaviour of words is that it enables us to meet a frequent type of objection against word statistics. The linguist's antipathy against the latter is mostly due to his doubts whether the basic frequency attached to a word has any real meaning. And, in support of this, he will advance the fact that a given word may have very different frequencies according to the content of the text or texts sampled.

It is the relation between the frequency of an atom at what we call "ground state or level" and that at various "excited states or levels" which enables us to clarify that point. The above distinction of states corresponds, according to our theory, to that between the global probability X_i of a word in a sample of "la parole", as an estimate of the basic λ_i in "la langue", and the probability of its appearance in one type of the *n*th-order classes of combination. In other words, *to the distinction between the word before the "spinning" starts, being statistically at rest, and the word "in action".*

According to its "angular momentum", the word will land in a particular type of the *n*th-order classes, its propensity for one or the other type of the *n*th-order classes being determined by the probabilities which for a specified number of segments are attached to a word according to the random partitioning function for appearing in the different types of the *n*th-order classes (see above, Sect. 19.1).

Now these different probabilities are what the linguist has in mind when he objects to the "reality" in the sense of uniqueness, of the relative frequency of a vocabulary item. For us, they are a sort of "relaxation feature" of the global frequency X_i, which enables us to bring the theory into accord with the facts. Let us assume we had combined the words from a number of different texts into one distribution and a particular word with global frequency X_i owed most of it to its prominence in one of the texts, or, if we had combined a number of samples from one text, to its prominence in one of the samples. The relative frequency of that word, i.e. the number of its occurrences in all parts divided by the total length of the text or text samples does, in this case, not give a true picture of the likelihood of its appearance. However, the range of probabilities which, according to the random partitioning function, are attached to words with not too small overall frequencies, which range increases quickly with the number of parts or samples combined, makes it perfectly feasible that a word with a specified overall frequency X_i should be one of those falling into a class of only very few combinations, if not into one particular class only. The definite probability according to the random partitioning function for that event is the answer to the objection raised by the linguist: *the global probability of the word not only cannot, but must not, always be considered as reflecting its relative frequency in particular texts.*

19.3   THE UNITS ('BITS') OF INDETERMINACY PER WORD

The far-reaching conformity in the mass behaviour of electrons and words, or, in other words, the conformity of structure between masses of electrons and masses of words, points to a better interpretation of the bi-variate entropy (Sect. 18.3) per word, and thus also of *R*.

In accordance with information theory, we regarded it as the amount of uncertainty attached to a word in a given sample if the transition probabilities between words are taken into account. This interpretation is still statistical. In the last sections, however, we have come to realise the part played by the linguistic analogue of the atomic and electronic spin in making the word appear in its proper place in the text, and this leads to a dynamic interpretation of the bi-variate entropy. As observed above, the electronic spin is connected with the quantum as the "unit of action". Considering the role which the spin plays in making a word occur in the right place at the right time, and considering that the bi-variate entropy gives the number of units needed for a word to "go into action", we interpret these units in accordance with quantum theory as *units of indeterminacy.*

In order to "go into action" as an instrument for expression, a word must make contact with other words. It must associate with them, and the entropy calculated as from Table 42 indicates the amount of uncertainty or indeterminacy in making such contacts in a given universe of discourse. R is the reduction in indeterminacy per word through taking the transition probabilities between words duly into account.

In the light of this result, and generally in the light of the nature of B-E statistics, let us examine in detail the partial values of H, i.e. those for each 5th-order class as entered in our table. Since H is also dependent upon the number of degrees of freedom (D.F.), that is, in our case, the number of frequency classes X_i which contribute to a class of combinations, the partial values of H must be divided by the appropriate H', i.e. the entropy calculated under the assumption of equi-distribution, $H' = \text{ld } N$, where N is the number of degrees of freedom, in order to make the partial H values comparable. The following table gives in the last column the ratios H/H'.

TABLE 43

Class	H	D.F.	H/H'
ABCDE	1.064	77	.170
ABCDε	.631	19	.149
ABCδε	.659	9	.208
ABγδε	.711	6	.275
Aβγδε	.735	4	.368

The values of the relative entropy increase, on the whole, as we pass from the class of words common to all parts, the words common to fewer parts, and reaches its maximum value for the word particular to a part. This is what we would expect if the bi-variate entropy was, as in our case, a measure of difficulty of making contact with other words, and thus of indeterminacy in the use of words. The words common to all parts which, in our example, are the nouns of most common use, and which in a complete word count would be primarily grammar words, have no difficulty in finding words with which to combine in sentences; the indeterminacy is therefore very slight and its numerical measure in terms of units of indeterminacy very small. As we pass to the less common words, i.e. words of less general use, the hesitation in combining with other words increases, and so does the number of units of indeterminacy which at an average attaches to these words. And this continues until we come to the rare words, occurring in one part only, which are recruited to a very large percentage from the hapax legomena of the text (G. Herdan, 1958); they are the least sociable among the words and consequently find it most difficult to find a suitable partner among the population of words in the universe of discourse, which is epitomised by the number of units of indeterminacy attached to them being a maximum for the series of such values.

In the terms used by Whittaker when describing B-E statistics: for the more gregarious among the words, such as grammar words, the amount of indecision when associating with other words is very slight and the number of units of action needed for finding their place in the universe of discourse is small; also, they show no preference for any of the nth-order classes and appear in all of them. The more selective among the words find it more difficult to choose their partners in the universe, the amount of indecision epitomised by the number of "bits" increasing with the selectivity of words; also, they are no longer entirely indifferent as to the nth-order class in which they appear; they will appear in some, but not in all parts. This continues until we come to the most selective words, the aristocrats, so to speak, in the community which find it most difficult to choose the company of other words; they also show now a distinct preference for one of the parts, and abhorrence for all the other parts, and therefore are peculiar to one part only; the indecision has here reached a relative maximum, epitomised by the greatest number of "bits" in the given series of H.

LANGUAGE IN THE LINE
THE UNIVERSES OF DISCOURSE

PART VI

THE UNIVERSE OF DISCOURSE AS A LINE
LINGUISTIC DUALITY

XX A

DISTRIBUTION IN THE LINGUISTIC SENSE

20.1 THE GENERAL STRUCTURE OF LINGUISTIC DISTRIBUTION

The principal difference between the manifold as given by the senses and experience and its representation in language stems from the fact that the former is a three-dimensional structure, with time as the fourth dimension, whereas the universe of language transmission is a line and, therefore, one-dimensional. Any text, no matter of what length, is fundamentally one line starting with the first letter in the text and ending with the last. Its arrangement in a great number of lines on a great number of pages is merely accidental and conditioned by the desire for transmitting the information in convenient form, but has nothing to do with the essential form of language. For the spoken language, the linear sequence is in time.

However, between the manifold of objects and their one-dimensional presentation in language, there is interposed the world of concepts as the universe of discourse content. Language is conceived to be two-fold: as comprising the "plane of content" and the "plane of expression", each of which has its own structure. In the plane of expression, structure means the hierarchy of relations between linguistic units, and therefore requires the continual comparison of distant parts, points and segments, of the linear sequence of linguistic forms. The frame-work of these relations in the plane of expression of a given language is called the structure of expression, and is not identical with the structure in the plane of content. Considering, however, that what is expressed immediately are not the objects of the three-dimensional manifold but the world of concepts, it is a safe guess that there must exist a close relation and similarity between the two structures. In fact, it is the working hypothesis adopted in Hjelmslev's Glossematics that the relational hierarchies in the two planes are identical as to principles. This is most strikingly confirmed in the mathematics of language structure as developed in this book.

20.2 RELATION BETWEEN THE PLANES OF CONTENT AND EXPRESSION

The close relation and similarity between the planes of content and expression is of great importance for the mathematics of distribution. If the structural principles of

content and expression are the same, then there must be operating in the latter a law
of duality corresponding to Boole's law of duality for concepts, this being declared
by Boole to be the fundamental law of symbolic logic.

G. Boole found that "the laws of the symbols of logic are mathematical in their
form, and that they are actually developed in the essential laws of human language"
(Boole, 1854, pp. 45, 46). As the fundamental law of thought he formulates what
he calls the law of duality

$$x = x^2 \qquad (1)$$

from which we have immediately

$$x(1-x) = 0 \qquad (2)$$

which is the algebraic expression of the logical principle of contradiction. For let us
give the symbol x the particular interpretation "men", and let 0 and 1 stand for
"nothing" and "universe" respectively, then $1-x$ will represent everything in the
universe which is not "men", or the class of "not men". Now the product of the
expression of two classes represents that class of individuals which is common to
both. Hence $x(1-x)$ will represent the class whose members are at once "men"
and "not men", and equation (2) thus expresses the principle that a class whose
members are at the same time "men" and "not men" does not exist. In other words,
it is impossible for the same individual to be at the same time a man and not a man.
Now let the meaning of the symbol x be extended from representing "men" to that
of any class of beings characterised by the possession of any quality whatever; and
equation (2) will then express that it is impossible for a being to possess any quality
and not to possess it at the same time.

Boole then arrives at the conclusion that the laws of logic are identical with those
of algebra, with the single addition that the symbols of logic are further subject to a
special law, $x^2 = x$, to which the symbols of mathematics are not subject. Thus in
common algebra it is not true that every x is equal to its square—it is true only for
$x = 0$ and $x = 1$—, whereas in the Boolean algebra of logic this is true. Boole
believes that if that law of thought had not existed, the whole procedure of the understanding would have been different from what it is.

It is thus a consequence of the fact that the fundamental equation of thought is
one of the second degree that we perform the operation of analysis and classification
into pairs of oppositions or, as it is technically said, by dichotomy.

20.3   THE LAW OF DUALITY AS OPERATING IN BOTH PLANES

The corresponding law of duality in the sphere of expression in its simplest form is
encountered in the gap distribution of linguistic units in a text. Let us suppose we
wanted to study the distribution of gaps between the successive occurrences of a
grammatical form, especially whether it differed from what could be expected on pure

chance. This requires the determination of the frequency of gaps of different length by chance only. We must start with an occurrence of the particular word, that is with a definite point along the line of text. Its "probability", p_0 say, is tantamount to certainty, and thus equal to unity. The probability that the immediate neighbour of that point be the same word, whose probability in the total text is p_1, say, is then

$$p_0\,p_1 = p_1 \tag{3}$$

On the other hand, the joint event of the word occurring in duplo as described is by the law of multiplication of probabilities and without regard to the line of discourse,

$$p_1\,p_1 = p_1{}^2 \tag{4}$$

which means that the same event can be described by both p_1 and $p_1{}^2$ which is the exact counterpart in the plane of expression of Boole's law in the plane of content. The first term of the gap distribution, p_1, is, from the language point of view, not distinguishable from the repeat rate $p_1{}^2$.

In order to generalise the law for all linguistic levels or units, we now ask what it is that makes it possible that Boole's law should have an exact counterpart in the sphere of expression.

The answer is that every distribution pattern must start, as we have done, with a definite point (linguistic unit) along the line of expression. In the simplest form, the point represents the unit in whose repetitions along the line we were interested. Insofar as the distribution pattern is one of linguistic quantities, the statistical parameters are calculated by starting with definite points on the line of discourse, which means that the frequencies of the variable-categories are partly pre-determined. This is characteristic for the consideration of any pattern along the line, and thus for distribution in the linguistic sense.

The relations describing linguistic distribution must always start with a definite point on the line, and are thus in the strict sense of the term point-line relations. Since by a celebrated theorem of projective geometry each such relation has a dual in the corresponding line-point relation, there arises the concept of *Geometrical Duality* as the general law of linguistic distribution. As will be seen, the point-line relations of linguistic distribution take on a different shape according to the language level.

A caveat! Here we are drawing the dividing line between the planes of content and expression so as to have Boole's duality in the former and geometric duality in the latter. But the demarcation line may be drawn differently without this having any influence upon the *relation* between the two laws, and it is only the relation which really matters. Such a possibility is to regard the two laws as belonging to different levels or stages of the plane of expression, but so that the level characterised by Boole's law is much closer to the plane of content than the level characterised by geometric duality.

This innocent looking mathematical formulation of linguistic distribution has important consequences. As will be shown, it reveals the purpose of linguistic duality as a means of communication along the line of discourse, it suggests the general law underlying distribution, it shows distribution as an important factor of linguistic development in time, and it reveals distribution as the general principle of conceptual combination in fields other than language.

20.4   DISTRIBUTION AND LIKELIHOOD

The parameters required in statistical linguistics in general were derived in Part I from the multinomial probabilities in the strict sense of the term, that is as complex probabilities comprising a combinatorial part and the likelihood part; in Part III the entropy as the characteristic parameter of information theory was shown to be the combinatorial part only of the multinomial probability; now we shall use the likelihood part of these probabilities in an analogous way and derive from it the characteristics of distribution in the linguistic sense.

Likelihood, in the sense in which the term is used in mathematical statistics is, however, a quantitative concept. In order to understand the relation between likelihood and linguistic distribution, we must emphasize that the mathematical presentation of language structure is a small-scale "map" describing language structure as a whole. Although a particular phonological opposition is a qualitative feature, the summation of oppositions of the same type gives a quantitative characteristic of the language. The probability patterns arrived at by contrasting the share which different types of phonological oppositions have in the phonemic system of a language are the likelihood patterns underlying the frequency distributions of phonemes.

We may, with Trubetzkoy, take it for granted that the phonemic system of a language consists of a vast network of phonological oppositions. If a phoneme count of dictionary material has been made, the resulting distribution (in the statistical sense) represents the accumulation of phoneme occurrence in phonologically relevant positions in the language (distribution in the linguistic sense), assuming, of course, that the dictionary is representative of the language. Thus, the statistical distribution of phonemes as parts of words in the dictionary is the result of the accumulated patterns of linguistic distribution in the language.

Insofar as we are here dealing with an accumulation or sum of phonological oppositions, we have before us again a numerical quantity built up from the probabilities of such phoneme types as we have taken into consideration.

These basic probability patterns we call the likelihood. Since it is derived from the network of phonological oppositions in the language (dictionary), it must be clearly distinguished from the phoneme distribution in running texts, which can be regarded as random samples of the dictionary count as the population.

In order to make the relation between the qualitative phonological opposition and the quantitative concept of statistical likelihood clearer, I recall a passage from the report by R. S. Wells in the Proceedings of the Eighth International Congress of Linguists, Oslo, 1958.

"Sapir, we are told, used to compare the description of a language with a map, and pointed out that a map may be on a larger or smaller scale. Any map purports to depict a certain terrain *as a whole*, but the smaller its scale the less it purports to depict *the whole* of the terrain. So far as the map is accurate, the abstractions it has carried out must be legitimate. Now in general the smaller the scale of a map the easier it will have been to make it; so likewise of language descriptions. The practice of giving small scale yet comprehensive descriptions of entire languages should be revived. If such a description is to be structuralistic, it is not enough merely to say something about each topic—phonology, morphology, syntax, lexicon, etc.—, it must show how the facts belonging to one topic relate to facts belonging to others; it must show, and not merely assert, that the language with which it deals is 'un système où tout se tient'."

20.5 DISTRIBUTION[1] VS. CLASSICAL PHONOLOGY

The relation between the two concepts in the headline of this Section is quite analogous to that between small sample theory and the classical large sample theory of statistics.

Probability theory, and with it statistics, is a method of drawing conclusions from incomplete evidence. It is just because we cannot follow the movement of *each* molecule in a gas that we need statistics, if we want to understand thermodynamics in terms of the movement of molecules. But even so, the information, although incomplete, must be sufficient, and this is guaranteed by the Law of Great Numbers (L.G.N.) if our sample is very large.

However, the greater extension of the application of statistics in the last 50 years or so, and the desire to get information quicker, or with less labour, that is from smaller samples, gave rise to small sample theory. The argument in favour of it is somewhat like this: since all statistics implies drawing conclusions from incomplete evidence, it should be possible by suitable modification of the basic formulae to apply it also to small samples.

Although it is true that the statistical argument is, by and large, the same whether applied to large or small samples, the results in the latter case may be afflicted by errors of such magnitude as to make them practically useless. Also, it is an open question whether statistics, which is based upon the L.G.N., really makes sense if applied to very small numbers. A mathematician of the rank of R. von Mises has expressed his doubts on this and his dislike of small sample theory in its application to experimental results.

Now in linguistics, the classical view of language study and description of living

---

[1] In this Section, the term is used in the sense in which some American linguists, known as Distributionalists, apply it.

languages was that only somebody with many years of experience among the natives speaking that language should undertake such a work. He was, moreover, supposed to collect, during the time needed for his acquisition of the language, all the relevant material needed for a thorough description. This applies to the phonetic aspect, the grammar and the vocabulary, and is truly comparable to the view that statistical results must be based upon large samples, giving full scope to the action of the L.G.N. This implies that there are no special precautions needed against bias either on the part of the investigator, or against misinformation on the part of one or the other informer, because the investigator is supposed to spend as long a time among the native speakers as to really get into the spirit of the new language, and to appreciate all the aspects in which it is different from his own, and because he has so many informants—everybody with whom he has come into contact during that time, apart from his teachers—, that the possible mistakes due to one or the other of them are levelled out by the correct information from the others.

All this is different when an investigator sets out to describe a language which he does not know, in the minimum of time. In this case, having only one, or a very small number of informants at his disposal which, moreover, must be solicited by him for information, all kinds of precautions have to be taken against mistakes and misinformation. The language has now to be acquired on the basis of a small sample, instead of under the working of the L.G.N., and the classical methods must be modified accordingly.

This is responsible, on the phonemic level, for the suppression of meaning—now the orthodox procedure—in the determination of phonemes. If the investigator has only a faint knowledge of the language, and if the informant cannot be relied on to give unbiased and exact information on the point of meaning (truly a case of "lucus a non lucendo"), and since it is not certain how well the investigator understands the informant, it becomes advisable to work only with purely formal—and fully patent— distinctions of word structure about which there could be no doubt or mistake.

Just as in the case of the small sample theory of statistics, the exclusion of possible bias on the part of the investigator and his informant have to be guarded against as far as possible. The methods which were developed with this end in view in linguistics during the last 30 years or so are characterised by the same detective-story type of feature as are the methods of small sample theory work in statistics. And here as there, it is the method as such requiring greater and greater attention, because of increasing difficulty, which has become the centre of interest, instead of the language to be described. In statistics this led to an avalanche of methods of increasing mathematical complexity, which tendency one of the foremost English statisticians, M. G. Kendall, has criticised as follows:

"We have reached a critical phase in the development of statistical methods, when pure mathematicians looking for something to research on are throwing up such a dust that the practical nature of the subject is being obscured and theoretical statistics is in danger of being discredited in the eyes of the medical man." ("The Statistical Approach". Inaugural Lecture given at the London School of Economics, January 17th, 1950).

Similarly in linguistics where the role of the pure mathematician throwing up much irrelevant dust is mostly taken by the mathematical logician.

The conclusion we must draw from this is that the elimination of meaning for linguistic procedures, with all the compensatory features of "distribution" this entails, is not to be regarded as an achievement in itself, but only as a faut de mieux, as something promoted by the lack of knowledge, by the lack of sufficient information, about the language one wishes to codify. No matter what the ingenuity of these formal procedures, our knowledge about the essential features of language structure benefits from them as little as does our knowledge of the external world profit by the procedures of small sample statistics.

XX B

THE UNIVERSE OF DISCOURSE AS A LINE

"Our inner consciousness, that is, our knowledge of the events in our mind, has as
its form not Space, but only Time; that is why the process of thought proceeds not,
as our experience of the outer world, in three dimensions, but only in one, and thus
in a line. This is the main source of the essential shortcomings of our intellect. We
are only able to perceive everything in succession, and to be aware of only one thing
at a time, nay, even this only under the condition that we forget everything else at
the same time. In this respect we can compare our intellect to a telescope with a
very narrow field of vision. The Intellect apprehends only successively and must,
for the sake of apprehending one thing, let everything else escape, retaining of it
nothing but traces which, by and by, also disappear. Incidentally, it is this short-
coming of the intellect which is responsible for the rhapsodical and often fragmentary
nature of our thoughts, from which arises the unavoidable dispersion in our thinking"
(after Schopenhauer, Die Welt als Wille und Vorstellung, II).

The conception of the universe of discourse as a linear universe has important
consequences.

20.6 A ONE-DIMENSIONAL UNIVERSE

Let us imagine a one-dimensional creature and its outlook on "life". He is confined
in motion and eyesight to that straight line which is his world. All vision is limited
to a point, and all movements to a straight line.

Each individual occupies the whole of the narrow path, so to speak, which constitutes the universe, and no one can move to the right or left to make way for passers-
by, from which it follows that no line-lander could ever pass another, or get bodily in
touch with another not immediately before or after him. Once neighbours, always
neighbours.

Only by sound could distant parts of the line be compared. The faculty of sound
and the sense of hearing makes literal proximity unnecessary for the "union" of
line-landers. Assuming the different individuals to be characterised by different sound,
or sound combinations, the repetition of sound in certain intervals makes the individual realise the existence of similar individuals along the line. If for "sameness"
of sound we substitute "harmony" between different sounds, then the occurrence of

such sounds in stated intervals would correspond here to what we call "the meeting of kindred souls".

It will not have escaped the attention of the observant reader that the above given conception of communication within the line universe introduces a new element. In fact, it is tantamount to trespassing the line limits. The comparison of distant points and segments of a line cannot be done within a line, but requires their arrangement in, at least, two dimensions, that is, in a plane. We have, in fact, made the step from the universe of language transmission to that of discourse, which is thus characterised by communication "within" in addition to that "between" the source and the target of the transmission, such "within" communication taking place by comparing distant parts, points and segments, of the line.

This, at once, reveals as the basic law of language that of geometrical duality. Since the comparison of distant points and segments of the line of communication must take place, at least, in a plane, it follows that the law of geometrical duality as the most general relation between points and lines in a plane must also govern the relations between what corresponds in the universe of language to the geometrical concepts, namely Type and Token. This is how we arrive at what I have called the Type-Token duality as the general law governing the relations between linguistic units. Thus, the conception of the plane or field of discourse paves the way for the Type-Token duality as a mathematical necessity (*TTM*, Chapter 17).

The *Statistical Universe* is the actual, or hypothetical, assemblage of items, also called the statistical population, and comprises the categories of a variable plus the probabilities attached to these categories or classes. In contradistinction to it, there are the samples from it, consisting of actual observations.

The statistical universe is not the sum of the random samples withdrawn from it without replacement, because these must largely overlap.

The *universe of discourse*, on the other hand, comprises the different texts dealing with the same subject, or the parts of one text, or samples from one text, or from different texts. It thus represents the sum of its parts, whatever they are. On the plane of content, the universe of discourse is the conceptual counterpart of the linguistic forms in the plane of expression.

20.7 DUALITY AS THE PRINCIPLE OF GRAMMAR

From what has been said in the previous Section it will have become apparent that the term "plane of expression" is more than a mere metaphor. The universe of discourse is a line whose points and segments are the Types and Tokens of language. The comparison, necessary for understanding, of the points (Type) and segments (Token) of the line of discourse requires their deployment in, at least, two dimensions, i.e. in a plane. This at once paves the way for introducing the law of geometrical duality as the basic law of the universe of discourse. That law, as the most general relation between points and lines in a plane, must govern the relation between the points and segments of the line of discourse when deployed in a plane, and if we let Type stand for point and Token for line it should also apply to the relation between Type and Token. In fact, this is what has emerged from the study of language: it was found to satisfy the law of geometrical duality (*TTM*, Chapter 17).

The great importance of that relation for the understanding of language structure lies in its being the basic principle of grammar. It was de Saussure's aim to conceive of language as a branch of semiology. But the peculiarity of the linguistic code as a code with an internal structure requires that, in addition, it should also be conceived as a branch of science using projective geometry.

The first, and perhaps the most complete grammar for any language was Panini's (4th. century B.C.) grammar of Sanscrit, which went far beyond the timid attempts of Attic Greece in this direction. Panini, and presumably his forerunners, were the first to take words to pieces in a systematic way, and to distinguish roots from affixes. In full agreement with this analytic procedure, the name of grammar in Sanscrit is *Vayakarani*, that is "*separation*", "analysis".

His work is characteristically mathematical. It consists of some 4,000 rules of the greatest brevity. This brevity is achieved by the use of an algebraical system of notation. But—and this is most important for our argument—the sequence, and distribution, of these rules is not organic in the sense of paradigmation, according to which method of arrangement the different forms of the same word are put together, but they are grouped according to either sameness of sound or function. It is very much the system advocated by Jespersen (1924) as that of *grammatical homophones*, which makes us proceed from the form to the meaning, and of *grammatical synonyms*, which makes us proceed from the meaning or function to the form.

In speaking of "grammar", it is the making of a grammar which I have here in mind, not the application of an already existing one, and this is why I use Panini's work as an illustration. What he—and his forerunners—had before them was just points and segments of the line of discourse, the segments being of rather different length. In order to get the 4,000 or so rules of grammar, they had to analyse, "separate", the parts of the segments into their significant elements, significant, that is, of their grammatical function or meaning. This lead to establishing both grammatical synonyms, i.e. different forms for the same grammatical function or meaning, and grammatical homonyms, i.e. different meanings or functions having the same form.

The separation of the segment into its significant parts has as its concomitant—I use this term to indicate that there is no temporal or causal relation between them—the *separation of the word from the underlying concept*, or of expression from content.

Now, such separation of words and concepts is the very essence of the geometrical principle of duality. As will be remembered, this principle is to the effect that any of the properties of plane geometry remains valid if we replace in it the points by straight lines, and the straight lines by points. As a consequence of the principle of duality, for each theorem that is proved, another theorem is obtained, and the latter is true, and does not require a new, direct proof. The number of theorems is thus automatically doubled. The importance of this principle for geometry is quite obvious. But its philosophical by-product is even more far-reaching. We have a theorem dealing with certain entities—points and lines. If this statement remains valid when these entities are replaced by lines and points respectively, then our original theorem is not specifically a statement about points and lines. This led to the more fundamental question of what we are talking about when we make statements in geometry.

The consequences which this had for the philosophy of mathematics do not concern us here. What does concern us is that a basic relation, like that between points and lines, remains unaltered if the entities between which the relation exists, are interchanged. This implies *the most complete separation of word and relation*, and may be regarded as the prototype of the separation needed for establishing rules of grammar. Be it observed that the separation between relation (concept) and word in projective geometry is ultimately based upon observation, as all geometry is to some extent, and that it is, therefore, a principle of empirical observation which is applied in grammatical separation.

As corroborating this conclusion, and as a piece of empirical evidence that grammar and separation are of the nature of geometrical duality, the following is an apt instance.

The simplest geometrical illustration of the principle of duality is this

(1) Two distinct points are   (2) Two distinct lines are
    on one, and only one, line   on one, and only one, point.

showing that two points are on a line, and two lines on a point. Now in his *Loom of Language* (1943), Bodmer stresses the surprising fact that so many of the syntactical rules of Chinese agree with rules of Western languages, i.e. English, and illustrates this by

I do not fear him.   WO PU P'A T'A.

 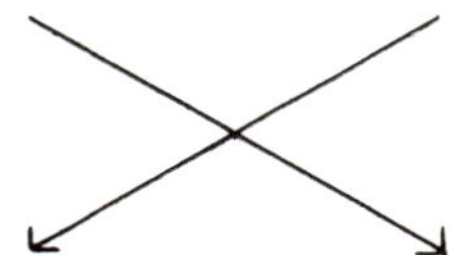

He does not fear me.   T'A PU P'A WO.

The change in word order from active to passive,—what was the subject in the active sentence and placed first became the object in the passive sentence and placed last, and vice versa—is identically the same for English and Chinese. In this illustration the verb relation represents the line with the nouns as its end points.

In our terms, the relation "do not fear" remains the same although the words for subject and object are interchanged. This is the essence of duality as grammatical separation. If we imagine either sequence of words as an undifferentiated whole, then only grammatical separation and separation of the relation from its 'end'-points, so to speak, enables us to express the relation in its opposite form, i.e. passive instead of active, or active instead of passive.

This little example also shows the value of describing grammatical separation in terms of duality. If duality is the prototype of *all* grammar, then it should be possible to trace it in such widely different languages as Chinese and English. The recognition of the mathematical concept underlying grammatical separation provides the explanation of grammatical isomorphy between genetically unrelated languages.

Moreover, it is the great benefit of establishing the essentially mathematical nature of separation as used in grammar, that it will enable us to trace the working of the same principle in phonology and in the structure of literary products, such as fiction, and thus lead to a unified idea of structure on different levels of language.

Another most important unification resulting from the conception of separation as the essence of the principle of geometrical duality, is that of the two "laws of duality": Boole's and Poncelet's (of geometrical duality). Boole's law which is the mathematical basis of symbolic logic is expressed as

$$x(1-x) = 0$$
$$\therefore x^2 = x \tag{1}$$

and formulates the logical Principle of Contradiction that it is impossible for any being to possess a quality and at the same time not to possess it, and which Aristotle has described as the fundamental axiom of all philosophy. It introduces into our empirical picture of the manifold the separation between a concept symbolised by x, and the rest of the universe symbolised by $1-x$.

This separation as such is not any more inherent in the manifold of objects than is the separation of expression (words) from content (relations, concepts) which is the essence of the geometrical law of duality. This explains the hitherto problematic parallelism between structure in the plane of content and in the plane of expression, or, in other words, it shows *the law of geometrical duality as the prototype of grammar, to be the correlate in the plane of expression of Boole's law of duality in the plane of content.*

XXI

DUALITY AND SEPARATION

21.1   PHONOLOGICAL OPPOSITION AS SEPARATION

The fundamental principles of linguistics stand in paradoxical contrast to the phonetic approach to language. Though language consists of sounds, what really matters is their distribution, in the linguistic sense. The locations and surroundings of distinct sounds are more important than the sounds themselves. This had led to the conclusion that the fundamental units of a language are not sounds, but categories or classes, namely the phonemes. A machine analysing minutely any utterance could give precise figures for the description of the sounds contained in it, just as it could for sounds from a tuning fork, a piano, their frequency, intensity and duration, but no machine yet devised can provide an analysis of language distribution, any more than a machine can analyse meaningfully a musical composition (W. P. Lehmann 1959).

Language is constructed around contrasting units, not physical sounds, and this may lead to interpreting different sounds as similar units, and also similar sounds as different units—phonemes—, or of different sounds as variants of *one* phoneme, and similar sounds as representing *different* phonemes. As a consequence, wherever a particular language, say English, is spoken, though the sounds themselves may differ and though the same sound may have different values, the contrasts are approximately the same and this is what matters for communication purposes. Since the speakers of English understand each other by noting the contrasting units—phonemes—, linguists must analyse English in terms of these units, and not in terms of the' sounds or letters. They do so, and the result is the phonemic system of the language.

What we are doing when ascertaining the phonemic quality of a sound, in contradistinction to its being only a phonetic variant, is to take the sound—a point on the line of discourse—as the starting point and put it into relation with segments of the line which comprise that sound but in either the same or different surroundings. This is the essence of the rules for determining the phonemes in a language as given by Trubetzkoy (1935). We have thus here again the basic principle of distribution in the linguistic sense. Accordingly, it can be shown that the principle of phonology is the precise equivalent in the expression plane of Boole's law of concepts in the content plane. The realisation of a phoneme may be, and mostly is, by different sounds. The repetition of a phoneme, say /a/, which according to Boole's algebra we would write as $/a/^2$, is not different from the phoneme itself, and therefore

$$/a/^2 = /a/. \tag{5}$$

It should be understood that in this equation a is not the *concept* of the sound comprising all individual occurrences of it, since (5) would then only be again Boole's law for content. $/a/$ is the phoneme whose manifestations are the different variants of the sound. To put this in different words: a concept is *secondary* to the individual events which are subsumed under it, whereas a phoneme is conceived to be *primary* to the different variants in which it manifests itself.

It is truly remarkable that this important similarity between Boole's law and Trubetzkoy's principle of phonology should have escaped notice. Most likely, this is due to narrowness in outlook as a consequence of specialisation. But it may be that no other method had the power to reveal this than the mathematical and, more precisely, the combination of both the mathematics of statistical and of linguistic distribution. This shows how fundamentally wrong Y. Bar-Hillel is when (Oslo, 1957) he recommended to keep the different types of mathematics relating to language in watertight compartments, and how little he understood the use of certain branches of mathematics, such as the mathematics of measurement and that of order and position, in linguistics.

21.2   GRAMMAR AS SEPARATION

Jespersen's proposal for a new grammar, i.e. one not based on paradigmatic arrangement, was based upon the idea of separation as the essential grammatical operation, which has the principle of duality as its mathematical prototype. In the paradigmatic arrangement all the forms of a particular word are placed together; there is thus no attempt to bring together the occurrences of the same ending if it is found in different paradigms. A consistent system of grammar must be permeated with the principle of separation. Starting from "without" (O →I), we take a form as given and then enquire into its meaning or function, listing all the different meanings or functions which may be conveyed by that form; starting from "within" (I →O), we take the meaning or function as given and enquire about its expression in form, listing all the different forms which may serve that particular purpose.

"We must never lose sight of the fact that one form may have two or more significations, or no signification at all, and that one and the same signification or function may be denoted now by this and now by that formal means, and sometimes by no form at all. In both parts of the system, therefore, we are obliged to class together things which are really different, and to separate things which would seem to belong naturally to the same class. But it must be our endeavour to frame our divisions and subdivisions in the most natural manner possible and to avoid unnecessary repetitions by means of cross-references... In speaking of the ending -s, for instance, with its three phonetically distinct forms (s, z, iz), we mention first its function as a sign of the plural in substantives, then as a genitive sign, then as a mark of the third person singular in the present tense of verbs, then in the non-adjunct form of possessive pronouns, e.g. in *ours*. The ending -n (-en) in a similar way serves to form a plural in *oxen*, a non-adjunct possessive in *mine*, a participle in *beaten*, a derivative adjective in *silken*, a derived verb in *weaken*, etc....

It will probably be objected that by this arrangement we mix together things from the two distinct provinces of accidence and word formation... The arrangement here advocated has the advantage that it brings together what to the naive speech instinct is identical or similar, and that it opens the eyes of the grammarian to things which he would otherwise probably have overlooked...

The arrangement here advocated is purely grammatical, treating together in its first part what may be called grammatical homophones (homomorphs), and in its second part grammatical synonyms. It will be remembered that we had the corresponding two classes in the two divisions of the dictionary". (O. Jespersen, The Philosophy of Grammar, 1924).

The following is an illustration of this principle in diagrammatic form:

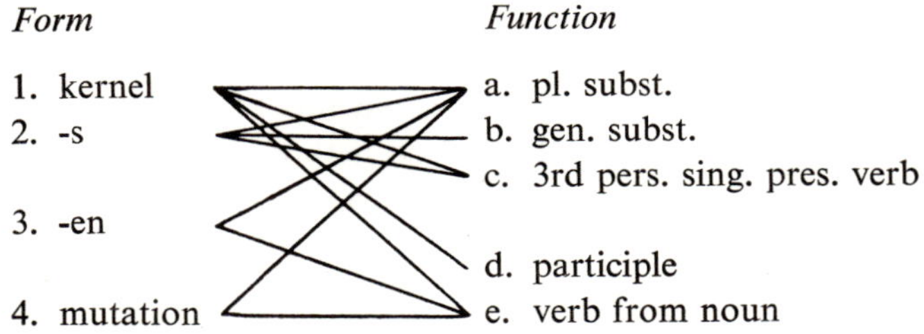

Examples:

1a... sheep;	1c... can;	1d... put;	1e... hand;
2a... cats;	2b... John's;	2c... eats;	
3a... oxen;	3e... frighten;		
4a... feet;	4e... feed.		

As another illustration of the principle of grammatical separation in preference to paradigmatic arrangement, we give below the distribution of forms (endings of nouns) according to case, singular and plural, masculine and feminine, and stems in Russian.

Denoting by

S ... Singular
P ... Plural
M... Male Gender
F ... Female Gender
N ... Nominative
A ... Accusative
G ... Genitive

D ... Dative
L ... Locative
I .... Instrumental,

the multiple function of three selected endings ь, и, e are shown in the following diagram.

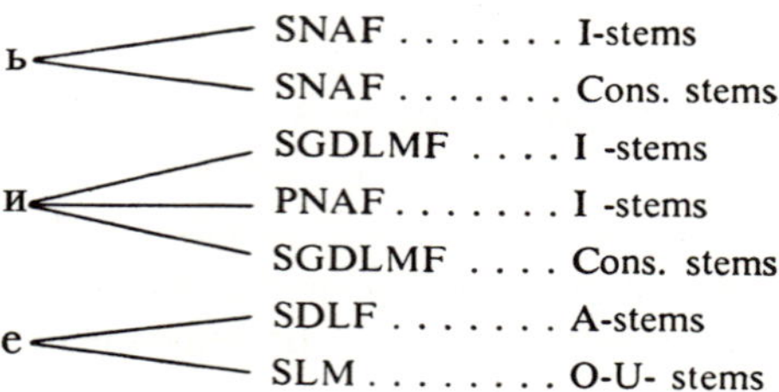

Observe the "democratic" structure of the pattern. In general, a given form has different functions, and a given function different forms. The illustration from Russian is such as to bring out the first aspect. The democratic structure is not brought out to such perfection as it applies to the points and lines of Desargue's theorem (a basic theorem of duality), nor could this be expected considering that point and line are idealisations not met with in nature. But even so, the reciprocity between form and function is of the same type as that between point and line. The linguistic reason or the cause of such reciprocity is, of course, the property of the linguistic code, according to which there must be grammatical homonyms and synonyms if the number of linguistic forms is not to be inordinately swelled. The conformity of the form-function pattern of grammar with Desargue's theorem has, therefore, its roots in the economy of linguistic coding.

In languages, like Chinese, which have no bound grammar forms, and where function is expressed by the order in which the ideograms follow one another, we should expect to find *sentence structure* in the sense of word order, to be patterned according to some law of duality. This is actually the case. Separation of grammar-category from grammar-function as noun, verb, etc. is typically Chinese.[1]

21.3   THE RESTLESS UNIVERSE OF LANGUAGE

It needs no emphasizing that concepts are not identical with words. But in spite of this, there is a close connection between concept and word. This, and with it the connection between expression and content, rests upon the following. Our whole consciousness with its inner and outer experience, has time as its form. Concepts, on the other hand, having originated through abstraction as completely general

[1]   This will be shown in a forthcoming publication.

entities different from individual objects, have a sort of objective existence which, however, is not part of the temporal sequence of events. Therefore, if they are to enter into the presence of an individual consciousness, and thus enter a temporal sequence, they must be "degraded", so to speak, to the nature of individual things, they must be individualised and connected with physical objects in order to enter our sensual experience. These physical objects are the words of language. They are, therefore, the physical signs of the concepts and, as such, necessary means for fixing the latter (Schopenhauer, *W.a.W.u.V.*, vol. II).

This is quite analogous to how we locate a physical event in space. In general terms, we specify the point of a physical co-ordinate system (Bezugskörper) with which that event coincides. This is true in scientific description as well as in everyday life. Analysing the topographical location (the "address") of an event as "in London at Trafalgar Square" we find that the earth is the co-ordinate system and "Trafalgar Square in London" is the specified point with which the event coincides. The term "coincidence" could be replaced by simply stating the distance between the event and the point.

Using these terms, we now see, and define, the connection between word and concept and between expression and content as fixing the event of thought (content) to the point (word) in a co-ordinate system (plane of expression) with which the word coincides, i.e. which it denotes. This at once makes us realise that the "fixing" implied is not such as to be once and for all, since there is no such thing as a unique point to which in a given body of reference the event may be referred to, nor is there such a thing as a unique body of reference to which an event may be referred. Since, therefore, what we mean by a thought finding expression is its being "fixed" by reference to specified words, it follows that this is not a matter to endure but one which is subject to change. Though word and language are absolutely necessary to clear thinking, yet like any other physical means, they also hamper thought by forcing it—for the time being, at least—into a definite mould through referring it to a particular point, or points, of a particular body of reference, i.e. certain words in a given language. This is partly remedied by acquiring more than one language (*LCC*, Sect. 14.2.1). But even in the same language, our thoughts do not remain fixed once they have been formulated. The conception of a physical world as a "restless universe" (Born, 1944) has its exact parallel in the restless universe of language. There is not only, on the part of our thoughts, a quest for expression, but an equally lively quest for change of expression, partly because of new aspects of the thought in question, partly because of inadequacy of the former "fixation".

Language consists in connecting word and concept. But having done so, we are, sooner or later, compelled to separate them again by changing the points or body of reference for the idea we wish to express. The most perfect separation takes place if the relation is reversed which, in our terms, means that the bodies of reference are moving against each other.

21.4   THE IMPORTANCE OF PATTERN IN GOETHE'S 'WAHLVERWANDTSCHAFTEN'

Goethe's "Wahlverwandtschaften" starts with the married life of Eduard (E) and Charlotte (C) as an ideal of this type of human relationship. However, soon we learn that each had been married before, and thus been a partner in conjugal life with another companion. Marriage as such is the relation between themselves, and also between each of them with another person.

A more fateful and complete separation of the marital relation from the two individuals, E and C, takes place, or rather is initiated when the "Hauptmann" (H) and Ottilie (O) enter the houshold. E's infatuation with O and C's with H lead to the "marriage through elective affinity" between E and O, on the one hand, and between C and H, on the other, with the child conceived by C from E as the incarnation of each parents infatuation with another partner. In appearance, it is the son of O and H. This means the complete duality separation of the original union between E and C: the parents by elective affinity, H and O, have been substituted for the legitimate parents, E and C, without alteration of the essential relation of marriage. Moreover, to make the inverse characteristic of duality complete, the elective father's, H's, contribution comes through C, and the elective mother's, O's, through E, as the parties in the act of conception. (Never mind about what the scientific geneticist with his x and y chromosomes would say to this).

The ever active and rightly so-called Mittler may be regarded as the symbol of the conventional view, incapable of separating word and concept.

The crucial event, the child's drowning, has also its duality precursor. This "casting their shadows in advance" by the important happenings is characteristic of the patterning device used by Goethe. It occurs not long after H and O have joined the household. At the festivities to celebrate the completion of a new building in the park, a boy falls into the lake, but is rescued by H. This happens on Ottilie's birthday. By contrast, her rupture with life originates in the event of the child, E's and C's son, falling into the same lake. This time, H is not present, and the child is drowned. Another instance of how Goethe lets the events "cast their shadow before": on Ottilie's birthday the house near the lake is completed, where the child is to drown; on Eduard's birthday the chapel is completed where Ottilie, and Eduard—the spiritual mother and the physical father of the child—are to be buried (Chpts. 15, pt. I, and 3, pt. II).

The idea of the human relation as a pattern which remains in spite of substitution of other words denoting the subjects of the relation, penetrates the whole novel. Goethe has expressed this himself in these words:

> "Was einem jeden Menschen gewöhnlich begegnet, wiederholt sich mehr als man glaubt, weil seine Natur hiezu die nächtste Bestimmung giebt. ... Und so finden wir die Menschen über deren Veränderlichkeit so viele Klage geführt wird, nach vielen Jahren zu unserem Erstaunen unverändert und nach äussern und innern unendlichen Anregungen unveränderlich." (Chpt. 17).

Another instance (the novel abounds with them), Ottilie remarks to Charlotte:

> "Zum zweitenmal ... widerfährt mir dasselbe. Du sagtest mir einst: es begegne den Menschen im Leben oft Aehnliches und auf ähnliche Weise, und immer in bedeutenden Augenblicken. Ich finde nun die Bemerkung wahr ..." (Chpt. 14).

Kneeling in front of Charlotte with her head in Charlotte's lap, she remembers having been in the same position before: *then* she had lost her mother, *now* Charlotte has lost her son.

Of the architect we hear:

> "Schon einmal hatte er so vor Belisar gestanden..." (Chpt. 18).

Another element of pattern is that three of the main characters have virtually the same Christian name: Ottilie, the Hauptmann and Eduard whose second Christian name is Otto; and Charlotte has, at least, the first syllable of Otto in her name.

In the pattern that constitutes the craft of fiction, the similarity of situation is used like, or is comparable to, the rhyme in poetry.

21.5 DUALITY AND POETICS

In *TTM*, Sect. 19.1, the attraction, if not the magic, of the rhyme in poetry was explained by according to it the power to create the impression that the ideas as expressed by the poet were already pre-formed in the language, and thus appear attested by language itself.

Since classical poetry does not use the rhyme, its appeal must rest upon other properties of the verse. As is well known, the classical form had a great fascination for Goethe who, for years, worked hard to realise his dream, namely to make it fit German. But in vain! In spite of producing such great poems as the Römische Elegien, Reineke Fuchs, and other works, he was not satisfied that his pet idea of a union between antique form and German content could ever be more than a brave attempt. We can infer this from a little poem of his:

> Ein ewiges Kochen statt fröhlichem Schmaus!
> Was soll all das Zählen, das Wägen, das Grollen?
> Bei alledem kommt nichts heraus,
> Als dass wir keine Hexameter machen sollen
> Und sollen uns patriotisch fügen,
> An Knittelversen uns begnügen.

To make us understand this failure, is one of the great achievements of analytical linguistics.

In the Latin, and indeed in the classical hexameter in general, the grammatically correct word order has to give way to the rhythm, and the word accent to the ictus, all in order to preserve the quantitative structure of the hexameter, that is, in order that the distribution of long and short syllables should be such as to fully satisfy the metric form, e.g.

Quis scit an adiciant hodiernae crastina summae Tempora di superi?

(Horace, Carm. IV 7, 17)

Infernis neque enim tenebris Diana pudicum Liberat Hippolytum, . . .

(Horace, Carm. IV 7, 20)

The crucial question for the understanding of the classical hexameter seems to be this: how could the Latin mind, being used to a logical word order, violation of which was felt to be something ungrammatical, not only submit to a change in the word order and in the word accent, but even glory in it, and regard the result as a great achievement of poetry?

This can only be if the transformation of the prose sentence into poetic form has something to compensate for the apparent violation of word pronunciation and word order. This "something" I maintain is the detachment of the thought from the words expressing it, or the separation of content and expression, which is necessary for making the thought or idea really the property of the mind.

Reading Latin verse, or still better, repeating it by heart, we realise the extent to which the order of concepts in the thought, and the word order in the verse, deviate from one another, and how very necessary it is to get the thought independent from the word order in the verse line. The aim of achieving such independence without making it too difficult to understand the verse, must have acted as a check on the divergence from the grammatical rules of word order.

But the detachment of thought and word we have found (Sect. 20.2) to be the very essence of geometrical, and, indeed, of linguistic duality. Strictly following the words in a Latin verse in their linear order would never enable us to understand the verse. The pre-requisite to its understanding is the deployment of points and segments of the line, the Type and Token, so as to bring out the grammatical connection. This means the application of the principle of duality. As a result, the thought becomes detached from its expression, which is required for its becoming part of our intellectual equipment.[2]

We can now attempt to answer the question put above: why does the classical verse form not fit a modern language like German?

A glance at Goethe's hexameters,—and they are the most natural ones that were

---

[2]   By the way, here we have the reason, revealed by the analytical method, why mechanical translation of languages has, so far, made so little progress beyond mere word-for-word translation. Translation requires the detachment of thought from word (*LCC*, 14.2.1), and this can only be achieved by using the method of duality. To instruct the machine to ape effectively the eminently human tactics of linguistic duality, even in its most primitive stages, has, so far, not been possible.

written in German—shows the reason. The German hexameter shows very little change in word order, and none in accent, from prose; such complete transformation of the prose sentence as in the classical verse we hardly find anywhere. Here are some examples of Goethe's verse, and they are quite typical in this respect:

> O wie fühl ich in Rom mich so froh, gedenk ich der Zeiten,
> Da mich ein graulicher Tag hinten im Norden umfing,
> Trübe der Himmel und schwer auf meine Scheitel sich senkte,
> Farb- und gestaltlos die Welt um den Ermatteten lag.
> . . . .
> Sternhell glänzet die Nacht, sie klingt von weichen Gesängen,
> Und mir leuchtet der Mond heller als nordischer Tag.
>
> (Goethe, *Römische Elegien*, 1788/93)

With very little change, or no change at all, these hexameters can be read as prose. Indeed, they are rhythmical prose. It follows that they have not the effect of the detachment of thought and word, which accounts for much of the fascination of the Latin verse. They read very nicely, and more than nicely, but they are not productive of thought as different from expression, in the way in which the Latin hexameters are. And with it, their main attraction has gone. The poetics of our modern languages seem to appreciate less such detachment, and more the anchoring of thought in the language, as I have shown in the passage quoted above from *TTM*. This is in very good agreement with the distinction which Goethe makes between the classical and the modern idea of tragedy, when he says: "Ovid blieb klassisch auch im Exil; er suchte sein Unglück nicht in sich, sondern in seiner Entfernung von der Hauptstadt der Welt." Analogously, the classical poet achieves his effect by making us proceed from language to thought, or from expression to content as something outside language, whereas the German poet, or the poet in any other modern language, achieves his effect by making us turn towards language itself, that is, by "bending back" to language as expression.

XXII

THE CALCULUS IN RETROSPECT—A SUMMARY

The reader might welcome a concise presentation of the Calculus of linguistic observations. Being a sort of gathering up of loose strands, it is not surprising that the exposition given in this chapter should start at "the other end", which explains the chapter heading. It brings out as a valuable property of the calculus that it provides a new criterion for the classification of, or discrimination between, languages, namely, the distance of the "plane of expression" from the "plane of content".

22.1 GEOMETRISATION IN THE PLANE OF EXPRESSION

1. According to de Saussure, language, being necessarily a discontinuous sequence of linguistic units, superimposes segmentation upon the continuum of the manifold of experience. Although this is not to be taken too strictly, as E. Haugen rightly observes (*Language*, 37, 1961), since the segments of language in terms of vocabulary items coincide, to a large extent, with empirically observed parts of the manifold, yet the dichotomy as such is justified and important. De Saussure puts language in opposition to the world continuum, thus leaving out the system of concepts which is interposed between the two ends of the opposition. However, since what the symbols of the language code stand immediately for are not the material objects, but the concepts as part of our inner experience, it is more correct to speak of the opposition between concepts and language symbols, which coincides, by and large, with that between "content" and "expression" in modern linguistic terminology.

Let us determine what it is exactly that constitutes the two members of the opposition. Since by "content" we understand what remains of language after we have abstracted from it everything that belongs to "expression", it is obvious that what we call "logic" will afford the purest possible view of "content", and we shall, therefore, for the purpose of our argument, use Boole's "Symbolic Logic" as a representative form of "content". By this we do not mean to identify symbolic logic with "content". As a sort of expression—not in words, though, but in mathematical symbols— symbolic logic already partakes to that extent of "expression". This is why I described it as affording only the purest possible view of content. This at once reveals Boole's Law of Duality as a fundamental law of expression:

$$x\,(1-x) = 0 \tag{1}$$

which is the Principle of Contradiction in algebraic form. Why do we regard (1) as a law of expression, and not of content? Because the form given to the Principle of Contradiction presupposes already the arrangement of the symbols in a line, and thus in a geometrical dimension which, as such, is alien to content:

The allocation of Boole's law of duality to the plane of expression is at the first glance in contradiction to its allocation to the plane of content in Sect. 20.2. However, we must not forget that the two planes are theoretical constructs, auxiliary structures (what in German is called Hilfskonstruktionen), and the difference between the two views may not mean so much. It all depends where the dividing line between the planes is drawn. What matters is the close relation between Boole's law and the other forms of the principle of duality, which is not affected by the difference in allocation.

2. This gives already an indication where to look for aspects of language belonging to expression: they are all of a geometrical nature. Expression by language requires arrangement of linguistic forms, standing for concepts, in linear sequences which we denote as the Line of Discourse.

The direction in which the symbols are to be read is, in general, immaterial and differs from language family to language family: in the Indo-European languages the linear arrangement is along the horizontal line and reads from left to right; in the Semitic languages it is also horizontal, but reads from right to left; in the Sino-Japanese languages it is in vertical columns and reads from top downwards, and the columns from right to left.

Boole's symbolic logic is built up in such a way that it considers only agreement and difference between concepts, without distinguishing whether the symbols stand for either nouns, verbs, adjectives etc. This is quite in accordance with logic as dealing with content only, not with expression. It is left to the mathematical symbolism to unravel the relations between the concepts, without any help from grammar. Accordingly, a concept is accorded in symbolic logic only two possible values, 1 for existence and 0 for non-existence. In this way all the possible relations between concepts are derived.

Considering now that, as remarked above, the symbolism of symbolic logic is already a form of expression, the characteristics of symbolic logic afford a criterion for the discrimination between languages with regard to their deviation from mere conceptual thought. If we understand by "structure of meaning" the system of hierarchy of conceptual categories, and by the structure proper of the linguistic code, its whole apparatus of linguistic oppositions on all its levels, then a language may be more or less conspicuous in either of these aspects. Languages may differ as to the extent of their having moved away from the plane of content through developing the symbolism of expression and obeying the laws of that symbolism in addition to the laws of logic.

3. Having established Boole's law of duality as the primary law of expression in language, we now enquire about other laws of expression.

I shall use what is known as the *Chinese Language Game*. Its essence may be expressed like this: starting from an original poem, the order of the sentences, and that of the words within a sentence, are systematically altered, i.e. reversed, so as to give a new poem. It should be clearly understood that what I call the "original poem" is not just any given poem, but must have already been composed with the subsequent operations in view. Since both the displacement of the original sentences (the columns of the poem in Chinese script) and the reversal of the characters within a column are mathematical operations, we may say that this shows a mathematical device as operative in transforming an original poem into its dual. For this is the desired result: the situation described in the original is, in the transformation, seen from another angle, the two poems being dual to one another, in content. The Game as such clearly has nothing to do with the conceptual basis, namely, the relations between the concepts denoted by the Chinese ideograms. The manipulations according to the Game are made possible by the linear sequence of the characters as language symbols. They consist in altering the order of the sentences represented by the columns of the original poem, and in the reversal of the ideograms within a column. As I have shown, the manipulations are those of the theory of groups, which thus appears to be applicable to Chinese expression.[1]

We have, thus, arrived at another law of linguistic symbolism, namely that linear sequences of symbols may, for some languages, be capable of being manipulated according to the theory of groups. This will, in general, be the case for languages with a minimum of distinct grammar forms, the grammatical function being indicated by word order.

Another variety of the "game" is most important for establishing the dichotomy between content and expression as being essentially one between language in the brain and language manifesting itself in the physical world as the spoken or written word. Four poems are obtained by first reading the ideograms of a 7×8 matrix of Chinese characters in an anti-clockwise direction, and then reading them in the opposite direction, each process yielding two poems consisting each of 28 ideograms of the matrix not occurring in the other, and all four poems standing to one another in the relation of group-theoretical transformations.

From the 7×8 matrix as the reservoir for the four meaningful arrangements of words there is no great jump to the general reservoir of word engrams in the brain. The fact of the matrix being already an artificial arrangement—true though this undoubtedly is—does not invalidate the comparison, because we cannot assume the word engrams in the brain to be a random assemblage, i.e. one without some order. Only, that order is not geometrical, but a hierarchy of conceptual categories.

---

[1]   The Chinese material referred to in this Chapter will be published as a separate booklet.

Be this as it may, we shall regard the matrix of Chinese ideograms as the nearest possible approach to, or at least simulation of, what we call "language in the brain" and the derivation of the four poems as the result of the concepts finding expression through their symbols being arranged according to a certain kind of geometry. By this we mean here a type of arrangement which by convention has become customary among the members of the speech community.

The manipulation previous to the group-theoretical transformations between the four poems consisted in a movement along and between the columns, which we recognised to be of the nature of movement on one-sided surfaces. Since it precedes the formation of the text in form of the four poems, it must be regarded as being fundamental for "translating" language in the brain into language in the plane of expression. The operations of uncoiling and winding up the ideograms in the matrix, which we described in terms of topology as movement upon a one-sided surface must be regarded as a simulation, at least, of the process in the brain when concepts are made available for expression in sentences.

4. Let us now look at a representative member of the family of Indo-European languages. As the mere word-order as a means for indicating grammatical function is abandoned in favour of definite grammar words and bound grammar forms, the linear sequence as such does not afford the possibility of comparison which is essential for that type of grammar, because we cannot move backwards, but only in one direction. The way out of the difficulty is the deployment of the line segments in two dimensions, at least. The relations between type and token become now those between point and line in a plane, and, herewith, subject to the basic law governing the relations between points and lines: the Law of Duality of projective geometry. The invention of the alphabet is a direct consequence of the analysis of morphemes as distant segments of the line of discourse, into the smallest units, the letters, through the operation of a law of duality. On the phonemic level the law of duality is known and appreciated as "linguistic duality". Both establishing and recognition of phonemes requires a pattern of opposition whose reciprocity nature marks it clearly as another instance of geometrical duality (Sect. 21.1) (see footnote on p. 242).

The peculiarity of Chinese sentence structure, especially the fact that a word belonging to a given grammatical category could be used, in general, in any grammatical function, is responsible for the fact that Chinese sentences can be fitted satisfactorily by certain theorems of geometrical duality, which makes projective geometry appear as the appropriate geometry also on that level (see footnote on p. 242).

The law of duality of projective geometry must be regarded as another form of the basic duality relation which is essential for any form of language expression, whatever the symbolism—or the language. Rightly understood, it originates, as observed above, in the very act of linear arrangement of the symbols, and is thus operating whenever conceptual relations are expressed in language. But its form changes according to the geometry of linguistic expression, and when it is a matter of comparing distant parts of the linear sequence, which requires deployment in two dimensions, at least, it naturally takes on the form of the law governing the relations of the basic geometrical elements, points and lines, and thus becomes the law of projective geometry.

The law operates not only in the comparison of distant segments of the line of discourse for a language whose grammar has been established, but, as explained, and stressed, in Section 20.6, in the very act of analysing the parts of the line of discourse with a view to establishing the grammar of a language. This was adduced as a reason why Panini chose the term *Vayakarani* meaning "separation" for grammar, separation of the line into segments being necessary for their comparison as a prerequisite for discovering the indicators of grammatical function. It should be noted that this segmentation with a view to describing grammar categories and function is different from that according to vocabulary items, or, broadly speaking, according to concepts, which is the very first form of segmentation. Now the segmentation cuts across the units of conceptual segmentation, and it may well be that this was particularly why Panini called it "separation".

It needs no emphasising that the differences between languages as regards both phonemic and morphemic (tagmemic) patterning are considerable. What may be the maximum required of either in some language may be quite insufficient in another.

5. Up to now there was no place in the linguistic geometries considered for anything like probabilities. The concepts from the plane of content found their appropriate expression on a one-to-one basis in the symbols of language. The geometries were those of arrangements of a finite number of elements in a line, subject to group-theoretical operations and certain topological laws, and when these elements were deployed in more than one dimension, they became subject to the law of geometrical duality.

As the knowledge of the manifold of experience increases, which means an increase, not so much in the number of concepts, and of vocabulary items, but in the number and complexity of the relations between them, and thus in the number of occasions for the use of words, the need for language statistics in the plane of expression arises, and this is responsible for a further increase in its distance from the plane of content. In fact, it is the discrepancy between the number of concepts and the frequency of occurrence of the symbols denoting them, which provides the occasion for the use of statistical methods. In other words, the comparison of a finite number—and a very small one, at that—of words can be effected without statistics; when considering great word masses, however, we must use statistical methods, and the geometry becomes that of the "sampling space" of the statistical universe, and, by and by, one of probabilities. This applies in a still higher degree to the smallest units of language, the letters and phonemes, into which the words have been broken up.

With the advent of statistics in the plane of expression, geometrical duality takes on a new, statistical aspect as connecting two frequency distributions, e.g. that of occurrence frequency of words according to the individual vocabulary items, and that of vocabulary items with regard to frequency of occurrence. (*LCC*, Sect. 12.9.1).

At the other end of the range of the languages considered, there are the Western languages, such as English. Here problems of telecommunication, e.g. telegraphy, of language teaching, of style in works of literature, and of information theory made it necessary to use statistical methods. Abstracting from any particular problem, and speaking in all generality, the use of statistics consists in this that we start with facts, be they qualitative or quantitative, facts or figures, and finish up with a table of probabilities for the occurrence of the facts. Let us consider the problem of style in the light of stylostatistics. We start with observations on the use of certain words or phrases by a given author, and—if we are successful—finish up by describing his style in terms of, say, the Characteristic K as an estimate of the Repeat Rate of the words constituting his vocabulary, i.e. the probability of two word occurrences withdrawn at random from the mass of words used being the same vocabulary item. To give another illustration, this time from statistical linguistics. In order to obtain information in the sense of information theory about the use of phonemes in the language, we start with the frequency distribution of phonemes. Their frequencies constitute our facts. From them the Entropy is calculated as the probable number of guesses needed for restoring a missing phoneme in the sequence of phonemes forming a message.

So far, it was only ill-defined concepts such as "style" or "information", something that depended upon the solidarity among the units in a great mass of linguistic forms, which statistical methods were successful in interpreting as the summary effect of a great number of unit events. The deeper, however, we penetrate into the structure and the use of language, the more do we find ourselves compelled to abandon the cause-and-effect idea for the use of words, and the doctrine of determinism has to give way in linguistics, as it has done in physics, and in science of today in general, to one of Indeterminacy. During the composition of a message of appreciable length, say a literary text, a particular word has different probabilities attached to it for occurring at certain points of the text. The appropriate geometry of linguistic symbols at this stage of estrangement of the plane of expression from that of content is that of the random partitioning distribution over the different segments of the message or text.

Thus, the at first rather modest degree of mobility which the geometry of linguistic symbolism superadds to language in the brain or to the concept in the plane of content, in the form of group-theoretical operations and certain topological movements of a finite number of symbols, and as the law of duality, has now become the decisive factor in the use of individual words by making them spin like snowflakes according to laws of probability before descending in the right place of a text according to their associations with the other words in the universe of discourse. The geometry is now that of Quantum theory.

22.2 THE 'DISTANCE' BETWEEN THE PLANES OF CONTENT AND EXPRESSION
AS A CRITERION FOR THE CLASSIFICATION OF LANGUAGES

This exposition of the calculus of linguistic observations has brought to light as a new criterion for the classification of languages, which might be of interest to both the historical and the anthropological linguist, the distance between the planes of content and expression.

That distance can be estimated by the type of geometry in the plane of expression. Its minimum is that inherent in Boole's symbolic logic of language expression. The group-theoretical operations of language, as possible in Chinese, denote a greater distance. Projective geometry epitomised by geometrical duality which we found to suit Chinese sentence structure, and grammatical structure in our Western languages, marks another increase in the distance. A very great increase in the discrepancy between the two planes is due to the need for statistical methods in the plane of expression (Eigenstatistics), which as the Quantum theory of language ultimately leads to the greatest estrangement, or distance, of expression from content.

Distance between the planes of content and expression as a criterion for the classification or discrimination of languages must not be confused with "development" as opposed to "primitiveness." Each of the geometries in the plane of expression is capable of development without going over into the next higher stage of geometrisation, that is, without a substantial increase in distance between the two planes. There appears to exist a significant correlation between language type and language geometry, which accounts for the persistence of particular language structures through the ages.

PART VII

LANGUAGE AND MATHEMATICS

XXIII

ON THE RELATION BETWEEN LANGUAGE AND MATHEMATICS

23.1   THE EIGENSTATISTICS OF LANGUAGE

In Chapter 22, *TTM*, the conception of "Eigenstatistics" was introduced as being needed for characterising the position of statistics in the field of language. The essence of what is meant by the term Eigenstatistics can be given in one sentence: *it is not only the study of language which requires statistics, but the very use of it.*

One might conceivably object that the relation between mathematics and linguistic observations was not different from that between mathematics and observations in any other field. In every case of application of mathematics to empirical data, it is implied that the events follow the mathematical law which seems to fit the data. Why then speak of "Eigenstatistics" as if it were something different from the normal procedure of fitting observations by mathematical formulae? The answer is briefly that in using language we already *apply*, not only *obey*, statistical laws.

We have a precedent for this in Boole's contention that "the laws of thought... in all those operations of which language is the ... instrument, are of the same kind as are the laws of the acknowledged processes of Mathematics. It is not contended that it is necessary for us to acquaint ourselves with those laws in order to think coherently... *Men draw inferences without any consciousness of those elements upon which the entire procedure depends.*" Boole means that the laws of thought are not just fitted by mathematical formulae, but that in thinking we already *apply*, not only *obey*, mathematical laws.

Analogously, we say that the laws of language are statistical in nature, and are of the same kind as the laws of the acknowledged processes of statistics. Since we cannot assume just accidental duplication of the laws in the two spheres of language and mathematics, one of them must have provided the pattern for the other. Which of them is to be regarded as prior to the other, this is the problem that will occupy us in this and the following sections.

If one were to criticise succinctly the philosophy of Kant and Schopenhauer—and indeed all philosophy leading up to that of Kant and Schopenhauer as the peak of European philosophy—one could say that it was deficient in the concept of evolution or development. For this it cannot be blamed, since it was six years after Schopenhauer's death that Darwin's "Origin of Species" appeared, which blazed a new trail for the exploration of the world and man's position in it.

It is this deficiency which is at the bottom of the contradictions in Schopenhauer's philosophy. The most glaring one is the conception of the "eternal" ideas in which the "Will" reveals itself to the "pure" subject of knowledge (Reines Subjekt des Erkennens), that is, to the intellect when temporarily freed from the task of its servitude to the Will of Life in its everyday contingencies. According to Schopenhauer, the intellect is a brain function, and thus, a temporary tool of the Will and, therefore, cannot very well be regarded, even in its "pure", i.e. detached action as a correlate of "eternal" entities. This contradiction is resolved by realising that the "ideas" are as little "eternal" as the apprehending intellect is "pure", i.e. toto genere different from the tool required by the will to cater for its everyday requirements.

Among the "ideas" are, for instance, the plant and animal species which, as we know since Darwin, are not eternal at all, but products of evolution. That entities which are subject to development in time should be the object of perception by the intellect in its more emancipated form, is then no longer a contradiction. Moreover, the intellect is itself, as an organ of the will, subject to development, and the stage of its development in the human species is a precise correlate to the development from the mere perception and use of the plants and animals by humans for their daily requirements to their becoming objects of scientific observation, and artistic contemplation and reproduction in works of art.

It is now for our subject most important to understand how Kant and Schopenhauer, having most ingeniously separated the contribution to our experience by the mind as time, space and causality from that by the senses, vitiated their great discovery by their being so hide-bound in their evolutionless view of the world as to transfer the idea of the "absolute" immediately to mathematics itself as embodying time and space.

Schopenhauer fully subscribed to this part of Kant's theory of knowledge, though he discarded Kant's "Kategorienlehre" and left only one category, that of causality, to join space and time as subjective contributions to experience. He regarded all conceptual knowledge as derived by abstraction from the "Anschauung" that is from experience, except the mathematical concepts or relations which he regarded as subjective. In this way he separated "Anschauung", "Begriff" (concept) and mathematical concepts. The salient point is that although he admitted that concepts were derived by abstraction from the objects of the manifold of experience, he did not contemplate even the possibility of mathematical concepts also being a product of development in time. This was, of course, quite in accordance with the epistemological principle (Kant) of mathematics being independent of experience. That the concepts of mathematics, and the relations between them which we call laws of mathematics, could be the product of a slow, and very slow, step-by-step evolution from the world of concepts—F. Klein's "Idealisierung"—did not even enter his mind. This is how the famous mathematician, F. Klein, puts it: "Die Raumanschauung ist zunächst etwas Ungenaues, welches wir zum Zwecke der mathematischen Behandlung in den sogenannten Axiomen *idealisieren*", and in his famous paper concerning the third volume of Lie's "Theorie der Transformationsgruppen" he says: "Die Ergebnisse irgend welcher Beobachtungen gelten immer nur innerhalb bestimmter Genauigkeitsgrenzen und unter partikularen Bedingungen; indem wir die Axiome aufstellen, setzen wir an Stelle dieser Ergebnisse Aussagen von absoluter Präzision und Allgemeinheit. In dieser *Idealisierung* der empirischen Daten liegt meines Erachtens das eigeliche Wesen der Axiome." (Quoted from L. Nelson, *Beiträge zur Philosophie der Logik und Mathematik*, 1960.)

In the light of this it is quite evident, though paradoxical, that Kant, the "Alleszermalmer", the virtual destroyer of Theism, had the "Absolute" so firmly in his mind that, having abolished an absolute God, could not but substitute for it an absolute mathematics as the eternal forms of our mind in which the ever-changing sensations of our senses appear. And in this Schopenhauer, though no admirer of mathematics, followed suit, but complicated the matter by vindicating eternity also for the ideas in which the Will as the 'Thing-in-itself' revealed itself to the 'Pure Subject of Knowledge' (Das Reine Subjekt des Erkennens). Schopenhauer himself was aware of the contradiction in his conception of mathematics as something toto genere different from experience, when he expressed astonishment that mathematics as a completely objective science should rest upon the subjective forms of the intellect (*Welt als Wille und Vorstellung*, ed. by P. Deussen, vol. 2, Munich, 1911, p. 98).

23.2 APRIORITY OF LANGUAGE

Our contention is that just as between the species of the organic world, the intermediate evolutionary stages between the world of language concepts and mathematics have disappeared, and the extremes of the evolution of symbolic thought, language and mathematics, are still to us what the organic species were to Schopenhauer: separate and immutable entities.

But can we blame Kant and Schopenhauer, the pre-Darwinian philosophers if today, a century later, we still find among philosophers and mathematicians the conception of mathematics as something toto genere different from all other activities of the mind firmly established, and the apriority of mathematics, its independence from anything connected with experience (Erfahrung) proclaimed as the very latest discovery? This has not a little contributed to the stagnation of philosophy in our time.

The interpretation of the concepts and relations of mathematics as being products of evolution from the manifold of concepts and the linguistic expression whose "idealisation" they are, could provide the stepping-stone to an amended Kant-Schopenhauer philosophy.

It makes no difference to the understanding of this work whether my theory of evolution of the system of mathematics from that of conceptual thought and its expression in language, is taken only provisionally and as an heuristic device, or whether it is regarded as a contribution to the solution of the age-long problem of philosophy about the apriority of mathematics or otherwise. Notwithstanding, it would be wrong not to point out from time to time the reasons for seriously considering the latter alternative. Pure mathematicians who adhere to the view of mathematics being altogether independent of experience, and of its structure being the necessary result of a few basic concepts and the axioms defining the relations between these concepts, all of which are regarded as free and, by and large, arbitrary creations of the mind only, ought to be reminded of the repudiation by the theologists of the pre-Darwinian era of the explanations of human moral behaviour by reference to the motives animating the creatures of the animal world, as an analogous case. Not only was man conceived to have a very special relation to God, who was supposed to keep full record of man's deeds, good and bad, but man's nature was believed to be so much akin to that of God himself that one man, Christ, was regarded as having directly descended from God, and others, the Saints, as more or less near relations.

To put it briefly: man's moral or ethical behaviour was considered to be the manifestation of his God-like nature. All these dreams suffered a profound shock when Darwin established the essentially animal nature of man. From that time on it is regarded as an anachronism to harp on man's God-like nature and to forget or discredit the springs and motives of all animals in their battle for life, when explaining man's ethical behaviour.

Similarly, mathematical logicians will be profoundly shocked at the suggestion of the concepts and their expression in language as being primary to mathematics—not in the bulk though, but so that each branch of mathematics is derived from some particular aspect of language.

If one only succeeded in exhibiting in one or the other instance the intermediate stages between language structure and mathematics, the connection would become as obvious, and even commonplace, as that between the primates and homo sapiens is today.

23.3   THE LINEAR ORDER OF LINGUISTIC FORMS AS THE PROTOTYPE OF THE LOGARITHM

1. In Chpt. 4 and also in *TTM* Chpts. 2, 9 attention was drawn to the prominence of skew distributions of statistical linguistics which could be transformed into lognormal ones. Apart from the frequent emergence of the lognormal distribution, there was the rectilinear relation between vocabulary and text length, between vocabulary ratios and text length (*TTM*, Sect. 1.4), between the frequency of species according to the number of individuals per species (log series) and between the frequency of genera according to the number of species per genus.

There is also the remarkable fact—though it did not seem to bother unduly the communication engineer or the statistician—that it is not only for the linguistic variable that we find the logarithmic transformation appropriate, but also for the probabilities themselves of the linguistic events. In fact, this is the essence of the formula for the information value of linguistic events which is defined as the negative logarithm of the probability of the event in question. As observed in Part IV, this implies that in information theory we work with the logarithmic distribution of the probabilities.   The reason becomes apparent when we remember that the most important variable quantity of the universes of statistical linguistics is frequency of occurrence. Other variables, such as length of linguistic form in terms of phoneme-, letter-, syllable- or word-number, or gap length between occurrences of the same form, are essentially of the same nature. Considering now that what we here call "the variable" is either identically or asymptotically the same as relative frequency or probability of occurrence, it is at once clear that a transformation which, like the logarithmic one, is appropriate for the variable—which, as shown above, is true in the field of linguistics—should also be appropriate for the manipulation of the probability in that field.

An explanation put forward by some writers, Brown and Aitchison (1957), is that linguistic events as phenomena of the mind could be supposed to obey the same law as the events of experimental psychology, and that the relation between object and symbol was analogous to that between stimulus and sensation, which, as is well known, is governed by the Weber-Fechner law and, by and large, conforms with lognormal requirements. This explanation is, however, little more than a guess. For one thing, the relation between "signifié" and "signifiant" is different from that between stimulus and sensation. A close examination shows that the relation between intensity of stimulus and sensation has no analogue in the language field. We must look for an immanent explanation, i.e. one truly appropriate to the field of language. Such an explanation is suggested by the nature of the universe of discourse.

As will be seen, the conception of the universe of discourse as one-dimensional has a most important consequence: the juxtaposition of linguistic forms which, like that of the segments of a line, is conceived as *addition* of information, denotes *multiplication* in the manifold, which corresponds to the relation between logarithm and numerus.

2. Boole remarks that the mathematical symbols of logic such as x, y for things as subjects of our conception, and $+$, $-$, $\times$ as signs of operation of the mind by which the concepts of things are combined, are in this sense subject to definite laws, *partly agreeing with, and partly differing from,* the laws of the corresponding symbols of algebra. He then sets up the various laws of symbolic logic, *l.c.*, pp. 29 ff.

A class of individuals to which a particular name or description is applicable is represented by a single letter, say x. If the name is "men", for instance, let x represent "all men" or the class "men". By a class is meant a collection of individuals to each of which a particular name or description may be applied.

Again, if an adjective such as "good" is employed as a term of description, let us represent it by a letter, say y. Boole now goes on "let it further be agreed that by the combination xy shall be represented that class of things to which the names or descriptions represented by x and y are simultaneously applicable. Thus, if x alone stands for "white" and y for "sheep", let xy stand for "white sheep", and in the like manner if z stands for "horned" and x and y retain the previous interpretations, let xyz represent "horned white sheep". If the symbols x, y are used in the above sense, they are subject to certain laws:

$$xy = yx$$
$$x^2 = x$$
$$z(x+y) = zx + zy$$
$$\text{if} \quad x = y, \quad \text{then} \quad zx = zy.$$

However, here the analogy of the present system with that of algebra, as commonly stated, stops (*l.c.*, p. 36). The rules of multiplication and division cannot be applied en bloc to the symbols if they stand for linguistic forms. This is a most important restriction in the use of the symbols, apart from the restriction that if they stand for language forms the variable is capable of taking on only the two values 0 and 1.

It is now of the utmost importance to realise the difference between the relation, when expressed in symbols, and both its algebraic meaning and its structure in the manifold. In language the mere sequence of symbols like xy means the simultaneous presence of two (or more) qualities, say "white", "sheep", and thus *addition*, whereas the algebraic meaning of the sign xy is multiplication, and as such reflects also the meaning of the combination in nature. When we say "white sheep", we mean all individuals comprised under the concept "sheep" provided they are also white. This is virtually a qualitative multiplication of "sheep" by "white". When we say 500, we mean every unit in 100 to be multiplied by 5. *The multiplicative procedure in nature, or in the manifold, is reproduced in language by a symbolic addition of qualities.* But this is the prototype of the logarithm or, as we might say, the idea of the logarithm which, however, must be quantified when applied to quantities.

This should make us realise the tremendous advantage of the linear arrangement of language symbols where the mere addition of symbols is used to describe complex multiplicative processes in the manifold.

Moreover, it accounts for the fact that whenever numerical features (or mass) of language forms are to be considered, their logarithmic transformation is indicated. It is the intrinsic linguistic nature of the logarithmic transformation which makes it so eminently suitable in language statistics.

23.4   EIGENSTATISTICS AS THE ERROR-REDUCING DEVICE OF LANGUAGE

Communication by language, as communication by any other means, is subject to error. The minimization of the error element in language through the adoption of error-reducing devices designed so as to render language a more and more efficient instrument of communication, this is what we call the development of language.

The calculus of linguistic observation exhibits clearly the means by which the reduction of error in language communication is achieved. This is perhaps one of its most valuable properties.

We have seen that the error-reducing devices of language have a far-reaching formal similarity with those used in statistical significance testing and in the modern statistical design of experiments, which was one of the reasons for speaking of the Eigenstatistics of language (*TTM*, Chpt. XXI). The purpose of these designs can be said to be the reduction of the experimental error to its minimal size by judicious interference with pure randomness. Neglect of reduction of the error element makes it more difficult to arrive at a decision as to significant differences between results.

23.4.1 *Transition probabilities between letters and phonemes*

What corresponds to this in language on the phonemic level is the reduction of the entropy per phoneme through taking the arrangement of phonemes in words, and thus their transition probabilities, duly into account. The entropy calculated from the global phoneme frequencies implies a purely random arrangement of phonemes. The actual uncertainty, however, in hearing the sounds of a language is less, because anybody who knows the language will automatically take the transition probabilities between the phonemes into account. It follows that to give the use of transition probabilities between phonemes for correctly understanding the sounds their due, the entropy must be calculated in the same way, that is by taking the transition probabilities into account, and will then be reduced against the entropy calculated originally from the global frequencies. For instance, for the German alphabet we find, for 32 letters, that the entropy for the single letter or, which is the same, under the assumption of an equi-distribution, is 5, whereas that calculated by taking not only the different frequencies of letters into account, but also their transition probabilities in digrams, trigrams, etc. is reduced to 1.3. From this we calculate the so-called redundancy as

$$R = \frac{5-1.3}{5} = .70,$$

which means that a German text would be understood if 70% of the letters were missing. It goes without saying that this percentage must derive from the letters used most often in the language, such as e, t, n. We see from this that *what corresponds to the reduction of the error element in statistics is in linguistics called the "redundancy"*. The latter is, therefore, to be regarded as the reciprocal of the standard error of statistics. It follows that the greater the redundancy concerning a given linguistic feature, the less the risk of error in understanding the language in that respect.

23.4.2   *Association between words as error-reducing device*

On the vocabulary level, errors in communication arise through words missing, or through their meaning not being properly understood.

The remedy lies again in taking the transition probabilities between the words into account. This, however, is much more difficult here than on the phonemic level, and we must proceed in an indirect way. It was shown above that the reduction in the correlation coefficient, r, between parts of a text, or between different texts, if calculated, not under the assumption of random sampling, but under that of random partitioning, is really due to our taking transition probabilities between words, their different association values, into account. By working with vocabulary connectivity between parts of a text or between different texts, the redundancy in the use of words is hereby increased. For instance, if under the assumption of random occurrence of words the correlation coefficient Q is .503 (Table 39a), and under the assumption of random partitioning it results as .122 (Table 41a), we can say that the redundancy equals $\dfrac{.503 - .122}{503} = .75$, which means that for about 75% of the words transition probabilities are active, and that these words, which comprise the most frequent ones, could easily be replaced when missing. This has the consequence that the error in understanding is reduced.

More generally, and apart from its effect upon vocabulary correlation, vocabulary connectivity is a means for reducing error (misconception) in content. It guards against loss or neglect of words through the different parts of the text being what I have called "variations upon a theme", each part carrying over some of the words—and therefore concepts—appearing in other parts, not haphazardly or repetitiously, but according to a judicious distribution of words. In this way a conceptual network is created, which acts, provided the netting is sufficiently or adequately fine, as a preserver of the content.

The two operating concepts required to make the judicious distribution of words in different parts of the text into such a net are the avoidance of mere repetition between parts and vocabulary connectivity. Conversely, the mere repetition of words in their association with other words needed for developing the subject, and the haphazard association of the key-words with other words, or briefly, mere repetition and mere randomness, can be regarded as the 'hall-mark' of bad language, i.e. language not employing its error-reducing devices in the use of words and thus increasing the error of communication, instead of reducing it.

23.4.3   *Language deterioration through systematic neglect of error-reducing devices*

This acquires great importance when judging the linguistic performance of individuals because it enables one to depart from a clear definition of what is meant by "good language", viz., language which adequately uses all the devices for reducing error, or the devices which make for an increased redundancy. A speaker or writer who complies with this requirement will express himself as clearly and unequivocally as possible. Observe that in contradistinction to all other definitions of "good language", this definition is not qualitative, that is, it is not connected with a particular *content* but is purely operative, and thus *formal*.

This enables us to define with equal precision, and to diagnose unmistakably, the mis-use of language, be it accidental or systematic. It consists in the occasional and accidental neglect of the error-reducing, or redundancy-increasing, devices of language or, in the deliberate and systematic abandoning of the principles which make language an efficient means of communication.

The difference between the occasional and accidental errors in language, on the one hand, and its systematical misuse on the other, cannot be too strongly emphasized, especially as it is something very little realized. It must have come as one of the greatest disappointments in the life of Karl Kraus, the incomparable master and critic of language when, after the take-over in Germany by the Nazis in 1933, the orgy of misuse of language that set in shortly after made him realise the abysmal difference between what he had been fighting his whole life against, viz., individual carelessness in speech and writing, and the systematic debauchery of language that was now taking place in Nazi Germany. Witness his question:

"Ist denn was hier dem Geiste geschah, noch Sache des Geistes?"
(Kraus, 1952).

So different appeared to him what he had criticised all his life and what was now happening to the German language.

But even that was not the worst that could befall language. Then it was restricted to one nation only. What if such debauchery of language were to be used on an international scale? And is not what we are witnessing today in diplomatic—lucus a non lucendo—utterances already the spectacle of a profound corruption of all that language ever stood for.

* * *

In speaking of error-reducing devices on the word level of language, it is evident that "truth" cannot be excluded from our considerations. We need only remember that the whole purpose of the statistical design of experiments with which, as I have shown in *TTM*, Chpt. XXI, vocabulary connectivity is in surprising conformity, is the discovery of the true relations between the variables included in the experiments.

It was quite right, and as a heuristic measure fully justified, to have excluded so far the question of truth from linguistics, because the subjective views of what is true and what is not could not but interfere with questions of what is "good language" and what is not. In other words, the latter question belongs to the plane of expression, and the former to the plane of content, and interferences between these aspects of language had to be avoided until the plane of expression had been thoroughly explored. However, now that analytical linguistics has led to a definition of "good language" completely independent of content, there is no longer a need for upholding the separation of the two planes of language, of expression and of content. Considering our definition of "good language" as one employing to the full its error-reducing devices, it is at once evident that what corresponds to it on the content level is that language statements should describe the true relations between concepts, and consequently between objects in the manifold.

XXIV

MATHEMATICAL LINGUISTICS VERSUS
LINGUISTIC PHILOSOPHY

1. In the light of mathematical linguistics, linguistic philosophy appears as one of the most grotesque misunderstandings of both philosophy and language which it has ever been the bad luck of philosophy to encounter. It has recently undergone severe criticism by E. Gellner (1960), who, from the philosophical angle, has exposed its weakness, but it has fallen to the lot of mathematical linguistics to provide, from the linguistic angle, irrefutable evidence for the travesty of philosophy which was perpetrated under the name of linguistic philosophy in Cambridge and Oxford.[1]

24.1 THE DECAY OF ENGLISH PHILOSOPHY

If we compare the style of English philosophers who, in the empiricists Locke and Hume, and in the idealist Berkeley, had shown so much philosophical genius, with that in some of the fundamental texts and papers on linguistic philosophy, we are struck by the cramped style of the latter. One cannot but have the impression that the writer was afraid of using his language as it ought to be used. This is somewhat reminiscent of S. Butler's remarking on the cramped expression of some clergymen, which he attributes to the habitual suppression of the intellect, because it might interfere with what they have to profess. It will be shown that the cramped style of linguistic philosophy is really due to the suppression of the most important feature of language as a means of expression.

---

[1] Of other criticisms, G. R. C. Mure's *Retreat from Truth* might be mentioned which is, however marred by Mure's adherance to Hegel and the consequent confusion inseparable from anything Hegelian. This did, however, not prevent the author from borrowing extensively from Hegel's antipode Schopenhauer, Chapter 2 on "The Pre-suppositions of Economic Action" being little else but a transcription of Schopenhauer's philosophy concerning the dichotomy between the individual intellect as a tool for the struggle of existence and the "Pure Subject of Knowledge" (Das Reine Subjekt des Erkennens). Mure has replaced Schopenhauer's philosophical terminology by such terms as "the economic agent" for the individual in its struggle to exist, and "the economic observer" for the pure subject of knowledge. That Mure does not acknowledge his debt to Schopenhauer is not so surprising as it might seem. How could a confirmed Hegelian admit that he owed the best part of his book to Hegel's greatest enemy and devastating critic, Arthur Schopenhauer.

24.2 THE TACTICS OF LANGUAGE

2. There is a linguistic feature of such generality as to govern the relation of linguistic forms on every level of language: the phonemic, morphemic, syntactic and stylistic, and that is the linguistic opposition. Linguistic forms do not mean anything by themselves, but only through their being parts of a system of solidarity, one for each language level, which is nothing but the sum total of linguistic oppositions on that level. De Saussure has expressed this by saying that linguistic forms are what they are only by contrast.

This contrasting element is a property peculiar to the linguistic code, and thus does not belong to the manifold itself. It constitutes what may well be called the *Tactics of Language*. It is something superimposed upon the manifold of experience for the purpose of linguistic expression, and thus, in a way, "falsifies" nature, by "exalting mere want of agreement into contrariety" (G. Boole).[2] This was quite rightly sensed by Wittgenstein, but only for the highest level of literary work, namely for the systems of philosophy, and made him suspect the objective truth of linguistic statements of that type. But the mistake he made was to restrict the working of the principle of opposition to the statements of philosophy, because the same principle is working in every part of the linguistic code, and thus on every level of language.

Moreover, he missed the most important property of that feature of opposition, namely that its proper use enabled us to counteract the "unnatural" condition imposed by it upon the manifold. The antipodal principle thus becomes the saving grace of language, and might well be regarded as the principal element of its tactics. In this respect, Wittgenstein's case is not unlike that of B. Whorf. Both were engineers by profession, who took language too literally. They were language-struck, which made them extol the power of language over thought to the skies.

Let us now follow the above argument in greater detail.

24.3 THE PRINCIPLE OF OPPOSITION IN LANGUAGE ON THE PHONEMIC, MORPHEMIC AND SYNTACTIC LEVEL

At every level of language we find the principle of opposition as quite essential for the linguistic code.

On the phonemic level, it was Trubetzkoy who regarded, not the phoneme, but the phonological opposition as the essential feature for the distinguishability of words and their meanings.

On the morphemic or word level, it was de Saussure who enunciated the principle of solidarity between the words of a language, according to which they had their meaning only as members of a solidarity system of vocabulary.

---

[2] G. Boole, *An Investigation of the Laws of Thought* (London, 1854).

In full agreement with this, but on the plane of content, is G. Boole's view that the law of duality, which is the algebraic expression of the logical principle of contradiction, according to which it is impossible for any being to possess a quality and at the same time not to possess it, was the fundamental law of thought.

On the syntactic level, it is again by opposition between grammar forms (bound and free) among themselves that grammatical meaning is established. The "new system" of grammar, as proposed by Jespersen (1924) based upon the opposition between form and function, clearly brings out the fact that the grammatical function of a given form is not uniquely bound to that form, nor does a certain form always denote the same function.

When we come to style as a characteristic of the literary work, we find the tactics of language permeated with what I call duality, and what G. Cambon (1961) calls "oppositional parallelism" or "antipodal similarity". On the highest level of literary work, the philosophical, it is known as the "antithesis". And it was there that Wittgenstein encountered it, and rightly recognised it as not to be inherent in the manifold of expression, but as something purely linguistical.

But Wittgenstein was not aware of the ubiquity of the principle of verbal counterpoint in language structure on all its levels, and thought that it could be avoided—and our philosophical statements be hereby made unimpeachable—if we restricted ourselves to the everyday use of language—whatever that means. This is why he would have liked to stop the use of language at the dictionary level, so to speak, and why his followers when, what they call, "thinking" about a problem, try to take their information exclusively from the word definitions in the dictionary.

Had Wittgenstein understood the tactics of language, as we know it today, he could not have escaped the conclusion that it was the very same principle of opposition which governed the use of words in both their everyday meaning and in the most general and abstract statements of philosophy, and that it was quite illogical to accept it in one, and exclude it in the other.

24.4   DICTIONARY MEANING OF WORDS AS PRECIPITATE OF THEIR USE
IN ALL WORKS OF LITERATURE

Moreover, it is almost inconceivable that a thinker like Wittgenstein, should never have thought about how the words in, say, the Oxford Dictionary of English—or in a representative dictionary of any other language—had acquired what he thought was their meaning for "popular" use. A little thought would have made him realise that their meaning was the precipitate (in the chemical sense) of their use in literary work throughout the centuries, and thus—as far as words denoting more general concepts are concerned—the result of their use by the very same philosophers whom he despised. It follows that in using the words in their everyday meaning, we use surreptitiously, or by second hand, the accumulated philosophical wisdom. All this under the assumption that there is such a thing as "everyday use and meaning of words", which—as I have shown—is at least open to the gravest doubts. [3]

It has been overlooked so far that Wittgenstein's philosophy rests upon an idea which is quite analogous to Hegel's disastrous misconception of the evolutionary process as a product of the mind.

According to the dialectic process (Die dialektische Selbstbewegung der Begriffe), every concept turns with metaphysical necessity into its opposite. This process is conceived to be not only one of philosophical thought, but, at the same time, the prototype of development itself in the manifold of experience. The laws of dualistic logic are, therefore, the laws of the world. Hegel had no respect for empirical knowledge (Erfahrung), and wanted to let everything appear as the product of the spontaneous movement of the mind (Die Selbstbewegung der Begriffe).

Wittgenstein went one better. Whereas for Hegel all the relations in the manifold of experience were the result of the "*Selbstbewegung*" *of the concepts*, for Wittgenstein all possible statements about these relations are the result of the "*Selbstbewegung*" *of the words*. For if, as he categorically stated, "the meaning of words is determined by their use—a sophism if ever there was one, and about as true as that the Tortoise must win the race from Achilles—, the words in their everyday use would tell us all that is worth knowing about the manifold of experience.

Wittgenstein's mistake can be traced to a statement by Kant who, more out of habit than deliberately and in a somewhat conventional way, once defined philosophy to be a science out of concepts, which Wittgenstein transformed into a statement of linguistic philosophy by substituting "words" for "concepts". Now, it is, of course, true that concepts and the words denoting them are the material of philosophy, but they are so only as the marble is the material of the sculptor: they don't *direct* thought, but conversely are *formed by* thought, and so invested with meaning. The concepts, and the meaning of words, are not something "given", but are the product of the work of the mind. Philosophy is a science *in* concepts (words), but not *out of* concepts (words). (Schopenhauer, *l.c.*, pp. 48, 90).

24.5   THE CORRECTIVE ACTION OF THE PRINCIPLE OF OPPOSITION

The greatest flaw in the Wittgenstein argument is due to his not understanding that the principle of opposition works so as to correct the unnatural "yes-no" or "all-nothing" form which it imposes upon the manifold. It is just by exalting mere want of agreement into contrariety, and thus a matter of difference in degree into an absolute difference, that it creates itself the occasion or the need for viewing the relation in question from other angles.

Linguistic coding—as different from other types of coding—has two stages, following closely upon one another. Hardly have we succeeded in finding expression by

[3]   "Linguistic Philosophy in the Light of Modern Linguistics", *Language and Speech*, Vol. 3.

referring our thoughts to certain code symbols, but the inadequacy of the chosen symbols makes us change the expression by selecting, partly at least, new words as another body of reference. This is, of course, to be understood cum grano salis, as being only the general rule and needed more for complicated thoughts, but in the long run it is true for all expression. Connecting thought and word, and separating them again, is the very soul of linguistic expression and style. It is due in the last instance to the fact that it is only the relations which matter, not the particular words expressing them, which fact finds its most characteristic expression in the inversion of the words forming the end-points of the relation, and which I have shown to be of the nature of geometrical duality. It is the most powerful element in the tactics of language.

The judicious application of the antipodal principle produces what we call the form of a literary work. A skilful writer does not start just anywhere and then proceed according to what the mathematician knows under the name of the "random walk", but his tactics make him view the subject from different angles, and use the interaction between these pictures as defining the track along which to proceed with the story, or generally with his subject. In this way, it is the *relations*, as different from the *words*, which are brought out, and with it thus the identity of the subject, no matter from what angle we prefer to look at it. This means that the very principle which makes the presentation of a subject in language differ from what it is like in the manifold of experience, has been instrumental in getting at the relations themselves in the manifold independently from the words used for their description.

24.6   THE LACK OF STYLE IN LINGUISTIC PHILOSOPHY

To summarise, Wittengenstein failed to realise that the tactics of language permeated the whole of it, and that what he objected to on the highest level—philosophical writing—was already inherent and essential on all other levels, and that the restriction of "truth" to the word meanings as given in a dictionary rested upon a mistake: they are in no way less subject to the general principle of opposition than are the statements of philosophy.

It is this mistake, and at the same time Wittgenstein's failure to understand the corrective action of the opposition principle in the tactics of language, which accounts for the cramped style of the writings of linguistic philosophers. They are afraid of making proper use of the tactics of language, and check themselves at every step to make sure they have not trespassed, hereby stifling every original thought and expression, all the time, of course, using surreptitiously—though they need not be aware of it—the very same tactics, but on a lower level. This is like planting a tree and uprooting it frequently so as to look at its roots. The reason why it does not work—in the sense of producing a philosophy—is that philosophy, having only language as its tool of expression, cannot be written with language at half-cock, so to speak. The result cannot fail to be as boring, if not ridiculous, as the outputs of linguistic philosophy mostly are. This fear of language, which they pretend to be the masters of, produces papers with titles like "On what there is", whose style is characterised by a ridiculous stultification of language. The result is a sort of Basic Philosophy, i.e. a philosophy in Basic English. Philosophy, where the tactics of language must be used to perfection, is thus starved of any except the most rudimentary display of it.

This is largely responsible for the boredom and the platitudes of linguistic philosophy such as Wittgenstein's basic principle "Die Welt ist alles was der Fall ist" (The world is everything which is the case) and must logically lead to its closing sentence: "Wovon man nicht reden kann, davon soll man schweigen" (What one cannot speak of, thereof one should be silent), at which G. R. C. Mure has rightly expressed surprise that Wittgenstein did not follow it up by "Sorry I spoke".

If one has become afraid of using language, the only way is not to use it at all, not to stop at using it "philosophically" by drawing an arbitrary borderline between "philosophical" and "everyday" use, which does not correspond to the facts.

BIBLIOGRAPHY

This is not a complete Bibliography of works concerned with mathematical linguistics, but rather a selection of such works as are referred to more particularly in this book. In addition to the items listed below, the reader is referred to the Bibliography in the author's *Language as Choice and Chance* (Groningen, 1956) and *Type-Token Mathematics* (The Hague, 1960), to the *Bibliographie Critique de la Statistique Linguistique* by P. Guiraud and J. Whatmough (Utrecht, 1953) and also to the *Bibliography on Information Theory (Communication Theory) and Cybernetics* by F. L. H. M. Stumpers.

Bodmer, F., *The Loom of Language* (London, 1943).

Bolinger, Dwight L., "Rime, assonance and morpheme analysis", *Word*, 6.117 (1950).

Boole, G., *An Investigation of the Laws of Thought* (London, 1854).

Born, M., *Atomic Physics*, 3rd ed. (London-Glasgow, 1944).

Brillouin, L., *Science and Information Theory* (New York, 1956).

Chambers, E. K., *"William Shakespeare"* (Oxford, 1930). Appendix II: "Metrical tables".

Chomsky, N., *Language*, 34 (1958), 100.

Chretien, C. D., "The quantitative method for determining linguistic relationships. Interpretation of results and tests of significance", *UCPL*, 1:2.11-20 (1943).

Cox, D. R., and Brandwood, L., "On a discriminatory problem connected with the works of Plato", *J.R.S.S.*, Series B, Vol. 21 (1959), 195-200.

Dewey, G., *Relative Frequency of English Speech Sounds* (Cambridge, 1923).

Driver, H., and Kroeber, A. L., "Quantitative expression of cultural relationships", *Un. Cal. Publ. Am. Arch. Ethn.*, 31.211-56 (1932).

Eddington, A. S., *New Pathways in Science* (Cambridge, 1935).

Einstein, A., and Infeld, L., *The Evolution of Physics* (Cambridge, 1938).

Ellegard, A., "Statistical measurement of linguistic relationship", *Language*, Vol. 35 (1959), 131-156.

Feller, W., *An Introduction to Probability Theory and its Application*, Vol. I, 2nd ed. (New York, 1957).

Fisher, R. A. et al., "The relation between the number of individuals and the number of species in a random sample of an animal population", *J. Anim. Ecol.*, 12 (1943), 42-58.

Fleay, F. G., "On metrical tests as applied to dramatic poetry", *New Shakespeare Society*, Vol. I (1874).

Galton, Sir F., and McAlister, D., *Proc. Roy. Soc.*, 29 (1879), 365.

Gellner, E., *Words and Things* (London, 1960).

Goethe, J. W., *Die Wahlverwandtschaften, Ein Roman* (1809).

Good, I. J., "On the population frequencies of species and the estimation of population parameters", *Biometrika*, 40 (1953), 237-264.

Gray, G. B., *The forms of Hebrew Poetry*, pp. 8, 24, 88, 244 ff., 267 ff.

Greenberg, H. J., "Patterning of Semitic Verbal Roots", *Word*, Vol. VI (1950), No. 2, and the literature cited there.

Halle, M., Review in *Kratylos*, III (1958), 20-28.

Hartley, R. V. L., "Transmission of information", *Bell System Technique Journal*, 1928, 535.

Herdan, G., "A new derivation and interpretation of Yule's 'Characteristic' *K*." *Journal of Applied Mathematics and Physics (Zamp)*, VI (1955), 332.

Herdan, G., *Language as Choice and Chance* (Groningen, 1956).

Herdan, G., "The mathematical relation between the number of diseases and the number of patients in a community", *J.R.S.S.*, Series A, 120, Pt. 3 (1957), 320-330.

Herdan, G., "An inequality relation between Yule's 'Characteristic K' and Shannon's 'Entropy H'", *J. Appl. Mathematics and Physics (Zamp)*, IX, Pt. 1 (1958), 69-73.

Herdan, G., *Type-Token Mathematics* (The Hague, 1960).

Herdan, G., "A critical examination of Simon's model of certain distribution functions in linguistics", *Applied Statistics*, Vol. X, No. 2 (1961).

Herdan, G., "Vocabulary Statistics and Phonology: A Parallel", *Language*, Vol. 37 (1961), 247-255.

Herdan, G., Review in *Language*, Vol. 37 (1961), 120-125.

Herdan, G., "The statistics of structured meaning", in *Information Retrieval and Machine Translation*, III, Pt. 2. Edited by Jesse H. Shera (New York, 1961), 993-1006.

Hillier, Sir W., *The Chinese Language and how to learn it* (London, 1929).

Jakobson, R., "Linguistics and Poetics", in *Style and Language*, edited by Thos. A. Sebeok (1961).

Jakobson, R., "Typological Studies and their Contribution to Historical Comparative Linguistics", *Proceedings of the VIIIth International Congress of Linguists* (Oslo, 1957).

Jespersen, O., *Philosophy of Grammar* (London, 1924).

Josselson, H. H., *The Russian Word Count* (para. 5 by B. Epstein) (Detroit, 1953).

Karlgren, B., *Sound and Symbol in Chinese* (London, 1923).

Karlgren, H., "Die Tragweite lexikalischer Statistik", in *Språkstatistika Symposiet 1962* (Uppsala, 1962).

Kendall, M. G., and Babington Smith, B., "Randomness and random sampling numbers", *J.R.S.S.*, 101 (1938), 147.

Kendall, M. G., *The Statistical Approach*. Inaugural lecture given at the London School of Economics, Jan. 17th, 1950.

Klein, F., Quoted by L. Nelson (see below).

Kraus, K., *Die Dritte Walpurgisnacht* (Munich, 1952).

Kroeber, A. L., and Chretien, C. D., "Quantitative Classification of Indo-European Languages", *Language*, 13.83-103 (1937).

Kroeber, A. L., and Chretien, C. D., "The Statistical Technique and Hittite", *Language*, 15.69-71 (1939).

Kullback, S., *Information Theory and Statistics* (New York, 1959).

Kupperman, M., "On comparing two observed frequency counts", *Applied Statistics*, Vol. 9 (1960), 37-42.

Landau, L., and Lifshitz, E., *Statistical Physics* (Oxford, 1938).

Lees, R. B., Review. *Language*, Vol. 35 (1959), 271-302.

Lehmann, W. P., *The Texas Quarterly*, II (1959), 23-36.

Levy, H., and Roth, L., *Elements of Probability* (Oxford, 1936).

Macaulay, T. B., *Critical and Historical Essays* (London, 1880).

Mandelbrot, B., "Structure Formelle des Textes et Communications. Deux Etudes", *Word*, Vol. 10 (1954), 1-27.

Matthews, C. W., *Chinese-English Dictionary* (Peking, 1930).

Meyer-Eppler, W., *Grundlagen und Anwendungen der Informationstheorie* (Berlin-Göttingen-Heidelberg, 1959).

Mises, R. von, *Wahrscheinlichkeitsrechnung und Ihre Anwendung in der Statistik und Theoretischen Physik* (Leipzig-Wien, 1931).

Morgenthaler, R., *Statistik des Neutestamentlichen Wortschatzes* (Zürich-Frankfurt am Main, 1958).

Morris-Jones, Sir J., *Cerdd Dafod (Welsh Poetic Art)*, pp. 290 ff.

Mure, G. R. C., *Retreat from Truth* (Oxford, 1958).

Nelson, L., *Beiträge zur Philosophie d. Logik u. Mathematik* (Frankfurt a.M., 1959).

Parry T., *The History of Welsh Literature* (Oxford, 1915).

Plath, W., "Mathematical Linguistics", *Trends in European and American Linguistics, 1930-1960* (Cambridge, Mass., 1961).

Pulgram, E., "Proto-Indo-European reality and reconstruction", *Language*, 35 (1959), 421-6.

Pulgram, E., "The nature and use of Proto-languages", *Lingua*, Vol. X (1961), pp. 18-57.

P'u Sung-ling, *Liao Chai*.

Ross, A. C. S., "Philological Probability Problems", *J. R. Statist. Soc. (B)*, 12 (1950), 39.

de Saussure, F., *Cours de linguistique generale*, 2nd ed. (Paris, 1922).

Schopenhauer, A., *Gesammelte Werke*. Edited by P. Deussen (Munich, 1911).

Schrödinger, E., *Statistical Thermodynamics* (Cambridge, 1946).

Sebeok, T. A. (ed.), *Style in Language* (1961).

Shannon, C. E., "The mathematical theory of communication", *Bell System Technique Journal*, Vol. XXVII (1948), 379.

Simon, H. A., "On a class of skew distribution functions", *Biometrika*, 42 (1955), 425-440.

Spang-Hanssen, H., *Probability and Structural Classification in Language Description* (Copenhagen, 1959).

Spearman, C., "General intelligence objectively determined and measured", *A.J.P.*, 15 (1904), 201-93.

Spearman, C., *The Abilities of Man* (London, 1932).

Sweet, H., *A New English Grammar* (Oxford, 1898).

Trubetzkoy, N. S., *Anleitung zu phonologischen Beschreibungen* (Brno, 1935).

Trubetzkoy, N. S., *Grundzüge der Phonologie* (Prague, 1939).

de Vries, M., Private communication (1962).

Waerden, B. L. v. d., *Science Awakening* (Groningen, 1954).

Walde, A., and Pokorny, J., *Vergleichendes Wörterbuch der Indogermanischen Sprachen* (Berlin, 1926-32).

Welch, B. L., "Note on discriminant functions", *Biometrika*, 31 (1939), 218-219.

Whittaker, E., *From Euclid to Eddington* (Cambridge, 1949).

Wilks, S. S., "The likelihood test of independence in contingency tables", *Ann. Math. Stat.*, 6:190-96 (1935).

Williams, C. B., "Yule's 'Characteristic' and the 'Index of Diversity'", *Nature*, 157. 482 (1946).

Williams, C. B., "The logarithmic series and its application to biological problems", *J. Ecol.*, 34 (1947), 253-273.

Wyn Roberts, E., Private communication (1961).

Yardi, M. R., "A statistical approach to the problem of chronology of Shakespeare's plays", *Sankhya, The Indian Journal of Statistics*, Vol. VII (1945/46), 263-8.

Yule, G. Udny, and Kendall, M. G., *Introduction to the Theory of Statistics*, 11th ed. (London, 1937).

Yule, G. Udny, *The Statistical Study of Vocabulary* (Cambridge, 1944).

Zipf, G. K., *Selected Studies of the Principle of Relative Frequency in Language* (Cambridge, Mass. 1932).

Zipf, G. K., *Human Behaviour and the Principle of Least Effort* (Cambridge, Mass., 1949).

INDEX

JANUA LINGUARUM

STUDIA MEMORIAE NICOLAI VAN WIJK DEDICATA

Edited by Cornelis H. van Schooneveld

SERIES MINOR

1. ROMAN JAKOBSON and MORRIS HALLE: Fundamentals of Language. 1956. 97 pp. Gld. 6.—
2. N. VAN WIJK: Les langues slaves. De l'unité à la pluralité. *out of print*
3. EMIL PETROVICI: Kann das Phonemsystem einer Sprache durch fremden Einfluss umgestaltet werden? Zum slavischen Einfluss auf das rumänische Lautsystem. 1957. 44 pp. Gld. 4.—
4. NOAM CHOMSKY: Syntactic Structures. Second printing 1961. 188 pp. Gld. 8.—
5. N. VAN WIJK: Die baltischen und slavischen Akzent- und Intonationssysteme. Ein Beitrag zur Erforschung der baltisch-slavischen Verwandtschaftsverhältnisse. 2nd ed. 1958. 160 pp. Gld. 15.—
6. BERNARD GEIGER, TIBOR HALASI-KUN, AERT H. KUIPERS and KARL H. MENGES: Peoples and Languages of the Caucasus. A Synopsis. 1959. 77 pp., map. Gld. 8.—
7. ERNST PULGRAM: Introduction to the Spectrography of Speech. 1959. 174 pp., 31 figs., 2 tables. Gld. 12.—
8. AERT H. KUIPERS: Phoneme and Morpheme in Kabardian (Eastern Adyghe). 1960. 124 pp. Gld. 16.—
9. A. ROSETTI: Sur la théorie de la syllabe. *out of print*
10. URIEL and BEATRICE WEINREICH: Yiddish Language and Folklore. A Selective Bibliography for Research. 1959. 66 pp. Gld. 6.—
11. E. and K. DELAVENAY: Bibliography of Mechanical Translation. — Bibliographie de la traduction automatique. 1960. 69 pp. Gld. 10.—
12. CARL L. EBELING: Linguistic Units. Second printing 1962. 143 pp. Gld. 12.—
13. SHELOMO MORAG: The Vocalization Systems of Arabic, Hebrew and Aramaic. Their Phonetic and Phonemic Principles. 1962. 85 pp., two folding tables. Gld. 15.—

14. DWIGHT L. BOLINGER: Generality, Gradience, and the All-or-None.
    1961. 46 pp.   Gld. 5.50

15. ALPHONSE JUILLAND: Outline of a General Theory of Structural
    Relations. 1958. 58 pp.   Gld. 7.50

16. Sens et usages du terme Structure, dans les sciences humaines et
    sociales, édité par ROGER BASTIDE. 1962. 165 pp.   Gld. 16.—

17. W. SIDNEY ALLEN: Sandhi. The Theoretical, Phonetic, and Historic
    Bases of Word-Junction in Sanskrit. 1962. 114 pp.   Gld. 16.—

20. FINNGEIR HIORTH: Zur formalen Charakterisierung des Satzes. 1962.
    152 pp.   Gld. 15.—

22. E. F. HADEN, M. S. HAN and Y. W. HAN: A Resonance-Theory for
    Linguistics. 1962. 52 pp.   Gld. 7.—

23. S. LEVIN: Linguistic Structures in Poetry. 1962. 64 pp.   Gld. 8.—

24. ALPHONSE JUILLAND and JAMES MACRIS: The English Verb System.
    1962. 81 pp.   Gld. 8.—

SERIES MAIOR

2. DEAN S. WORTH: Kamchadal Texts collected by W. Jochelson. 1961.
   284 pp. Cloth.   Gld. 58.—

3. PETER HARTMANN: Theorie der Grammatik.
   1. Die Sprache als Form. 1959. 144 pp.   Gld. 16.—
   2. Zur Konstitution einer allgemeinen Grammatik. 1961. 136 pp.
                                                                  Gld. 21.—
   3. Allgemeinste Strukturgesetze in Sprache und Grammatik. 1961.
      136 pp.   Gld. 21.—
   4. Grammatik und Grammatizität. 1962. 144 pp.   Gld. 24.—

4. GUSTAV HERDAN: Type-Token Mathematics. A Textbook of Mathematical Linguistics. 1960. 448 pp., 17 figs. Cloth.   Gld. 54.—

6. TATIANA SLAMA-CAZACU: Langage et Contexte. Le problème du
   langage dans la conception de l'expression et de l'interprétation par
   des organisations contextuelles. 1961. 251 pp., 5 figs. Cloth.
                                                                  Gld. 48.—

7. ALF SOMMERFELT: Diachronic and Synchronic Aspects of Language.
   Selected Articles, 1962. 421 pp., 23 figs. Cloth.   Gld. 54.—

8. THOMAS A. SEBEOK and VALDIS J. ZEPS: Concordance and Thesaurus
   of Cheremis Poetic Language. 1961. 259 pp. Cloth.   Gld. 58.—